The Civil Rights Movement

SEMINAR STUDIES IN HISTORY

The Civil Rights Movement

BRUCE J. DIERENFIELD

PEARSON
Longman

Harlow, England • London • New York • Boston • San Francisco • Toronto
Sydney • Singapore • Hong Kong • Tokyo • Seoul • Taipei • New Delhi
Cape Town • Madrid • Mexico City • Amsterdam • Munich • Paris • Milan

Pearson Education Limited
Edinburgh Gate
Harlow CM20 2JE
United Kingdom
Tel: +44 (0)1279 623623
Fax: +44 (0)1279 431059
Website: www.pearsoned.co.uk

First edition published in Great Britain in 2004

© Pearson Education Limited 2004

The right of Bruce J. Dierenfield to be identified as
author of this work has been asserted by him in accordance
with the Copyright, Designs and Patents Act 1988.

ISBN 0 582 35737 3

British Library Cataloguing in Publication Data
A CIP catalogue record for this book can be obtained from the British Library

Library of Congress Cataloging in Publication Data
A CIP catalog record for this book can be obtained from the Library of Congress

10 9 8 7 6 5 4 3 2 1

Set in 10/12.5pt Sabon by Graphicraft Limited, Hong Kong
Printed in Malaysia

The Publishers' policy is to use paper manufactured from sustainable forests.

CONTENTS

INTRODUCTION TO THE SERIES

Such is the pace of historical enquiry in the modern world that there is an ever-widening gap between the specialist article or monograph, incorporating the results of current research, and general surveys, which inevitably become out of date. *Seminar Studies in History* is designed to bridge this gap. The series was founded by Patrick Richardson in 1966 and his aim was to cover major themes in British, European and world history. Between 1980 and 1996 Roger Lockyer continued his work, before handing the editorship over to Clive Emsley and Gordon Martel. Clive Emsley is Professor of History at the Open University, while Gordon Martel is Professor of International History at the University of Northern British Columbia, Canada, and Senior Research Fellow at De Montfort University.

All the books are written by experts in their field who are not only familiar with the latest research but have often contributed to it. They are frequently revised, in order to take account of new information and interpretations. They provide a selection of documents to illustrate major themes and provoke discussion, and also a guide to further reading. The aim of *Seminar Studies in History* is to clarify complex issues without over-simplifying them, and to stimulate readers into deepening their knowledge and understanding of major themes and topics.

ACKNOWLEDGEMENTS

Many people and institutions have generously supported this study of the black civil rights movement. At Canisius College, I wish to thank the Rev. Vincent Cooke, president, Herbert Nelson, academic vice-president, Paula McNutt, dean of arts and sciences, and David Costello, my colleague in the History department, for a Peter Canisius Distinguished Teaching Professorship in the African American Experience. This award permitted me to test my writings in my course on the civil rights movement, bring such activists as Bernard LaFayette and C.T. Vivian to our Buffalo campus, and finance travel to movement sites. Canisius also provided fellowships and a reduced teaching schedule to complete this work. Ray Clough, director of the Center for Teaching Excellence, awarded me a laptop computer on which this book was typed.

I am particularly grateful to History department chairs Larry Jones and Nancy Rosenbloom, department secretary Dena Bowman, all of the reference librarians (Camilla Baker, Karen Bordonaro, Jessica Blum, Lisa Sullivan, Anne Huberman, and Betsey Higgins), interlibrary loan technician Sally DiCarlo, acquisitions librarian Barbara Boehnke, as well as my student research assistants (Anton Strgagic, Mark Muoio, Gail McDonald, Margaret Wood, Sarah Cosgrove, and Kathleen Kemp). Additional help came from librarians at the US Department of Justice, the John F. Kennedy Library, the University of Alabama, the University of Mississippi, and the state archives of Alabama. James Giglio, Lawrence Little, Michael Mayer, Michael Birkner, Jeff Patterson, Hilton Webb, Jr., Thomas Banchich, Henry Clark, and René de la Pedraja each read and commented on the text, a courtesy that I cannot repay. My good friend and colleague Bob Butler, a veteran of the Mississippi freedom movement, not only critiqued the text but brought SCLC co-founder Fred Shuttlesworth to our campus and team-taught a course with me in African American studies. Discussions with my former star student Dean Kotlowski – author of a revisionist study of Richard Nixon's civil rights policy – have been illuminating.

Several people have been constant sources of encouragement, including my former major professor Carl Brauer, an expert on the Kennedy administration; my gracious former colleagues, Martha Swain and Dorothy DeMoss; my old basketball teammate, Jim Anderson; Greg Russell, who reads Advanced Placement exams in US history with me each year; and Sababu Norris, director of the Canisius office of multicultural affairs. Gordon Martel, the series editor at Longman, and Casey Mein, the acquisitions editor, showed more patience than a dilatory writer had reason to expect.

An irreplaceable debt is owed to my family, especially to my supportive parents, Richard and Yvonne, my brother David, my uncle Charles, and my late uncle James. My heartfelt gratitude goes to my wife Kate, an incisive historian in her own right and an expert on white southern liberals in the civil rights movement. Once again, she put aside her own work to plow through mine. She also devoted much time attending to our effervescent 11-year-old daughter Elizabeth, the light of our lives. It is to Kate that this book is dedicated. Errors that remain are no one's fault but my own.

PUBLISHER'S ACKNOWLEDGEMENTS

We are grateful to the following for permission to reproduce copyright material:

Routledge/Taylor & Francis Books Inc. for an extract from a list of 'Telephone calls to and from Attorney General Robert Kennedy' 22 May 1961 as published in *Civil Rights, The White House and the Justice Department 1945–1968* by Michael R. Belknap © 1991; Writers House for the speech 'I have a dream' and 'letter from Birmingham Jail' by Dr. Martin Luther King Jr. by arrangement with the Estate of Martin Luther King Jr., copyright 1963 Dr. Martin Luther King Jr., renewed 1991 Coretta Scott King; and Zephyr Press for an excerpt from *Letters from Mississippi* edited with a preface by Elizabeth Sutherland Martinez © 2002 Zephyr Press.

Map 1 adapted from *Promises to Keep: The United States Since World War II, 1st Edition*, reprinted by permission of Houghton Mifflin Company (Boyer, P. et al. 1995); Map 2 detail from *Sweet Land of Liberty?*, reprinted by permission of Pearson Education Ltd. (Cook, R. 1998); Document 4 cartoon from *Herblock: A Cartoonist's Life*, pub. Times Books, reprinted by permission of The Herb Block Foundation (Block, H. 1998); Document 19 figure from *A Common Destiny: Blacks and American Society*, reprinted by permission of The National Academies Press (Jaynes, G.D. and Williams, R.M., Jr., eds. 1990).

We are grateful to the following for permission to reproduce photographs:

Plate 1 Brown Brothers, Sterling, PA 18463; Plate 2 News & Record; Plates 3 and 4 Associated Press Ltd.

In some instances we have been unable to trace the owners of copyright material, and we would appreciate any information that would enable us to do so.

LIST OF ABBREVIATIONS

ACLU	American Civil Liberties Union
ACMHR	Alabama Christian Movement for Human Rights
ADA	Americans for Democratic Action
AFSCME	American Federation of State, County, and Municipal Employees
AME	African Methodist Episcopal
BPP	Black Panthers Party
CCCO	Coordinating Council of Community Organizations
CIC	Commission on Interracial Cooperation
COFO	Council of Federated Organizations
COINTELPRO	Counter-Intelligence Program
CORE	Congress of Racial Equality
EEOC	Equal Employment Opportunity Commission
FBI	Federal Bureau of Investigation
FDR	Franklin D. Roosevelt
FEPC	Fair Employment Practice Committee
FOR	Fellowship of Reconciliation
ICC	Interstate Commerce Commission
IRS	Internal Revenue Service
KKK	Ku Klux Klan
LCCR	Leadership Conference on Civil Rights
MFDP	Mississippi Freedom Democratic Party
MIA	Montgomery Improvement Association
MOWM	March on Washington Movement
NAACP	National Association for the Advancement of Colored People
NOI	Nation of Islam
NSA	National Student Association
OEO	Office of Economic Opportunity
PUSH	People United to Save Humanity
RAM	Revolutionary Action Movement
ROTC	Reserve Officers Training Corps
SCEF	Southern Conference Educational Fund
SCHW	Southern Conference for Human Welfare
SCLC	Southern Christian Leadership Conference

SDS	Students for a Democratic Society
SNCC	Student Nonviolent Coordinating Committee
SRC	Southern Regional Council
UAW	United Automobile Workers
UNIA	Universal Negro Improvement Association
VEP	Voter Education Project
VISTA	Volunteers in Service to America
YWCA	Young Women's Christian Association

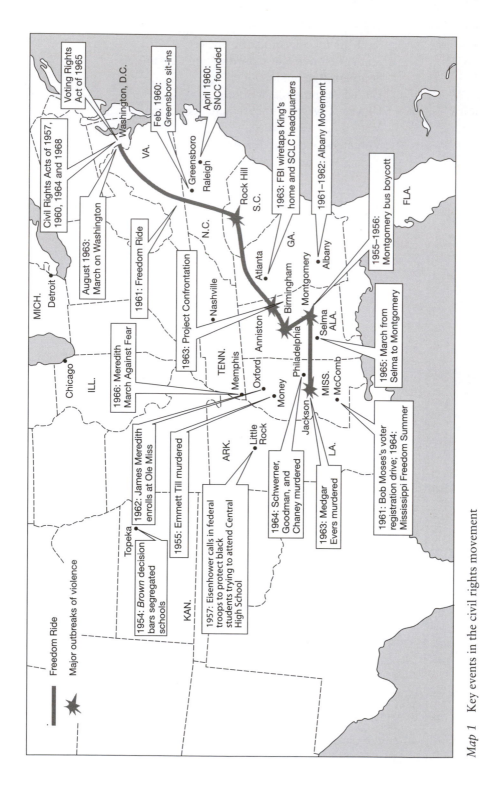

Map 1 Key events in the civil rights movement

Source: Boyer et al., *Promises to Keep*. Copyright © 1995 by Houghton Mifflin Company. Adapted with permission.

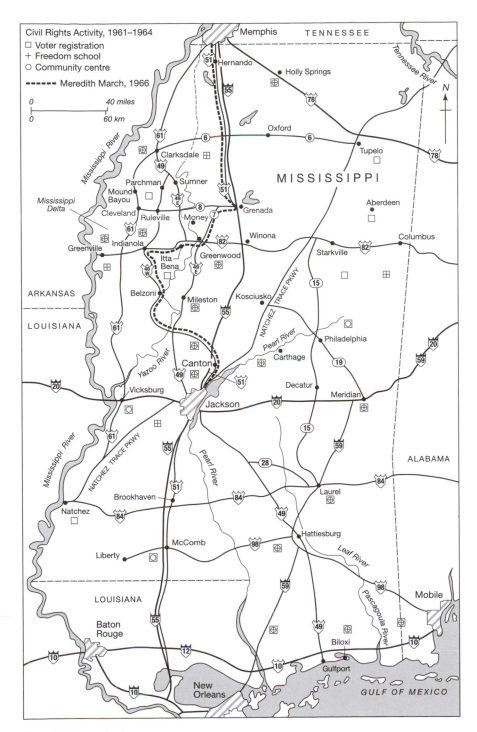

Map 2   Mississippi

Source: Adapted from Davis, T. (1998) *Weary Feet, Rested Souls*, pub. W.W. Norton & Company, Inc., p. 190. Detail from Cook, R. (1998) *Sweet Land of Liberty?*, pub. Longman, Map 3, p. 309, reprinted by permission of Pearson Education Ltd.

THE PROBLEM

Until the twentieth century, virtually every society that ever existed enslaved others. Early forms of slavery, like those of Greece and Rome, ensnared conquered nations without regard to race. By contrast, English colonists in the New World increasingly enslaved only black African laborers, a practice that was used to explain the latter's alleged inferiority. Such racism arose in a society professing strong belief in equality. As Protestant Christians, Englishmen believed that redemption was available to any convert; as revolutionaries, they believed that 'all men are created equal' and were therefore entitled to equal rights. Growing side-by-side with this notion of equality was the darker reality of racism that justified the degradation and enslavement of Africans. This anomalous situation arose for economic, cultural, political, and pseudo-scientific reasons, all of which reinforced each other.

While the origins of racism remain murky, it appears that prejudice against blacks was accentuated in the Middle Ages when light-skinned Arabs, Berbers, and Persians made sub-Saharan Africa the prime hunting ground for new slaves. These Muslim traders had to push beyond the Mediterranean world, which was rapidly converting to Islam, because Islamic precepts barred the enslavement of anyone who was already Muslim. A unique long-distance slave trade resulted in which millions of blacks were seized and sold to far-flung lands, where they worked as servants, concubines, soldiers, miners, and farmhands. In the process, Arabs lumped all dark-skinned peoples of Africa into one general category – 'blacks'. Negative stereotypes surfaced, with Arab intellectuals comparing 'ugly and misshapen' blacks to 'dumb animals' who 'dwell in caves . . . and eat each other'. Apes were said to be 'more teachable and more intelligent' than blacks. Muslims reinforced this racism with an Old Testament story in which the Hebrew patriarch Noah cursed the descendants of his son Ham to be slaves. Muslim (as well as Jewish and Christian) writers interpreted this ambiguous reference as a condemnation of black Africans. Indeed, the Arab word for 'slave' came to mean only a black slave. This said, slaves under Islamic rule were generally treated more humanely, were more likely to be manumitted, and were more readily assimilated than those who came to the New World.

Starting in the fifteenth century, Europeans followed the Arab lead in enslaving and dehumanizing black Africans, just as white serfs had once been stigmatized. Even though a rapidly growing European population could have sent enough of its own convicts, prisoners of war, and vagrants to satisfy its labor needs in the New World and done so at lower shipping costs, Portuguese, Spanish, English, Dutch, French, Swedish, Danish, and Prussian traders traveled long distances to acquire black Africans and market them like livestock. Europeans no longer enslaved each other because they gradually concluded their ethnicities were more alike than different and therefore above such debasement, because they came to value individual liberty for themselves (but not others), and because their advancing ship technology made it possible to procure distant peoples. In the race for national greatness, Europeans established trading stations in west Africa, solidifying the connection between skin color and slavery. Europeans regarded 'brutish' black Africans, such as the Igbo, Wolof, and Mandingo, as suited to slavery because they were reportedly pagans who wore little, if any, clothing and practiced torture, cannibalism, and cosmetic mutilation. Even when Africans adopted European cultural and religious forms, their apparently polluted skin color consigned them to an inferior place.

For the ethnocentric English, skin color mattered a great deal because in the mid-sixteenth century they were discovering themselves as a people and suddenly became aware of black Africans at the same time. To the English, black Africans were the antithesis of Englishness. Above all, the English regarded themselves as civilized, whereas they denigrated blacks as savage, dirty, and wicked. These attitudes were reflected in the works of well-known English writers, including Chaucer, Milton, and Shakespeare. Scottish philosopher David Hume maintained that 'There never was a civilized nation of any other complexion than white, not even any individual eminent in action or speculation. No ingenious manufactures amongst them, no arts, no sciences.' The English concluded further that their institutions, especially Parliament and the common law, and a purified Anglican church that had broken with Rome, made them superior to non-Anglo-Saxon peoples. In the middle of this rising prejudice, a Dutch ship captain named Jope sailed into Virginia's Chesapeake Bay in 1619 and swapped twenty 'Negars' for provisions. A fateful moment in American history had arrived a decade after the English founded Jamestown.

More than simple prejudice was involved in enslaving Africans over four centuries. A new consumer society in Europe developed an incurable sweet tooth and a penchant for tobacco that merchants and planters rushed to fulfill. To meet spiraling demand and to keep labor costs low, these modern entrepreneurs developed a novel kind of slavery whose distinguishing characteristics were its racist underpinnings, inexhaustible supply, and hereditary basis. All that mattered was the satisfaction of customers at the lowest possible price and the highest possible profit, not the shocking exploitation of labor. The slave trade itself, which packed Africans in ships like canned sardines, was immensely lucrative, with 100 per cent profits not unknown. Much of the wealth flowed back to mercantile houses, banks, shipping companies, and factories in England – the greatest of the slave-traders – helping to underwrite the Industrial

Revolution. The African kingdoms of Oyo, Dahomey, and Asante also enriched themselves in the slave industry by selling off rival tribes in exchange for glass beads, firearms, cloth, rum, tobacco, and cowrie shells.

When life expectancy in the New World increased in the mid-seventeenth century, buying slaves made more economic sense. African slaves possessed clear advantages over Indians and European indentured servants, including larger supply, resistance to deadly disease, greater farm productivity, and ready identification as slaves. Because labor in the New World was the scarcest yet most indispensable commodity, hereditary enslavement was required, lest slaves convert to Christianity and gain their freedom. The surest way to keep Africans in bondage was to change the law so that the children of slave women (including those fathered by white masters) would be slaves, producing a lucrative cycle. With enslavement came an ideology of racial oppression. Now Africans were inferior because they were slaves and slaves because they were inferior.

The English stripped African slaves of virtually all rights under English common law. Slaves were defined as chattel and were forbidden to speak their native tongue, practice their religion, or name their children. Their very identity as human beings was crushed. They could not move about freely, earn wages, marry whites, carry firearms, resist punishment, testify in court, or congregate in small groups. Teaching slaves to read and write was a crime, lest literacy arouse rebelliousness. In short, slaves were to be nothing more than servile beasts of burden. Free blacks represented a different kind of threat, and they were barred from voting and taxed at higher rates and imprisoned for longer terms than whites. Virginia ordered them to leave the colony within six months and Maryland prohibited their arrival altogether.

During the revolutionary period, American slavery represented a plain conflict between the promise and practice of liberty for all. While the colonists excoriated the British for enslaving them politically, the colonists enslaved Africans physically. During and shortly after the war for independence, northern states, which had few blacks and had little need of them, emancipated their slaves while southern states did not. Thomas Jefferson, the Virginia slaveowner who drafted the Declaration of Independence, called the institution of slavery an 'abominable crime'. But he felt trapped by the system that required him to be responsible for the welfare of his slaves while doubting their ability to succeed in a white man's world. Jefferson was hardly alone in thinking that blacks were hideous, child-like, inarticulate, lascivious, and suited only to manual labor. He concluded that blacks were inassimilable in a society that entrusted republican self-government to a 'natural aristocracy' of white Protestant men who owned substantial property. To avoid a convulsive race war, Jefferson proposed shipping the slaves back to Africa, a prohibitively costly plan. At the Constitutional Convention, the delegates temporarily resolved their differences over slavery by equating each slave with three-fifths of a free person and permitting a ban on slave imports when they were no longer needed.

Racism received a powerful boost in the eighteenth and early nineteenth centuries. European philosophers revived the Aristotelian notion that each human group had its own place, depending on how far it had degenerated from the original creation. This great chain of being hypothesis dovetailed with the typologies that European and American scientists developed to distinguish between animals. French naturalist Comte de Buffon first used the term 'race' to legitimize European claims of human biological superiority. Buffon believed that the white race represented 'the real and natural color of man' and regarded pale-skinned Europeans as close to the Greek physical ideal portrayed in statues. Europeans, in his view, were not only more handsome, but more intelligent and civilized than 'defective' Africans. He attributed the alleged inferiority of Africans to the theory that black women procreated with chimpanzees. Josiah Nott, an Alabama physician with a national reputation in ethnology, argued that blacks had been created separately from whites and that black skulls possessed smaller, inferior brains, which justified black enslavement. To these intellectuals, racial characteristics were distinct, inherited, and immutable.

These racial theories enabled southerners to stop apologizing for their 'peculiar institution' as white northerners and ex-slaves like William Lloyd Garrison, Frederick Douglass, and Henry Highland Garnet attacked it. Such attacks often represented rank hypocrisy, because slavery was unsuited to a region with rocky soil and unnecessary as labor-saving machines were introduced. Northern businesses, such as textile factories, shipping, and insurance, benefited enormously from slavery in the South. Moreover, northerners discriminated against blacks, segregating them in school and prohibiting more of them from settling in their states. Southern defenders of slavery noted that the Bible's Ten Commandments sanctioned slavery and that Jesus never said a word against it. Moreover, slaveholders claimed that all great ancient civilizations required a 'mudsill class' that did the dirty work. Roger Taney, a slaveholding chief justice, tried to end the debate over slavery. In the *Dred Scott* decision of 1857, the US Supreme Court declared that blacks were 'beings of an inferior order, and altogether unfit to associate with the white race'. Blacks, Taney wrote, possessed 'no rights which the white man was bound to respect'.

There the matter stood until Abraham Lincoln waged America's bloodiest war to preserve the Union and, secondarily, to free the slaves. In the end, the Union would be preserved, and the rebel government of the master race lay in ruins. But most whites on both sides could scarcely conceive of equality between the races. Navy secretary Gideon Welles captured the prevailing sentiment: 'Thank God slavery is abolished, but the Negro is not, and never can be, the equal of the White.' For a century, blacks wore their skin color as a badge of inferiority as they remained in the white man's wilderness. It would require an epic civil rights movement to exorcize the nation's original sin – racism.

CHAPTER ONE

JIM CROW SOUTH

For a few years after the Civil War ended in 1865, it looked as if 4 million blacks would enter the mainstream of society. In what amounted to a revolution in black status, the 13th, 14th, and 15th Amendments to the Constitution ended slavery, promised 'equal protection of the laws' to both races, and granted suffrage to black males [*Doc. 1*]. Congress used this authority to enact the nation's first civil rights laws, recognizing blacks as citizens with inviolable rights, prohibiting racial violence, and opening public accommodations and conveyances to all. As a consequence, many former slaves legalized their marriages, moved about without passes, attended school, testified in court, voted and held political office, and decided for whom and how long they wished to work.

To redeem the South from this 'nigger domination', whites terrorized and slaughtered blacks in what was called the Mississippi Plan. Vigilante groups, such as the Ku Klux Klan, castrated, raped, and lynched thousands of black men and women. In 1899, near Atlanta, Georgia, Sam Hose was accused of murdering his employer, Alfred Cranford, and raping Cranford's wife. Two thousand whites took the law into their own hands and disrobed 'this monster in human form', chained him to a tree, cut off his ears, fingers, and genitals, skinned his face, and plunged knives into his body before setting him ablaze. As his eyes bulged from their sockets and his blood sizzled, he cried, 'Oh, my God! Oh, Jesus.' The crowd fought over pieces of his heart, liver, and bones, which were sliced up for prized souvenirs. Although Cranford's widow told investigators that Hose killed her husband in self-defense and had never touched her, a local newspaper defended the lynchers as 'intensely religious, home-loving, and just'. Such sadistic 'Negro barbecues' amused whites and were intended as a grim warning to blacks never to seek equality. In this nightmare world, a black Mississippian recalled that 'to kill a Negro wasn't nothing. It was like killing a chicken or killing a snake. The whites would say, "Niggers jest supposed to die, ain't no damn good anyway – so jest go on an' kill 'em."' Appalled by the frequency of such attacks, writer Mark Twain called America the 'United States of Lyncherdom'.

Once blacks were intimidated, white politicians devised all manner of tricks to keep them from the voting booth. Whites claimed that removing blacks from politics would end electoral corruption and improve race relations as blacks accepted their proper place in society. Southern states imposed poll taxes that were payable in cash months before elections at a time when farmhands were cash poor. In Louisiana, the legislature effectively eliminated blacks from the political process by restricting the franchise to male descendants of grandfathers who could vote right after the Civil War. In South Carolina, officials set up eight ballot boxes – one for each office – and invalidated ballots that semi-literate black voters placed in the wrong box. In addition, the voting rolls were kept lily white by testing a black person's literacy, tossing out improperly completed forms, and, ultimately, just closing the registrar's office for days. These measures reduced black voting in the South to 3 per cent in 1900 and crushed all opposition to the white-controlled Democratic party. South Carolina governor Ben Tillman boasted, 'We have done our best. We have scratched our heads to find out how we could eliminate the last one of them. We stuffed ballot boxes. We shot them. We are not ashamed of it.' The federal government sat idly by as these outrages were perpetrated.

As the North retreated after Reconstruction, the South instituted a rigid caste system called Jim Crow, so named from a minstrel caricature of the 1830s. In the Black Codes, lawmakers barred blacks from attending white schools, marrying whites, testifying in court, having a gun, or owning property. Southern states rewrote their constitutions to separate the races from birth to burial. Signs appeared reading 'white' and 'colored' for drinking fountains, toilets, telephone booths, and bus stations. Each race had its own hospital and prison; theaters consigned blacks to the balcony, which was nicknamed 'the buzzard's roost'; libraries were for whites only. Racial mores permitted whites to call black men 'Boy' or 'Uncle', never 'Mr' or 'Sir'. Blacks were expected to walk in the gutter when whites came along. Except for family cooks, maids, and wet-nurses, not even in death could a black be near a white. Whites could mix with blacks, however. Because white men raped black women and fathered mulatto children – a crime called miscegenation – this color-conscious society defined a person with even one drop of black blood as black and thus forever barred from society's privileges. Incredibly, whites imagined that their black servants and farmhands truly loved them.

Stereotypes reflecting such prejudice proliferated and made black mistreatment seem logical. Racist artists depicted black adults with bulbous lips, bulging eyes, and vacuous smiles and black children eating watermelon and playing with jungle animals. These outlandish images appeared on cereal boxes, in advertisements, and as lawn ornaments. The theater staged popular minstrel shows that ridiculed blacks. In these productions, white men in blackface sang songs, such as 'All Coons Look Alike to Me'. Thomas Dixon demonized black men as crazed rapists of white women in his popular novel

The Clansman, which became the first modern film, *The Birth of a Nation*. The message from this stereotyping was that blacks were subhuman.

For a century, the US Supreme Court sanctioned white supremacy. After the Civil War, the Court invalidated attempts by the federal government to grant basic civil rights to the freedmen. In 1883, the Court robbed the 14th Amendment of much of its meaning when it barred racial discrimination by states, but not by businessmen who ran hotels and restaurants. The time had come, justice Joseph Bradley declared, for blacks to cease being 'the special favorite of the laws'. In the 1896 case of *Plessy* v. *Ferguson*, the Court subverted the meaning of the 14th Amendment still further to devise the 'separate but equal' doctrine that sanctioned segregated public facilities. With the Court's blessing, South Carolina segregated the races step-by-step, beginning with trains (1898) and proceeding to streetcars (1905), restaurants (1906), textile factories (1915), circuses (1917), pool halls (1924), and beaches (1934). Edgar Gardner Murphy, an Episcopal cleric and reformer from Texas, concluded that white supremacists had moved 'from an undiscriminating attack upon the Negro's ballot to a like attack upon his schools, his labor, his life – from the contention that no Negro shall vote to the contentions that no Negro shall learn, that no Negro shall labor, and that no Negro shall live'.

Blacks fiercely resisted this new social order. Tens of thousands escaped to the West, especially Kansas and Oklahoma, where they built homesteads and towns beyond the reach of white supremacy. More commonly, ministers, businessmen, and newspaper editors vigorously protested against violence and discrimination through equal rights leagues, lawsuits, and boycotts. T. Thomas Fortune of the *New York Age* formed the Afro-American League in 1890 to denounce lynchings, unequal schools, separate railroad cars, the leasing of black prisoners, and the exclusion of blacks from juries. Twenty-five southern cities experienced boycotts of the newly segregated streetcars. Blacks also searched for political allies, but the Republicans were too weak, the Democrats too hostile, the Populist third party too opportunistic, and all of them too racist. Given black poverty, illiteracy, and internal squabbling, as well as unified white opposition, such resistance was sporadic and short-lived. Before long, Jim Crow laws seemed unassailable, and many blacks survived by becoming 'good Negroes' known as Sambos, retreating from public life and praying for a better day.

CHAPTER TWO

ORIGINS OF THE MOVEMENT

Blacks were never reconciled to their inferior status and kept searching for the best approach that offered a way out. As stepchildren in American society, blacks alternately pursued assimilation with whites and independence from them. One school of thought was that blacks should accommodate themselves to overwhelming white power. Booker T. Washington, a former Virginia slave and the nation's most powerful black man, declared that agitating for equality was 'the extremist folly' and proposed that blacks accept temporarily their second-class citizenship. As the founder of Alabama's Tuskegee Institute for industrial training, he delivered a controversial speech before the Atlanta Cotton Exposition of 1895, in which he appealed to whites to accept blacks as partners in reviving the South's lagging economy. He thought that once blacks had proven their worth in the marketplace political equality and social integration would follow. With little fanfare, he pressed the black cause through northern philanthropy, patronage appointments, and lawsuits.

Other black leaders dismissed Washington's accommodationism as disastrous. Black patience did nothing to stop lynching, disfranchisement, and Jim Crow. William Monroe Trotter of the *Boston Guardian* called the Wizard of Tuskegee a 'skulking coward'. Ida B. Wells-Barnett, an outspoken journalist from Memphis, Tennessee, chided black leaders who remained silent after lynchings and warned that stopping such atrocities might require all-out race warfare. Washington's most persistent critic was W.E.B. Du Bois, the first black person to earn a Harvard doctorate. In his book *The Souls of Black Folk*, he charged Washington with counseling blacks to accept inferiority to whites. To chart a more militant direction, white and black progressives, including Du Bois and Wells-Barnett, founded what became the largest, most important civil rights organization of the twentieth century, the National Association for the Advancement of Colored People.

After Booker T. Washington died in 1915, gradualism subsided in favor of more forceful approaches to improve black life. Believing that bigotry could be overcome by ceaseless agitation, NAACP leaders W.E.B. Du Bois, James Weldon Johnson, and Walter White publicized the evils of lynching in their journal the *Crisis*, lobbied Congress for protective legislation, encouraged voting, sued in court to desegregate jobs, housing, and public facilities, and denounced European colonialism in Africa. A. Philip Randolph, the editor of a socialist magazine, ridiculed the NAACP's reformist ideology as elitist, condemned the black church as a business, and labeled obsequious black politicians as 'the worst enemies of the Negro race'. At the heart of Randolph's vision was his belief that exploitation was not a racial problem but an economic one. A well-paying job was the first step toward social and political freedom. To that end, he founded the Brotherhood of Sleeping Car Porters, which became the largest black union. Marcus Garvey, a charismatic Jamaican, believed that neither color-blind laws nor unionization would free black people from racism. His solution was black nationalism, in which blacks would control their own businesses and institutions within America. Better still, blacks would abandon efforts to integrate white society and go 'Back to Africa', their ancestral homeland. The unabashed racial pride of his Universal Negro Improvement Association made it the largest mass movement in black history until Garvey was deported for mail fraud.

When World War I broke out, a half million blacks joined the Great Migration in heading to Chicago, Detroit, New York, and other cities in the 'Promised Land'. They were weary of second-class citizenship, frightened by relentless violence, and attracted by higher-paying industrial jobs in the North. The migrants discovered their flight from Dixie was a mixed blessing. With the help of the Urban League, a new social welfare organization, the material well-being of blacks improved in the industrial cities, where they adopted a more cosmopolitan identity. Although blacks could vote for the first time and send their children to school for the entire year, they still held poor jobs and lived in rundown housing in segregated neighborhoods. Competition for jobs tightened when the veterans returned from war. Some blacks tried to become white, through expensive, painful processes of lightening their skin and straightening their hair. Others lashed back against whites in deadly riots that broke out throughout the Midwest in the Red Summer of 1919. The 'New Negro' would fight back when violence came his way.

When the Great Depression afflicted the nation in the 1930s, black America was flat on its back. Half of urban blacks had no jobs at all, and rural blacks lost money with every cotton harvest. Whites suddenly competed for 'Negro jobs' in foundries, garbage collection, and domestic service, and murdered black firemen and railroad workers who did not step aside. When president Herbert Hoover seemed paralyzed by the emergency, he was soundly defeated for reelection. His Democratic successor, Franklin D. Roosevelt, helped blacks in important ways. FDR developed relief programs for all Americans, relied on a black cabinet of advisers, and invited opera singer Marian Anderson to sing on federal property when she could not appear in a private concert hall. Under his leadership, the government hired many blacks for construction jobs, built the first subsidized housing, and taught black farmers how to read and how to diversify their crops. But his New Deal programs discriminated against blacks, and he did not lift a finger to outlaw lynching, the poll tax, or segregated neighborhoods. Although some blacks initially concluded that the 'new deal' was really a 'raw deal', most deserted Hoover's 'do-nothing' Republican party – the party of emancipation – and moved permanently to the Democrats.

In this hour of desperation, other blacks, including singer Paul Robeson, turned to the Socialist and Communist parties and the Southern Tenant Farmers' Union. These radical groups repudiated racial prejudice and helped black laborers, farmers, renters, and prisoners, including the hapless Scottsboro boys, wrongly convicted of raping white women. Blacks of all political persuasions celebrated when heavyweight boxer Joe Louis used his fists to lay low his white opponents, an implicit victory over segregation itself.

Because the president would not address civil rights directly, blacks used their considerable economic clout to force changes. Virginia Union University economics professor Gordon Hancock proposed a 'buy black' strategy in which blacks would spend 'black dollars' at black-owned businesses in order to recirculate that same dollar several times within the black community. Merchants, clerics, and teachers cooperated in this 'double-duty dollar' campaign. The flip side of this strategy was to boycott white stores in black districts that refused to hire black employees or else employed them only in menial positions. The *Chicago Whip*, a militant newspaper, promoted a 'Don't Buy Where You Can't Work' campaign against retail stores in the Windy City. The powerful 'Jobs for Negroes' idea spread quickly to thirty-five cities. In Harlem, Adam Clayton Powell, Jr., the charismatic minister of the Abyssinian Baptist Church, picketed and boycotted the hospital, department stores, utility companies, colleges, theaters, and mass transit so that black workers would be hired as something more than janitors, porters, and elevator operators. Some white businesses relented, especially the bus company, which established the nation's first affirmative action hiring plan for blacks.

After the outbreak of World War II, the forces of industrialization and urbanization created conditions from which the civil rights movement climaxed. A. Philip Randolph, America's top black union leader, pleaded with Washington officials to desegregate the military and to hire blacks in defense plants. When his plea went unanswered, Randolph threatened an embarrassing march on the nation's capital. FDR was furious at this war of nerves, but in exchange for canceling the march, he issued Executive Order 8802, which established the Fair Employment Practice Committee to prevent job discrimination in war mobilization. It was the most beneficial presidential directive for blacks since the Emancipation Proclamation. Two million black workers found jobs in munitions factories, giving them greater economic independence and the opportunity to organize politically. A million more served in the military, though it remained segregated. Randolph's approach – the all-black March on Washington Movement – showed that pressuring the president with a dramatic event could pay big dividends.

At the same time, a small group of young people living in Chicago was determined to confront racism directly but peacefully. As members of the Fellowship of Reconciliation, an interracial Christian pacifist group, James Farmer, George Houser, Homer Jack, and Bernice Fisher took inspiration from Indian nationalist leader Mohandas Gandhi, a Hindu who battled British colonial rule with nonviolent resistance (*satyagraha*), and from unions that launched sit-down strikes to win company concessions. Farmer, a black graduate of Howard University, asked FOR to endorse a relentless campaign of civil disobedience against racism, but its white officers demurred, leading the students to found the Congress of Racial Equality in 1942. With the South still too dangerous to reform, CORE employed the sit-in tactic in segregated restaurants and movie theaters in major northern cities. In the midst of all-out war, few noticed this new organization.

As World War II deepened, most blacks subscribed to the 'Double V' campaign, which stood for victory over fascism abroad and discrimination at home. In his influential 1944 book, *An American Dilemma*, Swedish economist Gunnar Myrdal underscored the idea that racism ran against the values that the nation was defending with its blood. Gains at home came uneasily. As blacks broke through the job ghetto, white strikers shut down factories and shipyards. When blacks moved into white neighborhoods, racial violence broke out in 47 cities in one year alone. Such racism did not deter black veterans, who returned to the South with a new spirit. A former army corporal from Alabama declared, 'I spent four years in the army to free a bunch of Dutchmen and Frenchmen, and I'm hanged if I'm going to let the Alabama version of the Germans kick me around when I get home. No sirree-bob! I went into the Army a nigger; I'm comin' out a *man*.'

Some white southern reformers, writers, and judges took courageous stands for civil rights. After race riots erupted following World War I, Will Alexander, a Methodist minister, founded the Commission on Interracial Cooperation, the South's first biracial reform group. Although Alexander did not challenge Jim Crow directly, he supported black voting rights, fair housing, and equal job opportunity. A CIC branch called the Association of Southern Women for the Prevention of Lynching launched petition drives, letter-writing campaigns, and conferences against racial murder. In 1944, CIC was succeeded by the Southern Regional Council, an organization of clergy and professionals that worked for the gradual elimination of segregation. Similarly, the Southern Conference for Human Welfare, a group of New Deal liberals, attacked poverty, opposed the poll tax, and promoted voter registration. When SCHW succumbed to McCarthyite charges of communist control, its work was carried on by the Southern Conference Educational Fund. Southern writers who attacked racism included sociologist Howard Odum, journalist Wilbur Cash, and Ralph McGill, editor of the *Atlanta Constitution*. Lillian Smith of Georgia probed the causes and costs of racism in *Strange Fruit*, a best-selling novel about an interracial love affair. When federal judge J. Waties Waring of South Carolina ruled against unequal teacher salaries, white primaries, and school segregation, he was hounded out of the state that his aristocratic family had lived in for eight generations. Most white southerners were either too afraid or unconcerned to join these brave few.

After World War II, blacks who moved North for defense jobs could no longer be ignored politically. Roosevelt's successor, Harry Truman, took unprecedented steps for racial equality. He was prodded by the cold-blooded murder of fifty blacks, the cold war competition for Africa and Asia, and signs that blacks might bolt from the Democratic party. In 1947, Truman's Committee on Civil Rights published a report titled *To Secure These Rights*, which recommended swift federal action to end lynching, segregation, and barriers to voting. Although most Americans opposed the report, an unrepent-ant Truman barred segregation in the military, ordered the promotion of more black officers, and prohibited job discrimination throughout the federal govern-ment. His Justice department supported the NAACP in court cases against segregated housing and education. Truman's bold strategy of embracing black voters paid off with the most unexpected electoral victory in American history. After the election, however, Truman's Fair Deal was stymied by a Republican Congress, and the president concentrated, not on civil rights, but on com-munism at home and abroad. In 1950, A. Philip Randolph helped organize the Leadership Conference on Civil Rights to implement the report that Truman disregarded.

While the federal government began to address racial injustice, a few areas of society, especially the entertainment industry, made more rapid progress after World War II. The entire nation followed the amazing exploits of Jackie Robinson, who integrated major-league baseball in 1947 when he joined the Brooklyn Dodgers. Robinson's breakthrough in America's pastime opened the door for blacks to enter professional football and basketball. At the same time, black musicians became widely popular, particularly jazz performers, such as pianist Thelonius Monk, trumpeter Dizzy Gillespie, and saxophonist Charlie Parker who ushered in 'bebop' music. Such 'race' music greatly appealed to white teenagers through Elvis Presley and other white rock 'n' roll singers. Before long, black performers Chuck Berry, Bo Diddley, and Little Richard developed their own following on white radio stations. As blacks became more visible to whites, they began to seem more deserving of their constitu-tional rights.

By mid-century, black southerners were on the cusp of achieving racial justice, but the task of defeating what amounted to a police state was herculean. To make America live up to its promises of equality and justice for all, the civil rights movement would have to develop black consciousness, mobilize black churches and colleges, enlist northern white opinion, divide the white southern elite, capture the national Democratic party, and win over the Supreme Court, the White House, and Congress. Ultimately, justice could be achieved only when urban blacks applied enough pressure to force the federal government to impose change from above. Such pressure would be developed by trial-and-error and demand steep sacrifices over many years. One of the early martyrs was schoolteacher Harry Moore, who was blown to bits by the Klan in 1951 as he slept. As Florida's NAACP executive director, Moore had filed anti-discrimination lawsuits, helped register an astounding 116,000 black voters, and demanded state investigations of police violence.

This Second Reconstruction was made possible by a remarkably changed black community. Racial pride received a boost from Carter G. Woodson, whose *Journal of Negro History* and Negro History Week trumpeted the unrecognized contributions that blacks had made in American history. Other scholars, including E. Franklin Frazier, Charles Johnson, and Ralph Bunche, knocked the intellectual underpinnings from segregation. As blacks migrated in large numbers from plantations to the New South's industrial cities, where segregation was overt and onerous, the region's caste system was questioned as never before. Boll weevils that destroyed the cotton crop pushed millions more to northern cities, where they found higher-paying jobs, joined the NAACP, and constituted a significant voting bloc. They were helped along by color-blind industrial unions, such as the United Automobile Workers and Congress of Industrial Organizations. Northern black publications, especially the *Chicago Defender*, the *Pittsburgh Courier*, *Jet*, and *Ebony*, reached the South, carrying bolder stories about injustice than timid local newspapers. Black southerners attended college in record numbers because of the GI Bill and scholarships from the United Negro College Fund, along with the postwar boom that doubled black income. A new crop of educated and articulate leaders emerged, notably Martin Luther King, Jr. Meanwhile, the NAACP won milestone legal victories in desegregating juries, housing, interstate transportation, and higher education, as well as removing impediments to black voting, especially the white primary in *Smith* v. *Allwright* (1944). The number of black voters increased to 1 million, a fourfold increase in a decade.

Other developments discredited racism in the eyes of many whites. The Nazi holocaust of innocents made the very idea of racism despicable. Scientists and social scientists demonstrated that educational achievement was directly related to one's environment, not to cranial capacity or genetic predisposition. Spurred by a growing revulsion against racism, progressive organizations, such as the American Civil Liberties Union, Americans for Democratic Action, American Jewish Congress, and National Catholic Welfare Conference, formed coalitions with civil rights groups to fight discrimination. In World War II, early Japanese victories against the British and French empires shattered the assumption of white superiority. After the war, the United States and Soviet Union competed for the allegiance of darker-skinned peoples in the Third World, making civil rights in America a necessity. The invention of television transformed domestic racial confrontations into a vivid morality play that was beamed into middle-class homes north of Dixie. In Dixie itself, the white elite divided as city businessmen came to realize that racism hurt their bottom line. Northern businesses that moved South to take advantage of low taxes and cheap labor reached the same conclusion – racism was bad for business. The affluent postwar society spawned a reaction that pulled many idealistic young people to a cause larger than themselves. All of these factors produced a change in leadership on the federal level, essential to dismantling the monstrous edifice of Jim Crow.

CHAPTER THREE

THE *BROWN* DECISION

Civil rights attorney Thurgood Marshall often asked black youngsters in the 1940s what they wanted to do when they grew up. When they answered that their ambitions were to become butlers, postmen, or maids, Marshall realized that these children were already defeated psychologically. Marshall blamed segregation for this crippling sense of insecurity and vowed to strike it down in the seventeen states that operated a biracial school system. To do so, he would have to use the white man's law to win justice in the white man's court.

Marshall learned the law at Howard University in Washington, DC, the capstone of black education. He knew firsthand how racism stymied black ambitions because he was denied admission to the University of Maryland. At Howard, he received his legal training from Charles Houston, a brilliant Harvard law graduate and the NAACP's chief legal counsel, and from Houston's equally brilliant cousin, William Hastie. Turning Howard Law from an unaccredited night school into a civil rights laboratory, Houston taught his protégés to become social engineers to abolish segregation.

Combining the skills of a shrewd legal strategist, community organizer, and raconteur, the tenacious Marshall scoured the South looking for suitable clients. Working for the NAACP's Legal Defense and Education Fund, Inc. (the 'Inc. Fund'), Marshall faced a daunting task, for the US Supreme Court had long been hostile to blacks. Marshall and his superb legal team – William Hastie, Robert Carter, Constance Baker Motley, Jack Greenberg, and Frank Williams – chipped away at the wall of segregation from the top down, starting with graduate schools, 'the soft underbelly' of Jim Crow. This was a key strategy because judges were familiar with what constituted a good law school. In addition, the NAACP attorneys demanded the equalization of teacher salaries and school facilities, rather than desegregation itself. By attacking segregation indirectly, Marshall hoped to forestall white fury and to make equalization too expensive. Angry whites stalked Marshall anyway. As he entered southern towns, he needed around-the-clock bodyguards and a different location to sleep in every night. Defying death threats, Marshall whittled away at Jim Crow through key cases in education, housing, transportation, and voting, earning him the sobriquet, 'Mr Civil Rights'.

Marshall's crowning achievement came in the momentous case of *Brown* v. *Board of Education*. First argued in December 1952, the case consisted of five lawsuits brought by black parents from across the country. These lawsuits exposed the vast inequities between white and black schools. In Topeka, Kansas, 8-year-old Linda Brown lived near the all-white Sumner Elementary School, but each morning she crossed a dangerous railroad yard to a dilapidated bus that carried her a mile away to a black school. Her father, a welder named Oliver Brown, sued to end the segregated school system, giving his name to the famous case. In Clarendon county, South Carolina, three-quarters of the students were black, but the all-white school board spent 60 per cent of its budget on whites. Black children walked long distances to school while whites rode new buses. When parents complained, the board chairman replied gruffly: 'We ain't got no money to buy a bus for your nigger children.' Once at school, black students crowded together in shanties without flush toilets, electricity, desks, or blackboards. Joseph Delaine, a local black pastor and schoolteacher, sued the school board, only to lose his teaching job and have his home and church burned to the ground. In the remote county of Prince Edward, Virginia, a fiery 16-year-old named Barbara Johns took matters into her own hands. She led hundreds of riled-up students on a two-week strike against broken-down toilets, classes in tar-paper shacks, and the absence of lockers, microscopes, a gym, a cafeteria, and an infirmary.

Marshall had to do more than show that black schools were substandard because Clarendon county finally equalized black teacher salaries, provided bus transportation for black children, and signed a contract for an expensive, new black high school, all to sustain segregation legally. Marshall therefore addressed the central issue – segregation itself. Calling on experts in social science and education, he argued that black children possessed the same ability as whites, but felt inferior in segregated schools, making learning nearly impossible. The most controversial testimony came from psychologists Kenneth and Mamie Clark, whose pioneering but flawed studies reported that most black children preferred white dolls over black ones, an apparent sign of black self-hate. One black child smiled when asked whom the black doll resembled: 'That's a nigger. I'm a nigger.' In his closing argument, Marshall challenged the Court to strike down school segregation laws and, by implication, all Jim Crow laws. He contended that the only way that segregation could be upheld would be 'to find that for some reason Negroes are inferior to all other human beings'. Four of the nine justices Marshall challenged came from states with Jim Crow schools. One justice had upheld white primaries, and two others fretted about white southern reaction. Chief justice Fred Vinson of Kentucky hoped that southern states would follow Clarendon county's lead in improving black schools in order to block integration.

The deliberations over *Brown* dragged on into the terms of a new president and chief justice. To succeed Harry Truman, Americans chose World War II hero Dwight Eisenhower, the first Republican president in a generation. In his first year, Eisenhower moved quietly against racism in several areas. Among his significant actions, he banned discrimination in federal employment and ended segregation in the armed forces and the nation's capital. His greatest contribution to civil rights was unintended. When chief justice Vinson died before *Brown* was re-argued, Eisenhower replaced him with California governor Earl Warren, to whom the president owed a political debt. Eisenhower believed that Warren was a 'statesman' with 'middle-of-the-road views'. As the Court reconsidered school segregation, the president was deeply concerned that the South would shut down its public schools if blacks were admitted, as several governors threatened. Moreover, having spent his entire life with whites, Eisenhower tried to influence Warren by defending white southerners, some of whom he knew from golfing and hunting outings. They only wanted to keep 'their sweet little girls' from sitting next to 'some big overgrown Negroes', the president remarked at a White House dinner. An outraged Warren recognized that a historic moment was at hand and so ignored the meddling Eisenhower to reverse *Plessy*.

On 17 May 1954, after months of cajoling his feuding colleagues, Warren calmly read the Court's ruling against segregated public schools. The unanimous opinion was short, unemotional, and non-accusatory. Drawing upon the 14th Amendment and studies showing segregation's damaging effects, Warren declared that legally enforced 'separate educational facilities are inherently unequal' [*Doc. 2*]. With most white southerners opposed to school desegregation, the Court let a year pass before requiring the compliance of local school systems with 'all deliberate speed'. Without an army of its own, the Warren Court felt it could not move too far ahead of the American people in pushing the races together. This ambiguous directive, known as *Brown II*, avoided a timetable and allowed district courts to decide how local desegregation should proceed. It was the first time that the Supreme Court deferred implementing a constitutional right.

The Court's stunning decision gave most blacks a jolt of confidence. A 16-year-old black girl burst into tears when her teacher broke the news. 'We went on studying history,' she remembered, 'but things weren't the same, and will never be the same again.' The *Chicago Defender* called the *Brown* ruling 'more important to our democracy than the atom bomb or the hydrogen bomb'. Thurgood Marshall predicted confidently that all forms of segregation would vanish by 1963, the centennial of Lincoln's Emancipation Proclamation. The South, after all, had not erupted in violence after earlier desegregation decisions involving interstate commerce, the all-white primary, and higher education. Marshall's prediction turned out to be wildly optimistic.

Many areas outside the deep South accepted *Brown* with the encouragement of white moderates. Three influential southern newspaper editors – Ralph McGill of the *Atlanta Constitution*, Hodding Carter of the *Greenville Delta Democrat-Times*, and Jonathan Daniels of the *Raleigh News and Observer* – insisted that the decision be obeyed. Southern church organizations, including the Methodists, Presbyterians, and Episcopalians, urged compliance with the ruling. Businessmen hoped the new social order would mean greater black buying power. Initial white acceptance of desegregation meant that 70 per cent of school districts in the border states of Delaware, Kentucky, Maryland, Missouri, Oklahoma, and West Virginia complied with *Brown* in a single year. In states where segregation was decided on the local level – Arizona, Kansas, New Mexico, and Wyoming – the schools integrated their classrooms quickly and peacefully.

Although attorney general Herbert Brownell strongly supported *Brown*, Eisenhower pledged only to enforce it, as the Constitution required. Privately, the president fumed that the decision was a serious mistake. He contended that *Brown* would '*set back* progress in the South *at least fifteen years*. . . . Feelings run deep on this, especially where children are involved. . . . And the fellow who tries to tell me that you can do these things by *force* is just plain *nuts*.' Eisenhower thought that school desegregation was inevitable, but recommended that it occur very gradually, starting at the top of the educational ladder. With his eye on the 1956 election, Eisenhower reached out to white southerners who traditionally voted Democratic. He denounced 'extremists on both sides' and declared that 'you cannot change people's hearts merely by laws'.

Eisenhower's neutrality on the day's leading moral issue and the Court's indefinite timetable on desegregation opened the door to the greatest defiance of the federal government since the Civil War. With many southern voices in the church, education, the press, and the bar keeping mum, white supremacists defended the 'southern way of life' against integration and miscegenation. They intended nothing less than to make the federal government back down through sheer stubbornness. Georgia governor Herman Talmadge summarily refused compliance with *Brown*, recalling his state's successful defiance of chief justice John Marshall's 1832 decision over Cherokee land claims. Talmadge also signed a bill redesigning the state flag to include the Confederacy's Stars and Bars. South Carolina governor James Byrnes, once a Supreme Court justice, accused his former colleagues of playing into communist hands and destroying southern civilization. In a vitriolic, widely disseminated speech, circuit court judge Tom Brady of Mississippi compared blacks to chimpanzees who would never learn that a 'cockroach is not a delicacy', much less how to become competent citizens. To protect 'blue-eyed, golden-haired little girls', Brady called for a separate territory for blacks, the election of Supreme Court justices, and the abolition of public schools. Alluding to the Civil War, Brady reminded northern whites that 'We have, through our forefathers, died before for our sacred principles. We can, if necessary, die again.'

Denouncing *Brown* as judge-made law, US senator Harry Byrd, Sr., and newspaper editor James J. Kilpatrick of Virginia called for 'massive resistance', which resurrected the antebellum doctrines of states' rights and interposition against federal interference. Such anger was encapsulated in the 'Declaration of Constitutional Principles' that was proposed and drafted by senators Strom Thurmond of South Carolina and Sam Ervin of North Carolina. This Southern Manifesto, which 101 southern members of Congress signed in March 1956, condemned the *Brown* decision and pledged to reverse it [*Doc. 3*]. In the Senate, only three southerners with presidential ambitions – Lyndon Johnson of Texas and Estes Kefauver and Albert Gore, Sr., of Tennessee – did not join this declaration of war against the Court.

To keep blacks out of all-white public schools, southern state legislatures declared *Brown* 'null and void'. Across the South, hundreds of laws and resolutions cut off state aid to desegregated schools, revoked the licenses of teachers in mixed classrooms, repealed compulsory attendance laws, empowered governors to close the schools, and provided tuition grants to white children who attended all-white private schools. New 'school choice' programs maintained segregation legally because blacks who applied to white schools were invariably dismissed from their jobs or evicted from their homes. The most effective device to resist desegregation was the pupil placement law. Ostensibly race-neutral, white school boards determined that black children's behavior and academic background were best suited to black schools. In the most extreme case of massive resistance, Prince Edward county, Virginia, shut down its schools for four years to prevent what governor J. Lindsay Almond, Jr., described as the 'livid stench of sadism, sex, immorality, and juvenile pregnancy infesting the mixed schools of the District of Columbia'.

Many politicians went after the NAACP, which initiated the *Brown* suit. If the NAACP could be destroyed, the argument ran, white supremacy could be maintained. Following Virginia's lead, several state legislatures required the NAACP to relinquish its membership lists or face large fines. State agencies spied on the NAACP, falsely imprisoned 'race-mixers', fixed juries, manipulated the media, and bribed 'Uncle Toms' to sell out black activists. The never-ending harassment cost the NAACP 246 branches and 48,000 members in the South. In many communities, the NAACP was supplanted by the black church, with its charismatic leadership and unequalled army of followers, meeting spaces, organizational skills, and fund-raising ability.

Encouraged by their leaders, angry white southerners joined segregationist groups and pasted defiant bumper stickers on their automobiles that read, 'Hell, No, I Ain't Forgettin!' The Ku Klux Klan was reincarnated, attracting 50,000 poor white farmers, mechanics, steel mill workers, loggers, and railroad men. One klansman explained his group's continuing mission: 'We are gonna stay white, we are going to keep the nigger black, with the help of our Lord and Savior, Jesus Christ.' More mainstream racists formed a new group, the White Citizens' Council, which first appeared in Indianola, Mississippi, in July 1954. Led by plantation manager Robert 'Tut' Patterson, businessman William Simmons, and US senator James Eastland, the councils aimed at driving all remaining blacks out of the state in a decade. This objective was popular among whites, and five hundred branches with 250,000 members spread across the South. Ostensibly, the councils shunned violence, thereby attracting a better class of bigots, including planters, businessmen, professionals, and politicians who wore suits, rather than sheets. The councils and similar groups, such as the Defenders of State Sovereignty and Individual Liberties and the National Association for the Advancement of White People, appeared respectable by forswearing violence, but Thurgood Marshall mocked them as nothing more than 'Uptown Klans'.

To keep the races apart, the Citizens' Councils retaliated against 'uppity' blacks and white moderates. One newspaper advertisement against black activists warned: 'Not the lash, not the rope, we'll starve them out.' Blacks who belonged to the NAACP or who registered to vote were evicted from their homes. When fifty-three black farmers in the Mississippi delta signed a petition to integrate the schools, the Citizens' Council ran a newspaper advertisement listing the farmers' names, addresses, and telephone numbers. The farmers lost their jobs and were denied credit for seeds and machinery. Ultimately, all the signatories erased their names from the petition or left the county. Such coercion reduced the number of black voters in Mississippi by two-thirds. Through economic reprisals, newspaper insults, ostracism by friends, and garbage dumped on front lawns, the councils also silenced white merchants, newspaper owners, ministers, and teachers who tolerated desegregation. National businesses that acted 'improperly' in the South, including Philip Morris and Ford Motor, were subjected to economic blackmail.

When reprisals failed, vigilantes used deadly violence to force blacks back into line. Mississippi witnessed at least seven gruesome murders during 1955. In Belzoni, white intimidation reduced the number of black voter registrants from one hundred to three. One of the three – the Reverend George Lee – died in his car, which was ruled an accident. After an examination of the body revealed shotgun pellets in Lee's mouth, the sheriff theorized that 'maybe they're fillings from his teeth'. Gus Courts, an NAACP organizer, ignored death threats and steep rent increases on his grocery store to keep his name on the voting roll, only to be felled by two shotgun blasts. He survived somehow and fled the state. The third registrant was Lee's widow, and she steered clear of the polling booth. In Brookhaven, Lamar Smith, a 63-year-old farmer who was teaching blacks how to vote by absentee ballot, was shot dead in broad daylight on the courthouse lawn in front of thirty witnesses. Such assaults went unreported by the national press corps, which viewed racial violence in the South as routine. Although no one was charged with these crimes, a new spirit was emerging, as local blacks armed themselves to the teeth, attended the funerals in large numbers, and boycotted merchants suspected of being citizen councilors.

It would take the brutal murder of a 14-year-old Chicagoan named Emmett (Bo) Till to expose the evil of lynching and spur the nascent civil rights movement. Before putting her cocky, chubby son on a bus to visit relatives in Money, Mississippi, Emmett's mother gave him a stern warning: 'Be careful. If you have to get down on your knees and bow when a white person goes past, do it willingly.' Emmett forgot all about the warning when local boys double-dared him to proposition Carolyn Bryant, a 21-year-old beauty queen and cashier in her husband's grocery store. Accounts differ as to what Emmett did. His cousin recalled that Emmett smart-mouthed Bryant by saying 'bye, baby' upon leaving, but Bryant insisted that Till grabbed her wrist, spoke lewdly, and wolf-whistled at her.

Enraged at such impertinence, Carolyn's husband Roy and his half-brother John Milam seized the youngster in the middle of the night, forced him to strip naked, and gave him one last chance to grovel to a white man: 'You still as good as I am?' Milam asked. When Emmett said he was, Milam blew his brains out with a .45 caliber Colt revolver and dumped his body in the Tallahatchie river with a heavy fan barb-wired around his neck. After Milam pocketed $4,000 in blood money from a reporter, he divulged his murderous motive: 'When a nigger even gets close to mentioning sex with a white woman, he's tired o' livin'. . . . "Chicago boy," I said. "I'm tired of 'em sending your kind down here to stir up trouble. Goddam you, I'm going to make an example of you – just so everybody can know how me and my folks stand."'

Emmett's mother shipped his battered corpse to Chicago and kept the casket opened during the funeral so that the entire world could see 'what they did to my boy'. Emmett's grisly face repulsed thousands of blacks who filed by the body and many more in a *Jet* magazine photograph. NAACP chief Roy Wilkins summed up the senseless murder for an angry crowd in Harlem: 'Mississippi has decided to maintain white supremacy by murdering children. The killer of the boy felt free to lynch because there is in the entire state no restraining influence of decency, not in the state capital, among the daily newspapers, the clergy, not among any segment of the so-called lettered citizens.' Mississippi teenager Anne Moody recalled that she had always known 'the fear of hunger, hell, and the Devil. But now there was a new fear known to me – the fear of being killed just because I was black.' Along with the black press, young, white southern reporters from northern newspapers helped make Emmett's murder a wake-up call in the civil rights era. Having fought against Nazi anti-Semitism during World War II, they were determined to use the Till case to end the grip that racial prejudice had on the mind of the white South.

For the first time, white men were charged with murdering a black man in Mississippi. The trial was a sham, however, because there was no investigation. Emmett's great-uncle, a 64-year-old sharecropper named Moses 'Preacher' Wright, fingered the abductors in a tense courtroom, but the sheriff speculated that Emmett was alive and well in Detroit. In his summation, the defense attorney expressed well-founded confidence that the all-white jury would close ranks with the accused: 'I'm sure every last Anglo-Saxon one of you has the courage to free these men.' The jury dismissed the charges after an hour of drinking soda pop. Immediately after the trial, the defendants lit victory cigars, kissed their wives, and mugged for the cameras. Angry blacks carried guns, joined the local NAACP, and boycotted the Bryant store until it folded, but black fury could not stop more lynchings. Fearing for his life, Wright fled to Chicago.

The racial onslaught largely intimidated the black community and paralyzed white moderates and liberals who either fell silent or beseeched blacks to return to their place. Many southern towns surrendered to mob violence in excluding blacks from public education. Far from cracking down on such lawlessness, many local officials either winked at or aided it directly. When Autherine Lucy enrolled at the University of Alabama in February 1956, a mob waving Confederate flags pelted 'the nigger whore' with rotten eggs and shouted 'kill her, kill her'. University officials expelled Lucy after she blamed them for not keeping order. When black children entered white schools in Clinton, Tennessee, and Clay and Sturgis, Kentucky, mobs calling for 'nigger blood' retreated only when confronted with machine guns, bayonets, and tanks. A bomb destroyed a new elementary school in Nashville, Tennessee, which had one black student out of four hundred. In Mansfield, Texas, a mob hung a black dummy above the school entrance and waved placards that read '2$ A DOZEN FOR NIGGER EARS.' Governor Al Shivers sent the Texas Rangers to keep blacks from enrolling in the white high school. Though such actions clearly violated *Brown*, the White House refused to act. A disgusted Roy Wilkins concluded that 'President Eisenhower was a fine general and a good, decent man, but if he had fought World War II the way he fought for civil rights, we would all be speaking German today.'

In Louisiana, governor Jimmy Davis vowed to go to jail before black children entered white schools in New Orleans. Nevertheless, in November 1960, 6-year-old Ruby Bridges was escorted to the William Frantz Elementary School by armed US marshals. As she ascended the school's steps, housewives and teenagers chanted and spat at her, shook their fists, threw eggs, and waved a baby-sized coffin containing a black doll. 'You wanna be white?' one woman screamed at Ruby. 'We'll make you white! We're gonna throw acid in your face!' Angry parents scurried into the building to withdraw their children. When the other teachers refused to teach Ruby, Barbara Henry, a young white teacher from Boston, made school fun for her only pupil. To force Ruby to quit, her father, who had saved a white soldier's life in Korea, was fired from his job, and her grandparents were forced off the land that they had share-cropped for twenty-five years. Eventually, some parents decided that education mattered more than segregation, and their children returned one-by-one to other classrooms. The next year, Ruby entered a fully desegregated class, but her first-grade teacher had been dismissed.

The Ruby Bridges story was the exception. Seven years after the Supreme Court ordered the desegregation of public schools, not a single black student sat next to a white one in Alabama, Georgia, Mississippi, and South Carolina. Less than one-tenth of 1 per cent of students in Florida, Louisiana, North Carolina, and Virginia attended desegregated schools. Arkansas and Tennessee had less than 1 per cent. At this rate, it would take the South 1,288 years to desegregate. In 1964, the Supreme Court finally acted. It canceled the decade-old order for 'all deliberate speed' and insisted that segregated school systems be merged 'forthwith'.

Some scholars have downplayed the importance of the *Brown* decision. The civil rights movement, critics point out, began much earlier, with NAACP lawyers winning important legal victories for twenty years before *Brown*. Moreover, the ruling sidestepped fundamental questions of school financing, which seemed more closely related to student performance than desegregation. The decision also did not touch de facto segregation, which became ever more pronounced in the North as black southerners migrated above the Mason-Dixon line. In fact, the mandate for desegregated schools oftentimes produced the opposite effect as whites fled to suburbia, leaving behind poorly funded, resegregated city schools. Nor did the decision declare that state-sponsored racism was illegal in all areas of American life, such as voting, housing, and interracial marriage.

Its shortcomings aside, *Brown* contributed mightily to the civil rights movement. It not only ended legal segregation, it deprived segregation of its moral validity. Most important, *Brown* meant that blacks would no longer wait for justice from the courts; they would demand it themselves, now that the law was on their side. The crucial questions remaining were whether and to what extent the federal government would enforce *Brown*, and those answers were not long in coming.

CHAPTER FOUR

LITTLE ROCK CRISIS

Little Rock, the capital of Arkansas, seemed an unlikely place for the gravest constitutional crisis since the Civil War. It was a New South community of 107,000 – a quarter black – in which both races lived next to each other with few incidents. Pressed by the local NAACP and professor Georg Iggers, a Jewish refugee from Nazi Germany, the city desegregated its library, parks, zoo, buses, hospitals, juries, and police force with little resistance. Harry Ashmore's *Arkansas Gazette*, one of the region's most respected newspapers, endorsed these integration initiatives. Still, there were limits to desegregation because the city's swimming pool, hotels, theaters, restaurants, drinking fountains, and toilets remained racially divided throughout the 1950s.

Little Rock's schools were slated for desegregation early on. A week after *Brown* was decided in May 1954, superintendent Virgil Blossom drafted plans for gradual desegregation, beginning with the elite Central High School. Blossom hoped that the governorship could be his if he handled the South's most difficult problem smoothly. His plan called for spending more money on black schools to siphon off demands for integration. Nearly all blacks would attend a brand-new $1 million Horace Mann High School on the east side while the children of community leaders could escape desegregation by attending the brand-new Hall High School in the growing suburbs to the west. One school board member remarked candidly that 'the plan was developed to provide as little integration as possible for as long as possible legally'.

Although only token blacks would be involved in school desegregation, the Blossom Plan was criticized by segregationists. Erving Brown, president of the Capital Citizens' Council, dismissed the plan as altogether unnecessary: 'The Negroes have ample and fine schools here, and there is no need for this problem except to satisfy the aims of a few white and Negro revolutionaries.' When blue-collar workers and fundamentalist pastors worried about the social consequences of school desegregation, the school board offered reassurances that there would not be 'love scenes in class plays featuring students of differ-ent races'. Such reassurances did not mollify white parents, who pressured the board to retreat. With the board dragging its feet, NAACP attorneys Wiley Branton and Thurgood Marshall sued to force immediate school desegregation. But the Eighth US Circuit Court of Appeals ruled that the Little Rock plan complied with *Brown*'s nebulous directive of 'all deliberate speed'.

The Blossom Plan delayed desegregation until September 1957 and sharply limited the number of black students. Seventy-five of the 517 black students who lived in the district sought admission to Central High. The selection process for 'good Negroes' winnowed the list to twenty-five, based on the intelligence, character, and health of the applicants. As the desegregation date loomed, the school board telephoned parents to pare the list still further: 'Your daughter has a magnificent voice . . . but if she goes over to the white school, and being new, she could get lost in the shuffle and won't get a chance to sing.' Several students took the hint and remained at the black high school. Those who pressed ahead – Minnijean Brown, Elizabeth Eckford, Ernest Green, Thelma Mothershed, Melba Patillo, Gloria Ray, Terrence Roberts, Jefferson Thomas, and Carlotta Walls – became known as the Little Rock Nine. Coming from middle-class families, they wanted to go to the best high school available – the all-white Central High.

This modest plan was undone by governor Orval Faubus. Raised in poverty by a father who condemned prejudice, Faubus appointed more blacks to state positions than any predecessor, integrated the state's colleges, and opposed lynching and the poll tax. After the *Brown* decision, however, Faubus faced the same problem that other bottom-feeding southern politicians faced – how to win reelection when white public opinion ran overwhelmingly against desegregation. He had seen the entire Arkansas congressional delegation run for cover by signing the Southern Manifesto, which lambasted the *Brown* decision. Faubus's task was made more difficult when several small Arkansas public schools admitted blacks. Compounding his troubles, Faubus had increased taxes and utility rates and was violating tradition in seeking a third term.

In the fall campaign of 1956, Jim Johnson, a fire-eating segregationist who was state director of the Citizens' Council, tarred Faubus as a communist traitor who let the 'ignorant nigger' demand 'integration in the white bedroom'. Fearing he would be destroyed politically, as well as financially, Faubus saw political gold in racial epithets. He vowed never 'to mix the races' while he was governor. He won reelection convincingly with racist support and signed several bills in early 1957 to preserve school segregation. The new legislation permitted parents to withdraw their children from integrated schools, authorized school districts to contest lawsuits for integration, required organizations challenging the state to report to state officials, and created a state sovereignty commission to resist the federal government's 'interference' in Arkansan affairs. Under the new laws, the Citizens' Council would receive state funding while the NAACP had to reveal its membership list, exposing its members to violence.

By stirring the racial pot, Faubus encouraged white supremacists to wage a last-gasp campaign to preserve school segregation. Over the summer, the Citizens' Council disrupted school board meetings and spread rumors that armed men would descend on Little Rock. Georgia governor Marvin Griffin poured gas on the fire, by telling a Little Rock rally that integration would never occur in his state and that fierce resistance from Faubus on down could block it in Arkansas as well. Speakers from Mississippi and Louisiana advocated bloodshed to keep blacks out. Such incendiary rhetoric led the KKK to target Daisy Bates, president of the state's NAACP, and her husband L.C. Bates, the crusading editor of the *Arkansas State Press*. Klansmen burned crosses on the Bates' front yard, fired gunshots at their house, and threw a rock through their living-room window. A note tied to the rock warned, 'STONE THIS TIME. DYNAMITE NEXT.'

Faubus worked hand-in-glove with white supremacists. He arranged surreptitiously for the Mothers' League of Central High, a Citizens' Council auxiliary, to petition a state court to postpone desegregation. In a surprise move, Faubus testified that the city's stores were selling out of guns and knives, 'mostly to Negro youths' planning gang warfare. Although FBI agents found no sign of impending conflict, a local judge accepted the governor's word and blocked the desegregation plan. Thugs drove by the Bates' home all night, honking their horns and shouting, 'Daisy, Daisy, did you hear the news? The coons won't be going to Central!' Federal judge Ronald Davies, who had been transferred temporarily from North Dakota, was not impressed by Faubus's unproven claims and ordered desegregation to proceed.

On 2 September, the night before the nine black students were to enter Central High, Faubus ringed the school with National Guardsmen and manufactured a crisis to justify the call-up. He encouraged his friend Jimmy Karam, a one-time football coach and anti-labor goon, to stir up trouble outside the school. In a disingenuous televised address, the somber governor insisted that the guardsmen were needed to prevent bloodshed and promised that they would act not 'as segregationists or integrationists, but as soldiers called to active duty to carry out their assigned tasks'. Their real task, a guardsman explained, was to 'Keep the niggers out!' Faubus had now gone far beyond race-baiting speeches, legislative roadblocks, and lawsuits to prevent blacks from receiving their civil rights. He now employed the armed might of the state to nullify a federal court decision, the most flagrant states' rights claim since South Carolina seceded before the Civil War.

When judge Davies again ordered desegregation to continue, the board advised the black students to go to Central High on 4 September without their parents to prevent a racial explosion. An explosion came anyway. Daisy Bates and several ministers escorted eight of the students to the school in police cars, only to be stopped in their tracks by guardsmen. The ninth student – 15-year-old Elizabeth Eckford – was not notified of the arrangements and faced the mob alone. As she alighted from a bus wearing a white dress and dark glasses, an angry throng screamed, 'Here comes one of the niggers! Lynch her! Lynch her!' Elizabeth expected the guardsmen to protect her, but instead, they used bayonets to block her path. After an old woman spat on her, a trembling Elizabeth sat on a bus stop bench nearby and sobbed openly. Fortunately, two whites came to her defense. Benjamin Fine, a *New York Times* reporter, consoled her, and Grace Lorch, an NAACP member whose husband taught at the all-black Philander Smith College, shamed the jeering crowd into backing away. 'Don't you see she's scared?' Lorch cried. 'She's just a little girl.' Elizabeth had nightmares for weeks that the mob was about to kill her.

In barring the Little Rock Nine, Faubus threw down the gauntlet before president Eisenhower. Faubus had good reason to believe Eisenhower would let Arkansas have its way in race relations because the president steered clear of school desegregation problems in Alabama, Tennessee, and Texas. Just two months before the Central High crisis, Eisenhower said that he foresaw no possibility of using federal troops to compel desegregation [*Doc. 4*]. Having won four former Confederate states in the 1952 election and five in 1956, Eisenhower was determined to avoid antagonizing white southerners who were turning to the Republican party. As a party worker recognized, 'This isn't South Africa. The white man outnumbers the Negro 9 to 1 in this country.'

To defuse the most serious domestic crisis of his presidency, Eisenhower worked behind the scenes. He sent FBI agents to investigate, spoke by telephone to Little Rock mayor Woodrow Wilson Mann, and met with Faubus on 14 September in Newport, Rhode Island, where the president was vacationing. The attorney general warned Eisenhower that Faubus was a double-crosser, but the president did not heed the warning. For two hours, Faubus vacillated between wanting to end the crisis and ranting about federal plots against him. When Eisenhower rejected a lengthy delay in desegregating Central High, Faubus seemed to cave in and issued a statement conceding that *Brown* 'was the law of the land and must be obeyed'.

Back in Arkansas, an obdurate Faubus reneged on his promise, keeping the guardsmen in place. When judge Davies ordered the governor to remove the guardsmen, Faubus replaced them with out-manned city policemen and promised to do 'everything in my power' to maintain order at the school. It was another bogus promise. On 23 September, Central High reopened with a thousand angry whites, including Faubus's friend Karam, waiting for the black students. Car licenses showed that a quarter of them came from nine other states, mainly Texas. 'Two, four, six, eight, we ain't going to integrate,' the menacing crowd chanted. With the police looking the other way, the mob broke school windows and assaulted black passers-by and 'Yankee' reporters. The black students circumvented the mob by using a delivery entrance. When the mob realized it was outsmarted, six white girls wearing ponytails and poodle skirts shrieked, 'The niggers are in our school. Oh, my God, they're in the school!' A ringleader shouted, 'They tricked us, the yellow bastards. Come on, let's go in the school and drag them out.' Other white teenagers jumped into their cars and threw bricks into black homes and businesses.

Meanwhile, the beleaguered black students barely survived. 'You want integration?' school officials taunted them, 'We'll give you integration', sending them to nine different classrooms. To get to her homeroom on the third floor, a terrified Melba Patillo kept her eyes straight ahead and recited the Lord's Prayer repeatedly. Before long, the school was overrun by the mob. When it seemed as if the black students might be lynched, they were rushed from their classes to the principal's office. Melba overheard panicked officials plotting how to escape: 'We may have to let the mob have one of those kids, so's we can distract them long enough to get the others out.' 'They're children,' another replied. 'What'll we do, have them draw straws to see which one gets a rope around their neck?' When firemen refused the mayor's orders to douse the mob, assistant police chief Gene Smith dispatched squad cars to extricate the black students. Smith told the embattled students to keep their heads down and advised the drivers to 'move fast and don't stop no matter what'. To make sure the black students had left, a Mothers' League representative searched the school and reported, with great satisfaction, 'we went through every room in the school and there were no Negroes there'. That night, the police intercepted a 100-car caravan loaded with guns and dynamite headed for the Bates home. As the situation worsened, prominent citizens persuaded the mayor, whose son went to Central, to cable Washington for federal troops.

The stand-off between state and national officials lured television crews to Little Rock, where on-site television reporting was pioneered. John Chancellor, a young reporter for NBC News, transmitted searing images of white mobs assaulting black teenagers going to school. Much of Chancellor's inside information came from Ira Lipman, a courageous 16-year-old senior, whose parents knew Ernest Green as an attendant at their country club. Furious at having their dirty secret exposed, segregationists threatened Chancellor and called his television network the 'Nigger Broadcasting Company'. But the networks knew a good story when they saw one, and television boosted the movement as a moral crusade.

Stung by Faubus's duplicity and the resulting violence, Eisenhower grudgingly took the side of integrationists, if only to uphold federal power against a wayward lieutenant. Moreover, the president had to defend the United States from harsh international criticism. Nigerian newspapers asked, 'What moral right have Americans to condemn apartheid in South Africa while still maintaining it by law?' The Soviet Union attacked the 'white-faced but black-souled gentlemen [who] commit their dark deeds . . . then these thugs put on white gloves and mount the rostrum in the UN General Assembly, and hold forth about freedom and democracy'. Although Eisenhower worried that the South might end public education if force were used, he crushed this insubordination with 1,200 paratroopers from the famed 101st 'Screaming Eagles' airborne division. It was the first time since Reconstruction that a president sent troops to protect black civil rights. Eisenhower's chief of staff remarked that the president carried out 'a constitutional duty which was the most repugnant to him of all his acts in his eight years at the White House'. Eisenhower also ordered 10,000 Arkansas National Guardsmen back to Central High, this time to protect the black students. Angry segregationists compared the soldiers to 'Hitler's storm troopers' and called for their states to secede from the Union.

As the troops arrived on 24 September, Daisy Bates waited for super-intendent Blossom's assurance that the black students would be protected. When the harried superintendent called after midnight to say that the students should come the next day, Bates replied that the parents left their telephones off the hook to avoid harassment while sleeping. Blossom insisted that the students come to school anyway, so Bates and two black school principals went door-to-door, knocking on each house after 1 a.m. The first stop was Gloria Ray's house. After repeated knocking, Gloria's father aimed a shotgun at the unwelcome visitors. 'What do you want now?' he growled. When Bates explained that the desegregation of Central High would begin in a few hours, he replied, 'I don't care if the President of the United States gave you those instructions! I won't let Gloria go. She's faced two mobs and that's enough.' At the appointed time, however, Ray brought Gloria over: 'Here, Daisy, she's yours. She's determined to go. Take her.'

As morning broke, the children were taken to Central High in a convoy of jeeps carrying machine guns. When the convoy approached the school, a mob blocked its path. An army major ordered the mob to disperse, but a man yelled, 'They're bluffing. If you don't want to move, you don't have to.' The army was not bluffing, and the mob scattered. As the students ascended the school steps, paratroopers surrounded them on the ground and helicopters hovered overhead. Faubus told a televised audience that 'we are now an occupied territory. Evidence of the naked force of the federal government is here apparent in these unsheathed bayonets in the backs of schoolgirls.' With the mob momentarily defeated, Minnijean Brown remarked that 'for the first time in my life, I feel like an American citizen'.

There was considerable turmoil inside the school as the Little Rock Nine headed for Central High. Almost 40 per cent of the 2,000 white students stayed away that first day. Inside the school, there was a mixed response. While many whites walked out when black students entered their classrooms, some whites ate lunch with them or invited them to join the glee club. Others shunned or abused them and their white friends. 'I'll show you niggers the Supreme Court can't run my life,' one white student declared. To guarantee the black students' safety, a trooper was assigned to each one. But the troopers were barred from locker rooms, lavatories, classrooms, and the cafeteria, where trouble awaited.

The paratroopers withdrew from Central by November, making it open season on the Little Rock Nine. The federalized guardsmen stayed until the following June, but they offered little protection. As a power vacuum developed, rabid segregationist students returned to school to force their black classmates to leave. The bullies spat on, tripped, and slugged the black students, and burned them in effigy. They wrote graffiti on the walls that read, 'Nigger Go Home.' They burglarized lockers and plotted to dynamite the school building. Gloria Ray was shoved down a stairwell and forced to 'dance' as firecrackers were thrown at her feet. Her assailant snarled, 'I'm going to get you out of this school if I have to kill you.' Melba Patillo was doused with raw eggs and nearly blinded by a chemical thrown at her eyes. The steady abuse reduced Elizabeth Eckford to tears, and she told vice principal Elizabeth Huckaby, 'I want to go home.' Huckaby counseled the black students that their continuing bravery would make it easier for the next group to enter Central High. Not even the dynamiting of Carlotta Walls's home could make them quit. Suspicions arose that only the governor could have orchestrated the campaign of terror.

In a year of 'trench warfare', only one black student retaliated. Minnijean Brown dumped a bowl of chili on her tormentor who kept shouting, 'nigger, nigger, nigger', and the delighted black cafeteria workers applauded. When Minnijean was suspended temporarily, she remarked bitterly: 'They throw rocks at you, they spill ink on you – and we just have to be little lambs and take it.' The suspension became expulsion in February, when a white girl and Minnijean took turns calling each other 'nigger bitch' and 'white trash'. After Minnijean left, cards appeared reading, 'One down, eight to go.' The remaining black students joked grimly that they were learning 'readin', writin', and riotin''. Through it all, Daisy Bates was a tower of strength, reassuring frustrated students and worried parents that the crucial experiment would turn out all right. Finally, graduation day came, and the police made sure that Ernest Green, the first black graduate of Central High, went unharmed. Rumor had it that there was a price tag of $10,000 on his head. No one clapped when Green crossed the stage for his diploma, but, as he said, 'I had accomplished what I had come there for.'

In August 1958, the US Supreme Court ruled in *Cooper* v. *Aaron* that Little Rock's public schools must integrate despite the threat of violence. Rather than obey the Court in this first test of *Brown*, Faubus defiantly shut down all four of the city's secondary schools. The governor's school closure was approved overwhelmingly in a popular referendum, 19,470 to 7,561. The main concern of some white parents was to keep Central High's championship football team playing, even when the school itself was closed. Overnight, the governor's wealthy supporters set up T.J. Raney High School, a private school in an abandoned building on the University of Arkansas campus, and 750 white students enrolled. Nearly 3,700 students – white and black – scrambled for schooling elsewhere.

The vote to close Little Rock public schools was too much for many whites. Now their own children's future was being damaged. All but one of the school board members resigned, only to be replaced by segregationists. The new board fired superintendent Blossom and forty-four teachers and school employees who supported desegregation. This wholesale sacking prodded many civic leaders into action, including Adolphine Fletcher Terry and the Women's Emergency Committee to Open Our Schools, a group of 1,500 white middle-class women. The Parent-Teacher Association, Arkansas Education Association, and chamber of commerce also demanded the reopening of the public schools. Within days, these groups formed an organization called STOP – Stop This Outrageous Purge – and recalled the segregationist board members in May 1959. The newest school board rehired most of the fired teachers. After a federal court struck down the law permitting public schools to be closed, the board announced that it would admit black students to the white schools that fall.

Surprised by this turn of events, the bitter-enders rallied. Several men and women lobbed tear gas into a school board meeting, dynamited the fire chief's car, and heavily damaged the school administration's building and a commercial building owned by the mayor. With the continuing turmoil, desegregation slowed to a snail's pace in Little Rock. When Central High reopened, only three blacks enrolled. Once more, Elizabeth Eckford faced a mob, but this time the police protected her as she entered school without incident. As late as 1964, just 123 black children out of 7,000 attended desegregated schools in Little Rock. Not until 1972 were all grades in the public schools integrated.

The Little Rock crisis left many casualties and an unfinished revolution. Dozens of blacks and whites lost their jobs or moved away. The public school system was devastated as teacher morale plummeted and whites fled the district to escape desegregation. As integration took hold, white flight left a black majority in Central High. In what became a national pattern, white parents enrolled their children in all-white private academies or suburban public schools. As the embarrassing violence over desegregation continued, Little Rock's industrial development ground to a halt. In 1957, the city attracted eight new plants worth $3 million; in 1958, there were no new plants. L.C. Bates lost his newspaper as subscriptions declined. Woodrow Mann, who tried to uphold the law as mayor, saw burning crosses on his lawn and fled to Texas, abandoning his insurance business and once-promising political career. Brooks Hays, Little Rock's Democratic congressman, was defeated for trying to resolve the crisis. The strain of implementing desegregation pushed assistant police chief Gene Smith to kill his wife and then himself. Across the South, only 49 more school districts desegregated in Eisenhower's last three years in office, compared to 712 in the three years after *Brown*.

Some benefited from, or at least endured, the crisis, especially Orval Faubus, who was identified in a 1958 Gallup poll as one of the world's ten most admired men. By dividing Arkansas along the color line, Faubus not only won a third term, which was unusual, but six in all. Other southern politicians like Alabama's George Wallace followed this racist recipe with similar results. All of the Little Rock Nine went to college, and most developed successful careers. The television networks, rocked by quiz show scandals, regained respectability with their captivating reports from Arkansas. Other southern cities, including Atlanta and Raleigh, learned that resistance to integration harmed business, and they avoided large-scale civil rights disturbances. Most important, the president's use of federal troops in Little Rock signaled that segregation in the South could not survive. But to make further gains against Jim Crow, blacks would have to fight community by community, beginning in Montgomery.

CHAPTER FIVE

MONTGOMERY BUS BOYCOTT

'Niggers, get back!' white bus drivers barked at black riders in Montgomery, Alabama, in the 1950s. Blue-collar blacks suffered such indignities twice daily because most did not have cars. Three-quarters of the bus riders were black, but no bus driver was black. Buses stopped at every corner in white neighborhoods and every other corner in black ones. Some drivers took perverse delight in speeding by blacks waiting at bus stops. All drivers compelled blacks to exit the front door after they paid and to re-board through the rear door. Occasionally, the drivers left blacks stranded after paying, cheating them out of their fares. Once on the bus, black riders had to stay out of the first ten rows, which were reserved for whites, and stand beside empty seats when the black section in the back was filled.

Not only could blacks not ride in the front of the bus, they lived their entire lives apart from whites. Blacks were born in separate hospitals, attended separate, inferior schools, and were buried in separate cemeteries. Blacks asked in vain for the city to provide adequate fire and police protection, pave the streets, extend the sewer lines, set aside playgrounds, and pick up garbage regularly in their neighborhoods. With little education and jobs limited to domestics and laborers, the median income of blacks was half that of whites. This poverty explains why blacks rode the buses so frequently.

A few Montgomery blacks and whites risked dismissal, arson, and murder to protest against such discrimination. The intrepid leader of the local civil rights movement was E.D. Nixon, a roughhewn railroad porter who had long led the NAACP's city and state branches. To change the lot of Alabama's blacks, he launched a voter-registration drive for the 93 per cent of them who could not vote. Rufus Lewis, an undertaker and former college football coach, likewise promoted black registration through the Citizens' Steering Committee. Jo Ann Robinson, a fiery English professor at Alabama State College, presided over the Women's Political Council, a group of educated black women that got out the black vote and pressured the police department to hire blacks. Both Lewis and Robinson belonged to the silk-stocking Dexter Avenue Baptist Church, where the Reverend Vernon Johns thundered against segregation and docile blacks who tolerated it. Such uncompromising rhetoric had inspired his niece, Barbara Johns, to protest against her inferior high school in Virginia, and she fled to him for safety after the NAACP sued the district to desegregate. A plain-spoken, young Baptist minister and World War II veteran named Ralph Abernathy also used his pulpit to demand racial equality. All of these leaders could count on Clifford Durr, a New Deal lawyer, and his wife Virginia, white southern liberals who belonged to the NAACP.

These reformers made little headway among a black community that was still cowed. One story illustrates this sense of futility. In 1950, when the Reverend Johns fumbled his dime while putting it in the bus coin box, the driver insulted him: 'Uncle, get down and pick up that dime and put it in the box.' Johns refused, and implored the black passengers to leave the bus in protest. None did. Days later, Johns saw a parishioner who was on the bus with him. Before Johns could chide her, she reproached him: 'You ought to knowed better.' Johns told a friend that 'even God can't free people who behave like that'. Johns bought a car to avoid the daily humiliation of bus-riding. Most blacks could not afford this luxury.

A new spirit surfaced among Montgomery blacks after the *Brown* decision. As disobedience on buses became more frequent, drivers threatened black men with pistols and called the police to arrest several black women and children. Claudette Colvin, a 15-year-old, refused a white passenger's demand for her seat, only to have a policeman kick her and knock her school books away. 'I done paid my dime, I ain't got no reason to move,' she screamed as she was dragged off the bus, handcuffed, and carted to jail. Colvin was willing to be the long-awaited plaintiff against segregated buses, but black leaders declined her offer upon learning that she was pregnant, which could doom a $500,000 challenge.

When Rosa Parks was arrested, she changed American history. Parks, a trim, soft-spoken, bespectacled 42-year-old seamstress at the Montgomery Fair department store, prepared for that decisive day all of her life. She married a civil rights activist and, at E.D. Nixon's suggestion, joined the NAACP during World War II. She became resentful when her brother was drafted into the army to protect a democracy in which neither of them could vote. As the city's NAACP secretary, she advised teenagers like Claudette Colvin and attempted to register voters and integrate the city's libraries. When James Blake forced her off his Cleveland Avenue bus in 1943, Parks vowed never to ride with him again, and she kept that vow for twelve years. In the meantime, she cultivated Fred Gray, a young black lawyer who was Clifford Durr's protégé, to use the courts against Jim Crow. In the summer of 1955, Virginia Durr arranged for Parks to attend a desegregation workshop at the Highlander Folk School in the mountains of east Tennessee, a civil rights training ground founded by Myles and Zilphia Horton. The workshop was led by Septima Clark, a born teacher whose creative pedagogy and infinite patience turned many illiterate blacks into potential voters. Parks was awed by Clark, but still had no idea that she would catalyze Montgomery blacks into challenging segregation.

On Thursday, 1 December, a weary Rosa Parks absentmindedly entered Blake's bus once more. Holding her purse and a grocery bag on her lap, she sat right behind the white section. As the bus filled, a white man was left standing. An indignant Blake yelled at Parks and three other blacks in her row to step to the rear: 'Move y'all, I want those two seats.' When no one budged, Blake sputtered, 'Y'all better make it light on yourselves and let me have those seats.' The three blacks sitting next to Parks moved immediately. Parks stayed put because she was 'tired of giving in' to racism, recalling how her grandfather had stood up to the KKK and how Emmett Till had died three months earlier. When Parks refused to move, a flustered Blake found two policemen who quizzed her motives. Parks held her ground: 'Why do you all push us around?' The policeman shrugged, replying, 'I don't know, but the law is the law, and you're under arrest.'

E.D. Nixon decided that the moment of truth had come. If blacks in Montgomery were no longer willing to accept second-class citizenship, they had to stand with Parks, a highly respected church member and veteran freedom worker. As someone who worked with her hands but possessed a middle-class demeanor, she appealed to blacks of different classes and seemed less alarming to whites. Although her protest terrified her husband Raymond – 'The white folks will kill you, Rosa' – she showed no fear. Nixon and Parks believed that they could duplicate the Baton Rouge bus boycott spearheaded by Baptist minister T.J. Jemison two years earlier. Although that eight-day boycott ended without entirely eliminating segregated seating, it served as a template for the bus boycotts that followed.

Boycott organizers had just four days to spread the word among blacks before Rosa Parks faced a judge. Jo Ann Robinson composed an unsigned leaflet calling for a bus boycott: 'We must stop these arrests now. The next time may be you, or you, or you. . . . We are, therefore, asking every Negro to stay off the buses Monday in protest of the arrest and trial.' Risking dismissal, Robinson stayed up until 4 a.m. to run off thousands of copies on a college mimeograph machine, and then enlisted volunteers to distribute them in schools, stores, churches, barbershops, factories, and bars. On Friday night, Nixon convened a meeting of black leaders to endorse the boycott. That Sunday, pastors called the boycott 'God's movement' and entreated their parishioners 'to walk in dignity rather than ride in shame'. When Nixon announced the boycott to the city's newspaper, most local blacks learned of the plan.

Before daybreak on Monday, 5 December, the bus boycott began despite the cold, lack of money, fears of retaliation, and cross-town commute that many blacks faced. One man waited at a bus stop beside a crudely lettered sign that read, 'Remember it is for our cause that you do not ride the buses today.' When the bus arrived, the door opened and the driver asked the man if he were 'gonna get on?' The man shot back, 'I ain't gettin' on until Jim Crow gets off.' Bus after bus sped by without black riders. Bus company records showed that 99 per cent of the usual 30,000 black riders walked, hitchhiked, and pedaled bicycles. At mid-morning, Rosa Parks, the demure woman who started it all, received a $10 fine.

That afternoon, Nixon assembled fifty ministers – the most influential leaders in the black community – to decide what to do next. Their response was disillusioning. Several ministers suggested timidly that one day had been enough. Another group endorsed a longer boycott if their identities could be concealed. A boiling mad Nixon reproached the clerics: 'What the hell you people talkin' about? How you gonna have a mass meeting, gonna boycott a city bus line without the white folks knowing it? . . . You oughta make up your mind right now that you gon' either admit you are a grown man or concede to the fact that you are a bunch of scared boys.'

Nixon's words splashed the preachers like a cold shower, and when the national NAACP hesitated to get involved, they formed a new organization called the Montgomery Improvement Association to coordinate the bus boycott. MIA drafted as its leader the 26-year-old Martin Luther King, Jr., who replaced Johns as pastor of the Dexter Avenue church. King seemed an ideal choice, given his prominent position as the city's highest-paid black minister and his singular intelligence and oratorical skills, as well as his independence from black factions and segregationist patrons who might have compromised him. Nixon just knew that King 'wasn't any white man's nigger'.

This modern Moses came to his civil rights calling from one of Atlanta's most prominent black families. His maternal grandfather, A.D. Williams, had built the famed Ebenezer Baptist Church almost from scratch a half-century earlier and, with his son-in-law, Martin Luther 'Daddy' King, Sr., turned it into the city's leading black congregation. In a day when most black ministers preached on heavenly salvation, Williams combated racism by becoming a charter member and president of the city's NAACP. He led a boycott that bankrupted a local newspaper that called blacks 'dirty and ignorant' and helped found the city's first black high school, which his grandson would attend. White officials did not intimidate Daddy King either, as he made Ebenezer a center for voter registration and led the fight to equalize teachers' salaries.

When the precocious Martin Luther King grew up, his father steered him to the ministry, a fateful decision reinforced at Atlanta's prestigious Morehouse College. President Benjamin Mays introduced the younger King to liberal Protestantism and persuaded him that the ministry could indeed produce social change. Thus inspired, King studied at Crozer Theological Seminary near Philadelphia and pursued a doctorate in theology at Boston University. Encountering a wide range of western thinkers, King was impressed by Reinhold Niebuhr, who maintained that evil was so powerful that it could only be defeated by coercion – including nonviolence – not by appealing to reason or the altruism of elites. In addition, King accepted Friedrich Hegel's dialectic model, which held that the truth would emerge from clashing opposites. Never an original thinker, King also borrowed heavily from the writings of radio preacher Harry Emerson Fosdick, *Christian Century* editor C.C. Morrison, Florida pastor J. Wallace Hamilton, and black mystic Howard Thurman of Howard University, who believed fervently that Christianity could transcend its own racism to bring social justice. In Boston, King met his wife, Coretta Scott, a student at the New England Conservatory of Music. She abandoned a singing career to help her husband pastor a church in her native Alabama, where whites had burned down her father's home and sawmill.

To break the back of segregation, King had to mobilize the black peasantry in the South. He appealed to their deeply held Christian faith by promising brotherhood with whites, not retribution. He reinforced Jesus' 'creative weapon of love' with Gandhi's tactic of nonviolence that helped the Indian masses win independence from Britain. Nonviolence promised the powerless a way – a painfully slow way – to end segregation by wielding the force of moral authority against the brutal oppressor who controlled every aspect of black life. But black southerners faced more forbidding obstacles than did the Indians: blacks were a minority; the white oppressors were native to the region; and the philosophy of nonviolence was unknown in the most violent part of the country. In view of these handicaps, King had to convert enough whites to support racial justice. He therefore pointed out that blacks were simply demanding their rights as American citizens. If such democratic appeals fell on deaf ears, King planned to provoke crises to force white southerners to reform their society.

In Montgomery, King despaired that blacks were incapable of changing the city. He saw that the poor had been abandoned by black leaders who fought among themselves and by the middle class bent on getting ahead. In his own church, King admonished parishioners to register to vote and join the NAACP, but he wondered whether he should challenge the status quo right away. He was, after all, a young man with a new family to support. More-over, he was inclined to follow the law, not break it. When black leaders anointed King, he had to convince the black middle class that their standard of living was too high a price to pay for segregation. By appealing to the deep religious faith held by many blacks, King united the lower and middle classes to challenge Jim Crow.

On the night the boycott began, thousands of plain folks attended a raucous revival at the Holt Street Baptist Church. King took fifteen hours to write his Sunday sermons, but this night he had twenty minutes to write the most important speech of his life. King proved equal to the occasion. 'We are here this evening,' he intoned in his powerful baritone voice, 'to say to those who have mistreated us so long that we are tired – tired of being segregated

and humiliated; tired of being kicked about by the brutal feet of oppression.'
Endorsing Christian nonviolence as the 'weapon of protest', King closed his
lyrical address with a paraphrase from the biblical prophet Amos: 'And we are
determined here in Montgomery – to work and fight until justice runs down
like water, and righteousness like a mighty stream!' The ecstatic crowd jumped
to its feet, applauding and shouting, 'Amen, brother, amen.' An elderly woman
said she 'saw angels standing all around him when he finished, and they were
lifting him up on their wings'.

The assembled then considered three modest objectives for the boycott:
(1) direct bus drivers to treat black riders courteously, (2) make seating
available on a first-come, first-served basis with blacks filling the bus from the
rear and whites from the front, and (3) hire black bus drivers for black routes.
The first two demands, as Coretta Scott King admitted, called for 'a more
humane form of segregation'. The third demand represented a negotiating ploy.
City officials might be willing to grant the first two demands, if they could
save face by denying the third. When Ralph Abernathy asked those who were
in favor to stand, no one moved at first. Then people stood in ones and twos
until everyone in the room was standing. A relieved Abernathy recalled that
'the fear left that had shackled us across the years – all left suddenly when we
were in that church together'.

White Montgomery ridiculed the boycott plan as too complicated for
local blacks. The city newspaper speculated that the real mastermind was not
King but Robert Graetz, the crusading young white minister of the all-black
Trinity Lutheran Church. Mayor W.A. 'Tacky' Gayle predicted the venture
would collapse before long. 'Comes the first rainy day and the Negroes will
be back on the buses.' Confident of an early victory, the bus company flatly
refused every demand, even though it operated desegregated buses downstate
in Mobile. The bus company attorney ruled out any compromise because blacks
'would go about boasting of a victory they had won over the white people,
and this we will not stand for'. A shocked King saw that white supremacists
never intended to be reasonable. The boycott, he now realized, would take
months, not days. The prospect was disheartening, for there had never been
such a sustained, highly organized black protest.

The black community proved far more resilient than white officials
believed possible. Working-class blacks walked miles to their jobs, sometimes in inclement weather. Others needed cars because they were enfeebled
or because the distance was too great. Black taxis lowered rates to the same
dime fare that buses charged and crammed riders in. When the police commissioner blocked the fare reduction to render the taxi fleet useless, King
set up a private taxi system that made thousands of trips a day. Funds for the
$3,000-a-week operation poured in from local blacks who contributed as much
as 20 per cent of their income at mass meetings on Monday and Thursday
evenings. Women sold sandwiches, cakes, and sweet potato pies to raise money

for the cause. Additional monies came from churches, the NAACP, UAW, SCEF, Jews, anonymous white southerners, and elementary schoolchildren. The donations allowed the MIA to purchase a fleet of fifteen new station wagons to transport the boycotters. Each new car was turned over to a different church, so collectively they were dubbed 'rolling churches'. Thanks to military-like discipline, the operation succeeded spectacularly and raised black confidence. A janitor explained, 'The world knows we are right, and we is gonna win our cause. . . . White folks don't scare us no longer.'

As the bus company, downtown businessmen, and city lost $1 million, local politicians tried to destroy the boycott. Mayor Gayle urged more whites to ride buses to stem the financial hemorrhaging. He also asked white Montgomerians not to chauffeur their black maids. Angry women wrote letters to the paper saying that 'If the mayor wants to do my wash and wants to cook for me and clean up after my children let him come and do it. But as long as he won't do it I'm certainly not going to get rid of this wonderful woman I've had for fifteen years.' The city commissioners then tried a ruse to end the boycott. To bypass King, they placed a newspaper advertisement reporting that prominent black ministers had called off the boycott. Worried MIA officials quashed the hoax before the workweek resumed. A furious mayor cut off discussions with black leaders and announced that every city commissioner had joined the Citizens' Council.

White supremacists went after the boycotters themselves. Insurance companies refused to insure the car pool, a serious problem until Lloyd's of London covered the black drivers. Rosa Parks was fired from her job and left for Detroit, where her brother lived. To stop attorney Fred Gray, the local draft board reclassified him as eligible for military service. The police adopted a get-tough policy on drivers for the boycott, checking headlights and ticketing drivers for going too fast and too slow. Jo Ann Robinson received thirty traffic citations. Young whites in speeding cars shouted obscenities, tossed rotten eggs, and squeezed balloons filled with urine at black pedestrians. Dynamiters blew up car pool stations, black churches, and E.D. Nixon's lawn. Despite beatings, job dismissals, home foreclosures, and arrests, most boycotters carried on. 'They can bomb us out and they can kill us, but we are not going to give in,' Nixon declared resolutely.

As the stakes rose, King became the logical target. False rumors spread that King embezzled enough money to buy a new Cadillac. To defend himself against such charges, King lived modestly throughout his life. When he received personal threats, King applied for a gun permit and accepted around-the-clock volunteers to guard his home. He rescinded his permit application and dismissed the guards after northern pacifists from FOR tutored him on the finer points of nonviolence. King's faith in nonviolence was tested almost at once as his parsonage was bombed with his wife and infant daughter inside. Maintaining his composure, King told blacks bent on revenge to put their guns away and 'love our white brothers no matter what they do to us'. Terrified, Daddy King drove through the night from Atlanta to demand that his son give up the fight. 'Better to be a live dog than a dead lion!' the senior King roared to no effect. Weeks later, a hundred boycotters, including King, were indicted for violating the state's anti-boycott law. Although King was found guilty and fined $500 or a year at hard labor, the decision was overturned on a technicality. As King left the courthouse, a crowd of boycotters sang, 'We ain't gonna ride the buses no more, Ain't gonna ride no more. Why don't all the white folk know That we ain't gonna ride no more?'

When compromise was impossible, the NAACP filed suit in federal court against bus segregation itself. Montgomery blacks no longer sought to modify segregation on the local level. In June 1956, a three-judge panel, including Frank Johnson, Jr., an Alabama native and Eisenhower appointee, ruled that segregated buses violated the 14th Amendment. It was the first of several trail-blazing decisions for Johnson during the civil rights era. To intimidate 'the most hated man in Alabama', the KKK bombarded Johnson with death threats, burned a cross in his yard, and later dynamited his widowed mother's house.

Judge Johnson's ruling was a serious defeat for white Alabama. The city appealed the decision to the US Supreme Court. State attorney general John Patterson demanded the NAACP produce its membership list, which would have meant even greater reprisals against blacks. When the New York-based organization refused to identify its members, a state court fined it $100,000 and shut it down in Alabama. As bus revenues dropped by two-thirds, the company offered to desegregate its seating, but the mayor said no. He did not care if blacks ever rode a city bus again 'if it means that the social fabric of our community is to be destroyed'. The city of Montgomery finally sued the MIA to stop the car pool as a business without a license.

As the city's suit was being heard in November 1956, the US Supreme Court ruled in *Gayle* v. *Browder* that Montgomery's segregation laws were unconstitutional. By then, the bus boycott had outlasted 381 days of intimidation, bombings, and court challenges and resulted in a major civil rights victory. Black Montgomerians shouted and wept as they voted to end the boycott. A janitor said proudly, 'We got our heads up now, and we won't ever bow down again – no, sir – except before God.' A few whites like Virginia Durr expressed 'pure, unadulterated joy' at the news. 'It was as if a great burden had fallen off us.' Though some southern cities resisted the Court's decision for years, *Time* magazine predicted accurately that 'Jim Crow would never again be quite the same.' Montgomery, once the cradle of the Confederacy, had become the cradle of the civil rights movement. At 5.45 a.m. on 21 December, King, Nixon, Abernathy, and Gray climbed aboard the first integrated bus and sat in front.

Most whites accepted bus desegregation with resignation, but some retaliated. A whites-only bus line was formed but soon failed. A drive-by sniper fired through King's front door and dynamite with a burned-out fuse was found on his porch. Snipers also fired on two buses, wounding a pregnant black woman. Five white men beat a 15-year-old black girl as she left a bus. Citing the violence, city officials shut down the bus service for two weeks, forcing blacks to walk because whites ordered it. Then, bombs pulverized four black churches and the homes of King and Abernathy. When Abernathy wanted to see what remained of his ruined church, a policeman threatened him: 'If you go inside, I'll blow your brains out.' Frustrated that no one had died, the Klan targeted a black truck driver who was dating a white woman. They got the wrong man. A substitute driver was forced at gunpoint to jump from a bridge to his death.

Although the city remained mostly segregated for years, the Montgomery bus boycott demonstrated several lessons for the larger civil rights struggle. The smug white belief that blacks were 'happy' with their subservience was an obvious lie. Moreover, black unhappiness was not stimulated by outside protesters. Nor was it true that blacks were incapable of organizing themselves for any substantial goal or that they possessed little economic clout. The boycott catapulted to the front of the movement a new leader of the first rank, Martin Luther King, Jr., whose noble goals, soaring rhetoric, and extraordinary courage would inspire many black southerners and white northerners to join the civil rights crusade. Most important, the boycott showed that protesters needed to create sufficient internal pressure to compel intervention from outside the South. The MIA's interlocking strategy of local boycott, nonviolent protest, and federal lawsuit, would prove successful time and again. The victory in Montgomery led the Reverends Joseph Lowery of Mobile, Alabama, and C.K. Steele of Tallahassee, Florida, to initiate their own bus boycotts. Altogether, more than twenty cities desegregated their bus lines.

Building on the success in Montgomery, King and other black ministers formed the Southern Christian Leadership Conference in January 1957 to harness the untapped power of the church against racial discrimination. King surrounded himself with talented allies and lieutenants – some with elephantine egos – including Ralph Abernathy, an earthy Baptist preacher and King's closest companion; Andrew Young, an articulate young Congregational minister from New Orleans; Wyatt T. Walker, a tall Baptist preacher with an aristocratic air from Petersburg, Virginia; Fred Shuttlesworth, a wiry, sharp-tongued Baptist preacher from Birmingham, Alabama; C.T. Vivian, an intense, outspoken Baptist preacher from Illinois; Hosea Williams, a firebrand from Savannah, Georgia, who would be jailed a record 135 times; James Bevel, a mystical preacher from the Mississippi delta with a skullcap that adorned his shaved head; Bayard Rustin, an urbane, chain-smoking Quaker from FOR and CORE; Ella Baker, a passionate, no-nonsense former NAACP field secretary; Glenn Smiley, a white Methodist minister and FOR's national field secretary; and Stanley Levison, a wealthy New York lawyer, speechwriter, and fundraiser for a philanthropic group called In Friendship. 'To redeem the soul of America', SCLC (sometimes pronounced 'slick') encouraged the black masses to over-throw Jim Crow themselves. By fomenting crises, blacks could persuade whites that segregation was so evil that it should be dethroned, opening the way to 'reconciliation' within a truly integrated 'beloved community'. The increased demands on his time compelled King to leave Montgomery for Atlanta, where he headed SCLC and co-pastored his father's church.

SCLC's first action was to pressure the federal government to remove hindrances to black voting. In May 1957, Martin Luther King led a Prayer Pilgrimage to Washington, which attracted an enthusiastic crowd of 30,000. 'Give us the ballot,' King implored in endless refrains. To avoid direct federal government involvement in racial disputes, Eisenhower had formulated a multifaceted civil rights measure, which was then stuck in Congress. The admin-istration hoped to divide the Democratic party into northern and southern wings, stymie Texas Democrat Lyndon Johnson's presidential ambitions, and showcase the Republicans as the party of Lincoln. In Eisenhower's reelection, the Republicans polled 39 per cent of black voters, the highest total since the Depression began. King promised that the bill would put many new blacks on the southern rolls, and they would likely vote Republican.

The administration's bill was a political minefield for presidential aspirants. Lyndon Johnson, the Senate majority leader, cautiously lobbied for the bill after two drastic changes were accepted. The attorney general could not seek injunctions against Jim Crow and local juries would hear criminal contempt cases concerning voting rights. Since jurors were selected from nearly all-white voting lists, white defendants would likely get off. Vice president Richard Nixon fought the crippling jury-trial amendment while Democrat John F. Kennedy of Massachusetts supported the change, which succeeded. The emasculated measure passed in September 1957 and established a temporary US Commission on Civil Rights to monitor, rather than redress, alleged racial complaints. In addition, the civil rights section of the Justice department was upgraded to a division that could investigate and litigate allegations against local officials for impeding voting rights. The measure was so weak that Richard Russell, an arch-segregationist from Georgia, described it as 'the sweetest victory in my twenty-five years as a senator'. Under the law, only 3 per cent more blacks registered, leading the NAACP and SCLC to demand more than a 'phony' civil rights bill.

One of the earliest complaints to the Civil Rights Commission came from Charles Gomillion of Tuskegee, Alabama. When blacks made remarkable gains in registration after World War II, Gomillion testified that the state redrew an electoral district that zigzagged twenty-eight times to exclude all but four of the city's 500 black voters. He also noted that the officials resisted black registration by hiding behind desks, working slowly, and arbitrarily failing blacks in the literacy test. Gomillion and his Civic Association fought back with a devastating boycott against local white merchants. In 1960, the US Supreme Court struck down the state's gerrymandered district as unconstitutional.

The rising civil rights movement and election-year politics forced the enactment of a second civil rights act. This 1960 corrective required that local voter registration records be open to federal inspection and provided criminal penalties for interfering with the right to vote. Federal courts could appoint referees when local electoral districts obstructed voter registration. In the short term, few additional black southerners managed to vote, but once the legislative logjam was broken, more significant bills would be enacted.

Eisenhower took important steps to implement desegregation but his actions were often too little and too late. He failed to use the moral authority of his office on behalf of justice for all. A Civil Rights Commission official observed that under Eisenhower the rights of blacks had become a 'White House orphan'. This slow pace sparked a dramatic shift in the movement, with students taking charge.

CHAPTER SIX

SIT-INS

In Greensboro, North Carolina, the Woolworth's department store management allowed black patrons to buy merchandise and to eat at a stand-up snack bar, but refused them service in the sit-down diner. After a late-night 'bull session', four black freshmen from North Carolina A & T College decided in early 1960 to challenge the store's demeaning and hypocritical policy. Joseph McNeil, a studious physics major; David Richmond, who contemplated a future in the ministry; Air Force ROTC student Franklin McCain; and Ezell Blair, Jr., son of an industrial arts teacher, goaded each other to start their own boycott. They had read black protest literature in high school, been active in NAACP youth groups, attended a presentation by the Little Rock Nine, and heard Martin Luther King give a heart-pounding sermon. Their incipient rebelliousness was encouraged by Ralph Johns, a clothier of Syrian descent who belonged to the NAACP. Steeling themselves for trouble, these middle-class students agreed that 'We've talked about it long enough. Let's do something.'

'All of us were afraid,' Franklin McCain admitted, of having 'our heads split open with a night stick and hauled into prison', but 'we went ahead and did it' anyway. At 4.30 p.m. on Monday, 1 February, the neatly dressed teenagers entered Woolworth's and bought toothpaste, notebooks, and pencils to show their good intentions. Then they sat quietly on stools at the formica-topped, L-shaped lunch-counter, waiting to be served. When Ezell Blair asked politely for coffee, a white waitress scolded the Greensboro students, 'I'm sorry. We don't serve colored here.' Most white customers turned their heads and cursed the 'nasty, dirty niggers', but a couple of old white women encouraged them with a pat on the back and told them that they 'should have done it ten years ago'. The manager, Clarence 'Curly' Harris, rushed over to tell the students that store policy forbade serving blacks. When the students showed their receipts from the merchandise counter and stayed on, Harris tried unsuccessfully to have the well-behaved students arrested. Outside the store, McCain was relieved that he escaped violence and gratified at gaining his 'manhood'. The Greensboro Four thus launched the student phase of the civil rights movement. Like Rosa Parks, the students remained in their seats to claim full citizenship.

Word of the Greensboro Four's sit-in traveled quickly, especially after a local radio station broadcast the story. Brimming with the confidence of a 'Mack truck', thirty-one young black men and women returned the next day to Woolworth's. On the third day, students filled almost all sixty-six seats and did their homework, wrote letters, or read the Bible. By Saturday, hundreds of black students from A & T, the all-women's Bennett College, and Dudley High School plus whites from three area colleges jammed Woolworth's and Kress's five-and-dime stores. Others filled drugstores, shopping centres, and drive-ins. Eventually, 90 per cent of A & T students participated in the sit-ins, which thrilled one woman: 'We older people didn't have the guts to do it, but the young people didn't care even if they died.'

Although twenty sit-ins had taken place in southern cities in the late 1950s, the Greensboro sit-in ignited the largest of all black protests. The civil rights movement was in a lull ever since Little Rock, and the sit-ins provided a much-needed tonic. According to historian William Chafe, the Greensboro 'coffee party' was a 'watershed' in American history, a 'volcanic' event comparable to the Boston Tea Party before the Revolution.

A & T students told their dramatic story to family, friends, and fraternity members. Within a week of the Greensboro sit-ins, like demonstrations appeared in other North Carolina cities, including Raleigh, Durham, High Point, and Winston-Salem. Black colleges and churches combined with the NAACP, SCLC, and CORE to coordinate the students who demanded an end to Jim Crow. Under the direction of Floyd McKissick – the first black admitted to the University of North Carolina law school – a sit-in headquarters provided eager students with training and legal assistance and then transported them to other sit-in sites. When SCLC executive director Ella Baker heard of the sit-ins, she challenged students at other southern colleges to act. White university students at Michigan, Swarthmore, Berkeley, and Harvard picketed Woolworth stores to express their support. The sit-in movement had unexpectedly caught on fire.

Again, television was instrumental in helping the civil rights movement. Images of the sit-ins transfixed young blacks who regarded *Brown* as a failure and showed them the new tool to dismantle Jim Crow. The sit-ins gave Cleveland Sellers, a teenager in Denmark, South Carolina, 'a shot of adrenalin' when he saw students 'beaten and dragged through the streets by their hair'. The televised student revolt inspired Robert Parris Moses, a young Harlem high school mathematics teacher, to join the southern crusade. He discerned a new militant attitude in the Greensboro activists, one that was no longer 'cringing' but 'sullen, angry, determined'. 'They were kids my age,' Moses observed, 'and I knew this had something to do with my own life. It made me realize that for a long time I had been troubled by the problem of being a Negro and at the same time being an American. This was the answer' [*Doc. 5*].

When James Lawson, a 31-year-old Vanderbilt University divinity student, heard the news from Greensboro, he was well prepared to join the sit-in movement against segregation. As a pacifist, Lawson went to jail rather than fight in the Korean war and, upon his release, studied Gandhi's nonviolent formula in India. Back in Nashville, Tennessee – the 'Athens of the South' – Lawson and fellow ministers Kelly Miller Smith and C.T. Vivian conducted weekly nonviolent workshops that were sponsored by FOR and King's SCLC affiliate. For two years, seventy-five Nashville participants met in Smith's First Colored Baptist Church and role-played sit-ins to anticipate the verbal and physical abuse that would surely come. The workshop participants resented the daily humiliation of entering stores that would not let them eat at lunch-counters, try on clothes, or let their children use the restrooms.

At the forefront of the local movement was a stellar group of young people that included American Baptist seminarians James Bevel, Bernard LaFayette, and John Lewis, Fisk students Diane Nash and Marion Barry, and high school student Cordell Reagon. These Christian idealists became prime movers in the national student movement. Nash, an articulate beauty queen from Chicago, recalled her conversion to the movement: 'I had a date, and we went to the Tennessee State Fair. . . . I started to use the ladies' room, and those were the first signs I had really seen in Nashville, and they were "WHITE WOMEN" and "COLORED WOMEN", and I just got furious.' To practice for full-fledged sit-ins, the Nashville students went to segregated restaurants, spoke to the managers when service was refused, and then left the premises. Always, Lawson graded their performance. 'You have to do more than just not hit back,' he reminded the students. 'You have to *love* that person who's hitting you.'

The Nashville sit-ins were the largest of all, taking place in a city where black customers spent $50 million annually in white businesses. A fortnight after the Greensboro sit-ins, a hundred Nashville students entered the Kress, Woolworth, and McClellan discount stores shortly before noon. After making some purchases, they sat at lunch-counters waiting for service. A middle-aged waitress at Woolworth's froze at the sight. 'Oh, my God,' she said to herself. 'Here's the niggers.' The white customers soon left. Then, the lights went out, and the students sat in the dark for hours until the store closed. Once safely outside, the students regaled each other with sit-in stories. Two black girls told how they entered the 'whites only' ladies' bathroom to the astonishment of an elderly white woman. As the woman fled in tears, she shouted, 'Oh! Nigras, Nigras *everywhere!*'

When the Nashville police chief announced that student demonstrators would be arrested, John Lewis, an Alabama sharecropper's son, hurriedly composed a set of 'do's' and 'don'ts' for his peers: 'Do be friendly and courteous at all times. Do sit straight and face the counter. Do remember the nonviolent teachings of Jesus Christ, Mohandas Gandhi, and Martin Luther King. Don't strike back or curse if abused. Don't laugh out. Don't leave your seat without permission. Don't block store entrances or aisles.' The guidelines came just in time. Thugs spat on the protesters before pulling them off the stools and beating them. The well-coached students did not retaliate. One co-ed even smiled after a lighted cigarette was crushed in her hair. After the beatings, a policeman said, 'Okay, all you nigras, get up from the lunch counter or we're going to arrest you.' No one moved, so the police dragged the students away on charges of trespassing and disorderly conduct. Another wave of protesters replaced those who were arrested. When the next round of arrests came, a third wave of protesters occupied all the lunch-counter seats. To boost their spirits, the Nashville demonstrators sang one song over and over: 'I'm gonna do what the spirit says do, If the spirit says sit in, I'm gonna sit in, If the spirit says boycott, I'm gonna boycott, If the spirit says go to jail, I'm gonna go to jail, I'm gonna do what the spirit says do.'

Nearly every arrested Nashville student followed the new dictum – 'jail, no bail'. Civil rights organizer Bayard Rustin explained why this strategy was crucial to the movement's success: 'There are not enough jails to accommodate the movement. This is an important strength. . . . Only so many can fit into a cell; if you remain here, there can be no more arrests! Imprisonment is an expense to the state; it must feed and take care of you. Bails and fines are an expense to the movement, which it can ill afford.' Bail was set at $100, but lowered to $5 when the students refused to pay the higher amount. Still the students would not pay, leaving the officials no choice but to release the students into the custody of their college deans. The jail, no bail strategy had worked perfectly. To end the sit-ins, a mayoral committee recommended that stores divide the lunch-counters into white and black sections. The students flatly rejected the proposal, and the sit-ins resumed. Black adults offered food, money, and prayers for their new leaders – the students.

The black community helped out in an even more effective way – a boycott of downtown merchants. Those who defied the boycott were roughed up by black enforcers. As the boycott took hold, a bomb destroyed the home of Z. Alexander Looby, a black city councilman and defense attorney for the students. Although Looby and his family were uninjured, 4,000 angry blacks marched on city hall in what was the first large-scale march of the civil rights movement. They walked silently as whites watched in amazement. On the steps of city hall, Diane Nash asked for mayor Ben West's opinion of racial discrimination. Backed into a corner, West agreed 'as a man' that discrimination was morally wrong. The mayor's concession marked the turning point in Nashville. Three weeks later, the Greyhound bus terminal served blacks food on the same basis as whites, making Nashville the first major southern city to begin desegregating its lunch-counters. Lawson's highly trained demonstrators worked miracles.

As always, there was a price to be paid for racial progress. The four blacks who ate the first meal at an integrated counter were badly beaten, and bombs were discovered in the terminal. James Lawson was expelled from Vanderbilt, prompting the divinity school dean to resign in protest. It would take four more years of sit-ins, marches, beatings, and arrests before blacks in Nashville could desegregate hotels, movie theaters, and fast-food restaurants.

In Atlanta, which civic boosters called the 'City Too Busy to Hate', Morehouse College football star Lonnie King was concerned that Greensboro 'would again be another isolated incident in black history if others didn't join in to make it become something'. He wondered, 'Why don't *we* make it happen here?' He recruited Julian Bond, a published poet and the handsome son of an eminent scholar, to be the voice of the students. At exactly 11.00 a.m., on 15 March, two hundred protesters occupied the dining areas of city hall, the state capitol building, the county courthouse, two office buildings, and the bus and train stations. When the manager said he could not serve them, Bond replied, 'The sign outside says the public is welcome and we're the public and we want to eat.' The demonstrators then refused the lieutenant governor's plea to leave, prompting the police to put them in jail, where lunch was served. Once released, the students organized as the Committee on Appeal for Human Rights and called on merchants and institutions to desegregate. Spelman student Ruby Doris Smith took on Grady hospital because it admitted blacks as patients but compelled them to enter the building through separate doors. When the receptionist insisted Smith leave because she was not sick, Smith vomited all over the receptionist's desk. 'Is that sick enough for you?' Smith demanded to know.

By the end of 1960, sit-ins had occurred in all southern states but Mississippi. All told, a citizen army of 70,000 crossed the color line in 150 cities to desegregate many different public venues. They not only sat at segregated lunch-counters, they waded in segregated pools, knelt in segregated churches, lay on segregated beaches, read in segregated libraries, rode segregated buses, bowled in segregated bowling alleys, skated on segregated ice rinks, slept in segregated motel lobbies, sat in segregated theaters, walked into segregated parks and museums, washed clothes in segregated laundromats, and applied for 'whites-only' jobs. Greensboro's Joseph McNeil explained why sit-ins broke out in so many places: 'I guess everybody was pretty well fed up at the same time.'

At first, whites ignored the sit-ins, the traditional response to black demands. Retaliation was not long in coming because, unlike federal court decisions, sit-ins and boycotts hurt white businesses. Greensboro merchants lost a third of their profits. Elsewhere, storekeepers unscrewed or roped off lunch-counter seats, so that every customer had to stand. To nip the practice of sit-ins in the bud, local officials across the South pressured black college presidents to expel the protesters, and two hundred students and faculty were removed. Expulsion proved to be an insufficient deterrent, so the police charged 3,600 demonstrators with trespassing, disturbing the peace, or inciting a riot.

The police allowed thugs to pummel the protesters with bats and torment them with cigarette smoke, scalding coffee, and ketchup. In Atlanta, a demonstrator's face was doused with acid. In Houston, three masked white men kidnapped a demonstrator, beat him with a chain, carved 'KKK' on his chest, and hung him upside-down from an oak tree. A firebomb destroyed a gymnasium at a black college in Frankfort, Kentucky. In Biloxi, Mississippi, a white mob shot ten blacks on a segregated beach.

Not all blacks welcomed this new student activism, especially older folks who had long witnessed intimidation and violence when Jim Crow was challenged. Because the livelihood of many blacks depended on white good will, the students' brash demands for 'freedom now' invited dismissals, bombings, and murders. NAACP chief legal counsel Thurgood Marshall believed that the students had embarked on a foolish and costly plan to go to jail to break the back of segregation. He vowed not to represent 'a bunch of crazy colored students who violated the sacred property' of whites. This very caution alienated black youngsters. When Cleve Sellers organized a sit-in in his hometown, his father chided him: 'This demonstrating and rallying is no good. If you keep on, you're going to destroy everything.' The younger Sellers thought to himself, 'Goddammit, nigger, you're scared . . . of what those candy-assed white crackers will do to you!' Enthusiastic black students led the way in this new facet of the civil rights movement because they were less constrained by family or career concerns.

After the heady first weeks of the sit-in movement, the Highlander Folk School held its annual workshop for college students. The theme in March 1960 was 'The New Generation Fights for Equality', which reflected the generational shift in the civil rights movement to young blacks and whites. In the Smokey Mountains retreat, folk troubadours Guy Carawan and Pete Seeger introduced the students to 'freedom songs' adapted from slavery and the labor movement. 'We Shall Overcome', which was based on a spiritual ('No More Auction Block for Me') and Charles Tindley's 1900 gospel song ('I'll Overcome Some Day'), became the movement's anthem [*Doc. 6*]. With hands held and bodies swaying, the idealistic singers avowed that 'deep in my heart I do believe, we shall overcome some day'. The training was so effective that Highlander was forced to close, the victim of constant police harassment, FBI surveillance, IRS audits, and state investigations.

To accelerate the movement, SCLC's outspoken director Ella Baker convened a meeting of student protesters in April at her alma mater, Shaw University in Raleigh, North Carolina. Baker believed that the sudden success of the sit-ins rendered Martin Luther King's cautious strategies obsolete. Two hundred participants attended, mostly from elite black colleges and high schools, including Fisk and Morehouse. The 'Nashville All-Stars' included James Lawson, C.T. Vivian, James Bevel, Diane Nash, Bernard LaFayette, and Marion Barry. Julian Bond led the Atlanta contingent. Stokely Carmichael, a

Trinidad native, and Courtland Cox headed up the Nonviolent Action Group from Howard University. Sympathetic observers arrived from liberal and leftist organizations, including FOR, CORE, SCEF, YWCA, the National Student Association, the Students for a Democratic Society, the Young People's Socialist League, and the ecumenical National Council of Churches in Christ, the largest religious organization in the United States. The 55-year-old Baker recognized that 'the younger generation is challenging you and me. They are asking us to forget our laziness and doubt and fear, and follow our dedication to the truth to the bitter end.' She challenged the students, in turn, to find larger targets – 'something much bigger than a hamburger or even a giant-sized Coke' – especially voting, housing, jobs, and health care.

King was the chief draw at the Shaw meeting, but it was James Lawson who struck a responsive chord among his listeners. He, not King, had been on the frontlines of the sit-in movement. After praising sit-ins as the optimum way to end segregation, Lawson criticized the NAACP for its 'middle-class conventional, half-way efforts' that left blacks as a whole 'victims of racial evil'. He predicted that 'all of Africa will be free before the American Negro attains first class citizenship'. Even as Lawson spoke, sixteen African nations, including Chad, Senegal, and Nigeria, became independent of European colonialism. Lawson warned that 'until America honestly accepts the sinful nature of racism, this cancerous disease will continue to rape all of us'.

At the close of the meeting, the participants formed an important civil rights organization – the Student Nonviolent Coordinating Committee (SNCC), pronounced 'snick' – that spurned formal ties to King's SCLC. SNCC welcomed white allies, refused to follow a prophetic leader, and distinguished itself by its piercing internal debates, democratic procedures, and ventures into the most dangerous areas of the deep South, especially the small towns of McComb, Mississippi; Albany, Georgia; and Selma, Alabama. Its fearless, even reckless, workers became known as the 'shock troops of the revolution'. As SNCC's work grew in importance, the civil rights establishment tried to hijack the student organization. The NAACP, CORE, and SCLC each wanted the students to become a youth wing, but the Atlanta-based SNCC rejected such paternalism by these mainstream groups. After all, the impatient students were 'probably as much experts at this as anybody else', as Franklin McCain observed pointedly. Even so, it soon became obvious that to make their mark the cash-strapped students needed the NAACP's financial aid and legal know-how.

The students pressured two hundred cities in twenty states to integrate their lunch-counters and theaters. The Greensboro Woolworth's caved in after losing $200,000 – 20 per cent of its business. A black female employee – not the Greensboro Four – ate the first meal, an egg-salad sandwich she made herself that morning. Although the entire Woolworth's chain changed its racial policy by the end of 1961, desegregation proceeded unevenly. In

Greensboro, most white businesses kept blacks out of restaurants, motels, and theaters, until North Carolina A & T student council president Jesse Jackson led a thousand protesters in the spring of 1963.

The sit-ins signaled a decisive shift in who would lead the struggle for racial justice. For a half-century, the NAACP and Urban League used lobbyists and the law to end Jim Crow, but they were increasingly eclipsed by students impatient with the direction, speed, and scope of the civil rights movement. By transforming segregation from a legal to a moral issue compelling immediate action, the sit-ins attracted thousands of new activists, black and white, and spawned new movement leaders, notably John Lewis, Bob Moses, Julian Bond, and Stokely Carmichael. They had tasted success and demanded the whole house of Jim Crow be destroyed. 'Nothing can stop us now,' one insisted optimistically. Moreover, the sit-ins greatly broadened the civil rights movement. Instead of an occasional demonstration orchestrated by prominent civil rights leaders, students organized many protests throughout the South. As the movement gained ground, prominent entertainers Harry Belafonte, Sammy Davis, Jr., Dick Gregory, and Sidney Poitier joined the students. When Gregory was told by a lunch-counter waitress, 'We don't serve colored people here', the comedian quipped, 'That's all right, I don't eat colored people. Bring me a whole fried chicken.'

A new round of sit-ins in Atlanta propelled civil rights into the presidential election of 1960. The students singled out Rich's, the city's largest department store, where the King family and Ebenezer church members had shopped all their lives. Their slogan was: 'Close out your charge account with segregation, open your account with freedom.' On 19 October, King joined the sit-in, despite serious misgivings. It was the first time that a black leader of national stature courted arrest, and he would end up going to jail thirteen times. When the protesters refused bail and the Klan began marching, the mayor saw that charges were dropped against the students. King's arrest was a different matter. He had violated his probation for not getting a Georgia driver's license after moving to Atlanta and was sentenced to four months of hard labor with dangerous criminals and violent deputy sheriffs.

The White House was inundated with calls for King's release. The heat was especially intense for the presidential candidates, Richard Nixon and John Kennedy. With white southern voters up for grabs, the Republican Nixon kept mum about King. With Nixon remaining sphinx-like, Kennedy saw an opportunity to do the 'decent thing' that would also attract black voters. In a brief telephone conversation after midnight, he told an overwrought Coretta Scott King: 'I want to express to you my concern about your husband. I know this must be very hard for you. I understand you are expecting a baby, and I just wanted you to know that I was thinking about you and Dr King.' Robert Kennedy, the president's brother and campaign manager, was steamed up over the political predicament that King's arrest posed. He applied tremendous pressure on the judge who jailed King, and the judge saw the wisdom of releasing King the next day. Although Daddy King had favored Nixon because Kennedy was Catholic, he announced from the pulpit that 'because this man was willing to wipe the tears from my daughter[-in-law]'s eyes, I've got a suitcase of votes, and I'm going to take them to Mr Kennedy and dump them in his lap'.

The Kennedy campaign milked the incident fully, distributing millions of pamphlets in black churches and neighborhoods that described the candidate's telephone call and King's release. The pamphlet read, *'No Comment' Nixon Versus a Candidate with a Heart, Senator Kennedy*. Kennedy also praised the sit-in movement as within 'the American tradition to stand up for one's rights – even if the new way is to sit down'. He told audiences that 'if the President does not himself wage the struggle for equal rights, if he stands above the battle, then the battle will inevitably be lost.' As a sign of his resolve, Kennedy pledged to prevent job discrimination and to end segregated public housing 'with the stroke of a pen', meaning by executive order.

Impressed by Kennedy's call for a New Frontier in civil rights, 68 per cent of blacks voted for the Democrat, 7 per cent more than the party received four years earlier. In the key states of Illinois and Texas, blacks abandoned the Republican party to vote overwhelmingly for Kennedy. Black votes nationwide were crucial to Kennedy because Nixon captured 52 per cent of white votes. Blacks had high expectations of the new president, and they pressed him to respond. The first challenge was a bus ride through the deep South.

CHAPTER SEVEN

FREEDOM RIDE

Growing up in Texas, James Farmer saw whites humiliate his father. J. Leonard Farmer was a college professor with a doctorate, but whites in the Lone Star state still looked down on him. One day, while Dr Farmer was driving his family to a picnic, his car struck a stray pig crossing the road. He drove on, he explained, because 'out in these rural parts, Negroes are killed for less'. A pickup truck caught up to the picnickers, and a tall white man carrying a shotgun yelled at Dr Farmer: 'You done kilt mah hawg, nigger. . . . Ah wuz gon show that hawg in the county fair. Y'all gon pay a purty penny fer that hawg.' To spare his family, Dr Farmer adopted a Sambo pose. He held his straw hat in his hands and looked downward while he apologized and asked how much the hog was worth. When the white man claimed the absurd figure of $45, Dr Farmer handed over his entire paycheck, which the white man let fall to the ground. 'Pick it up, nigger,' he ordered the professor. When his father bent over to retrieve the check, Jim vowed angrily, 'I'll never do that. . . . They'll have to kill me.'

To wage war on racism after the sit-ins lagged, James Farmer led a decisive phase in the civil rights movement. A burly, good-humored man with humanist convictions and Shakespearean diction, Farmer had pursued racial equality in pacifist and socialist groups, including CORE, which he co-founded. Farmer quit CORE over an internal squabble and became a union organizer. Years later, he returned to the civil rights cause as program director of the conservative NAACP, but grew frustrated when he could not interest the association in the sit-in tactic that he pioneered. When CORE invited him back, he jumped at the second chance. His former boss, Roy Wilkins, remarked wistfully that Farmer would be riding a mustang pony while he was riding a dinosaur.

As CORE's national director, Farmer read stacks of letters from black southerners complaining that whites abused them for sitting in the front of buses and using terminal facilities. Such harassment in interstate travel was barred by the US Supreme Court in two cases – *Morgan* v. *Virginia* (1946) and *Boynton* v. *Virginia* (1960). CORE therefore organized a bus trip called the Freedom Ride that was patterned after its little-remembered Journey of Reconciliation through the upper South in 1947. Like this earlier journey, the Freedom Ride of 1961 would test compliance with a court decision by sending an interracial group traveling through southern cities. The Ride would go further and ignore 'white' and 'colored' signs hanging by toilets, lunch-counters, and waiting rooms in the deep South. Moreover, if the riders were arrested, they vowed to remain in jail to make Jim Crow prohibitively expensive. 'We planned the Freedom Ride', Farmer revealed, 'with the specific intention of creating a crisis. We were counting on the bigots in the South to do our work for us. We figured that the government would have to respond if we created a situation that was headline news all over the world.' The two-week, 1,500-mile trip was to end in New Orleans on 17 May, the anniversary of the *Brown* decision.

Farmer made elaborate preparations for the risky Freedom Ride. Because CORE had a small budget, SCLC and NAACP branches would provide food and lodging along the way. To ensure protection, Farmer forewarned the federal government of his plans and enclosed a map outlining the journey's route. The Ride, he noted, was not civil disobedience, because segregated bus stops were unconstitutional. President Kennedy, attorney general Robert Kennedy, the chairman of the Interstate Commerce Commission, and the bus companies, ignored CORE's correspondence and hoped that the demonstration would go away. FBI director J. Edgar Hoover passed on the Ride's itinerary to Alabama officials, some of whom were known to be violent klansmen.

On 4 May, thirteen obscure CORE volunteers – seven black, six white – set out from Washington in Greyhound and Trailways buses. To challenge prevailing custom, blacks sat in the front of the bus and whites in the back. At first, the Ride experienced few difficulties. But when John Lewis, a short, slightly built veteran of the Nashville sit-ins, approached the white waiting room in Rock Hill, South Carolina, hoodlums in leather jackets and duck-tail haircuts blocked his path. 'Nigger, you can't come in here,' they sneered. Lewis cited the *Boynton* decision and tried to pass by, only to be slugged and kicked until he fell to the ground, bleeding. When another rider, Albert Bigelow, a Harvard-trained architect and ex-Navy captain, shielded Lewis, the thugs attacked Bigelow until he collapsed. A policeman then told the gang, 'All right, boys. Y'all've done about enough now. Why don'cha all go on home now?'

More bloodshed seemed likely in the Klan state of Alabama. The long-anticipated violence erupted on 14 May in Anniston, sixty miles east of Birmingham. As the Greyhound bus pulled into the station, the driver yelled to the mob of two hundred, 'Well, boys, here they are. I brought you some niggers and nigger-lovers.' With that invitation, the enraged mob surrounded the bus, dented the sides, smashed the windows, and slashed the tires. To complete the lynching in a deserted area, the driver drove out of town, where the mob pummeled the bus again. When someone hurled a smoke bomb through a smashed window to force the riders out, the seats caught fire, forcing the choking passengers to lie on the floor to breathe. Delighted by this turn of events, the mob cried, 'Fry the goddamn niggers!' Henry Thomas, a Howard University student from Florida, decided that the asphyxiating smoke on the bus would kill him, so he might as well face the bloodthirsty mob. He was almost killed, as his head was clubbed with a bat. When the rest of the coughing riders stumbled out, they too were assaulted while the bus burned then exploded. The lynching was interrupted by, of all people, an undercover Alabama state patrolman, who brandished his pistol and badge and shouted that he would kill any assailant. When the grievously wounded riders reached a hospital, the mob threatened to burn it down. In the nick of time, Fred Shuttlesworth sent a caravan from Birmingham to rescue the injured. Except for the embarrassing media coverage, Kennedy's Justice department regarded the bombing as nothing more than 'a pain in the ass'.

The Trailways bus arrived in Anniston an hour later. As four policemen stood by, hoodlums entered the bus with brass knuckles, blackjacks, and pistols. One of them gave an ultimatum: 'I ain't movin' this bus another foot until the niggers get into the back of the bus where they belong.' The black freedom riders ignored the demand and were thrown to the rear. When two white riders – James Peck, a wealthy 46-year-old white pacifist, and Walter Bergman, a retired professor with socialist sympathies – intervened, the hoodlums savagely turned on them too. Peck ended up face down on the floor, bleeding profusely, and Bergman's head was kicked until his brain hemorrhaged and he was confined to a wheelchair for life. One observer described the bloodshed as a 'hog killing'.

This same Trailways bus reached Birmingham later that day. Shuttlesworth warned the riders that it was an open secret that a mob would be waiting for the buses. The mob was encouraged by the notorious commissioner of public safety, Theophilus Eugene 'Bull' Connor, a high-school dropout, union buster, and former sports radio announcer, who wanted the riders stripped naked and beaten until 'it looked like a bulldog got hold of them'. Gary Thomas Rowe, an 8th-grade dropout and divorced father of four who had just joined the Klan, forewarned the FBI that the police would let the KKK do its dirty work. Rowe had overheard sergeant Tom Cook tell imperial wizard Robert Shelton of the United Klans of America that 'you can beat 'em, bomb 'em, maim 'em, kill 'em, I don't give a — —. . . . You can assure every Klansman in the country that no one will be arrested in Alabama for that fifteen minutes.' J. Edgar Hoover, who ran the FBI as his personal fiefdom for a half century, did not pass Rowe's warning to his titular boss, Robert Kennedy.

No policemen were in sight as the buses arrived, Connor claimed, because they were visiting their mothers on Mother's Day. As the bloodied Peck looked out the window next to the loading platform, he saw thirty men, including

Tommy Rowe, carrying bats, bicycle chains, and lead-lined bats. Resigned to their fate, the riders disembarked only to be beaten senseless. Peck was left for dead and needed fifty-three stitches to close the gashes. By the time the police arrived, the thugs had vanished in waiting cars. Governor John Patterson had no sympathy for the riders, because 'when you go somewhere looking for trouble, you usually find it'. Although the FBI had photographic proof that Rowe participated in crimes that he was supposed to prevent, it paid him $22,000 over a five-year career as an informant.

The sickening violence put pressure on the president, but Kennedy hesitated to act, beyond requiring an anti-discrimination clause in federal contracts. With his wealth and Harvard education, the Boston-bred Kennedy was far removed from powerless black southerners, and he regarded civil rights as a minor irritant that could divide his party and cost him reelection. Unreconstructed southern Democrats like James Eastland, Richard Russell, and Howard W. Smith hated the very idea of civil rights – 'civil wrongs', in their view – and they had a stranglehold on Kennedy's program in Congress. To curry their favor, Kennedy withheld civil rights legislation, delayed desegregating public housing, kept the Civil Rights Commission on a short leash, and appointed racist judges to the federal bench. Kennedy cynically believed that such actions would not alienate black voters from the Democratic party as long as he cultivated black leaders with money, patronage, and sympathetic words. Moreover, the president believed that the principle of federalism assigned law enforcement to local officials. Most important for Kennedy, national survival came first, and he fretted that black demands during the Cold War sent the wrong signal to Moscow when Berlin and central Europe were threatened. He ordered an aide to 'tell [the riders] to call it off. Stop them!'

Although the Kennedy administration feared that more racial violence was likely, it wanted to avoid using army troops in Alabama in a repeat of the Little Rock crisis. Robert Kennedy explained his reluctance to use force in the deep South: 'Now maybe it's going to take a decade; and maybe a lot of people are going to be killed in the meantime. . . . But in the long run . . . it's the best way to proceed.' That left the administration with two choices. Ideally, governor Patterson would protect the riders, but if not, US marshals would be sent in. When the attorney general called to discuss the matter with Patterson – 'our great pal in the South' – the governor's aide said he had 'gone fishing'. Exasperated, Kennedy reached the Greyhound superintendent in Birmingham and barked at him: 'Somebody better get in the damn bus and . . . get these people on their way.' Finally, the attorney general sent an emissary, John Seigenthaler, a native Tennessean, to talk turkey to Patterson. Although Patterson warned Seigenthaler that there would be 'blood in the streets' if the president sent US marshals, Seigenthaler held his ground until state public safety director Floyd Mann promised to protect the riders.

Instead of quitting, frantic SNCC leaders in Nashville continued the Ride, lest mobs conclude that violence could preserve segregation. Farmer warned SNCC that the trip might be 'suicide', but an iron-willed Diane Nash was undeterred. 'If they stop us with violence,' she insisted, 'the movement is dead. We're coming.' She dispatched ten riders to Birmingham, where the police put them in protective custody. In the middle of the night, public safety commissioner Connor drove the students to the Tennessee line, where they were dumped on the side of a road in Klan country. John Lewis said he was never 'so frightened in all my life'. Fortuitously, the dazed students found a shack owned by a frightened old black couple who took them in. The students called Nash for food and a car and headed back to Birmingham immediately.

The students wanted to continue the journey, but fearful bus drivers would not drive them. When blacks boarded a bus to leave Birmingham, a white driver nervously told them, 'I understand there is a big convoy down the road and I don't have but one life to give and I don't intend to give it to CORE or the NAACP.' With that, the driver disappeared. Governor Patterson nonetheless advised the riders to 'get out of Alabama as quickly as possible' because 'the state . . . can't guarantee the safety of fools'. The bus company produced the missing white driver after the attorney general threatened to send down a black driver in an Air Force fighter plane. As policemen surrounded the bus to protect a new group of twenty-one freedom riders bound for Montgomery, Fred Shuttlesworth was delighted: 'Man, what this state's coming to! An armed escort to take a bunch of niggers to a bus station so they can break these silly old laws.'

The police protection vanished when the bus entered Montgomery. The moment the riders got off the bus all hell broke loose as Tommy Rowe and hundreds of klansmen went ballistic, shouting, 'Go get the niggers!' They went first for the news photographers who could rally support for the riders. Thugs then seized John Lewis and beat him bloody with a Coca-Cola crate. While James Zwerg, a Wisconsin exchange student attending Fisk University, prayed that God would forgive the assailants, he was knocked out and had his teeth kicked in. After watching the sordid beating on television, Zwerg's father suffered a heart attack and his mother a mental breakdown. The thugs broke another boy's leg and set a man on fire with kerosene. When John Seigenthaler offered to assist two women who were being beaten, he was sucker-punched from behind with an iron bar and lay unconscious until Floyd Mann and his troopers arrived. Mann fired his gun into the air and yelled, 'There'll be no killing here today.' When a white attacker raised his bat against 19-year-old Nashville seminarian William Barbee, Mann put his gun to the attacker's head. 'One more swing,' he shouted, 'and you're dead.' Barbee lived, but was paralyzed.

The next day, a large rally was held in Ralph Abernathy's Montgomery church. As the rally began, angry whites waving Confederate flags surrounded the church and tossed stones, bottles, and Molotov cocktails at it. The ministers pleaded for calm, but some men pulled out knives and guns to defend their families. Martin Luther King angrily called Robert Kennedy for help, and the attorney general dispatched 400 US marshals to disperse the mob with tear gas. It was the first federal show of force to protect blacks since the Little Rock crisis. Unfortunately, the chemical wafted inside the church. Just as it looked as if the trapped crowd would capitulate, governor Patterson surprisingly declared martial law and sent in the police and Alabama National Guard.

The president hoped that this latest disturbance would persuade the riders to accept a cooling-off period. He did not want any domestic embarrassments before his upcoming summit meeting with Soviet premier Nikita Khrushchev in Vienna. Kennedy had been humiliated a month earlier in the Bay of Pigs fiasco, leading Robert Kennedy to pressure Farmer to stop the Ride. An insulted Farmer replied heatedly that 'We have been cooling off for 350 years. If we cool off any more, we will be in a deep freeze. The Freedom Ride will go on!'

New riders arrived from southern cities, and the Ride resumed days after the mob attacked Abernathy's church. Despite several entreaties, Martin Luther King did not become a rider. He explained that, if he survived, the ride would violate his probation in Georgia and send him to prison for six months. Moreover, he wanted to pick the time of his own Golgotha, a reference to Jesus' crucifixion. The student riders derided King for his lame excuse, pointing out that they were on probation too. '*De Lawd!*' they called King for comparing himself to Christ. The Ride's instigator, James Farmer, was likewise petrified by the trip's obvious peril and intended to stay behind. He went to the bus station and shook hands with the riders, telling 17-year-old Doris Castle to 'have a safe journey'. Dumbfounded, Castle implored him to rejoin the Ride. Farmer regretted his cowardice and climbed on board.

As the buses sped toward Mississippi, which Farmer called 'bigotry's main den', the riders received protection from planes and helicopters, as well as National Guardsmen and dozens of police cars. Before long, the buses passed by two ominous billboards at the state line: 'WELCOME TO MISSISSIPPI THE MAGNOLIA STATE' and 'PREPARE TO MEET THY GOD.' 'Everyone on the bus was prepared to die,' a rider admitted. The riders took the precaution of writing down the names and addresses of kinfolk who could claim their bodies. To banish their fear, they sang one song with gusto:

I'm a-takin' a ride	Hallelujah, I'm a travelin'
On the Greyhound bus line.	Hallelujah, ain't it fine?
I'm a-ridin' the *front seat*	Hallelujah, I'm a travelin'
To Jackson, this time.	Down freedom's main line.

As the Ride continued, Robert Kennedy decided that his brother's political fortunes mattered more than the constitutional rights of the students to travel where they wanted. After a flurry of telephone calls, the attorney general made a Faustian bargain with James Eastland, the rock-ribbed segregationist who chaired the Senate Judiciary committee [*Doc. 7*]. The riders would be arrested in Jackson for their own safety, provided there was no mob violence. Eastland kept his promise. When the riders entered the bus station's white cafeteria and restrooms, they were promptly pushed in paddy wagons, charged with disorderly conduct, and fined $200 each. State officials told klansmen that arrests were more effective in stopping Freedom Rides than burning buses.

Farmer announced that the riders would not pay the fines, which meant three weeks of jail time. The riders were crammed into small cells where they were given urine-soaked blankets. To relieve overcrowding in the county jail, the police moved the riders to the dungeon cells of Parchman penitentiary. In 'Little Alcatraz', the riders were subjected to a nearly unbearable routine. They ate overly salted food covered with bugs and were denied books, exercise, and cigarettes. The guards regularly abused them with electric prods and wrist-breakers and subjected women to humiliating body searches. Some riders were so stressed that they sang songs, began hunger strikes, and punched each other. The songfest irritated the guards, who confiscated the bedding and blasted the riders with pressurized water. Hank Thomas hollered, '*Take my mattress! I'll keep my soul!*' When the riders still refused to cooperate, they ended up in sweatboxes or solitary confinement.

Farmer urged others to keep the pressure on apartheid by flouting Jim Crow laws and going to jail. A thousand people, mostly young black men, but also white clergy, Quakers, professors, communists, and union members, crossed the color line in Dixie. The push to desegregate bus bathrooms spread to other interstate facilities, including railroad depots and airport terminals, and the jails filled to overflowing. Their sacrifice paid off. At the attorney general's behest, the ICC required interstate carriers and terminals to display signs saying that seating was available 'without regard to race, color, creed or national origin'. In three hundred southern terminals, signs segregating the races in waiting rooms and restrooms were taken down that fall. It had taken the federal government fifteen years to enforce the Supreme Court's ruling for desegregated interstate travel.

To steer the movement into less confrontational activities, Robert Kennedy promoted a Voter Education Project to register blacks who would use the polling booth to dissolve segregation. He gave VEP tax-exempt status and lined up liberal philanthropies, including the Taconic, Field, and Stern foundations, to pay $900,000 to run it. Donors would get tax deductions, and activists draft exemptions. Many black activists accused the administration of a 'trade-off' bordering on 'bribery'. They suspected correctly that the Kennedys wanted to shut down direct-action campaigns in favor of a quiet, orderly crusade for ballot-box power. The president saw black voter registration as a highly beneficial activity for him and his party that would take the media spotlight off the protesters, enroll more voters for Democratic candidates, and make southern Democrats in Congress more reasonable.

The offer of federal money was too good to pass up. That fall, the NAACP, SCLC, CORE, SNCC, and Urban League launched VEP under the Southern Regional Council's auspices. To coordinate their activities in Mississippi, these rival organizations formed an umbrella group called the Council of Federated Organizations. Although the bulk of the project's funds in the first two years went to the Magnolia State, next to no gains were made there. Across the South, VEP raised black voter registration from 29 to 43 per cent, primarily in safer urban areas.

At the end of 1961, CORE pressed president Kennedy to end discrimination in public housing as he had promised. Thousands of civil rights supporters mailed ballpoint pens to the White House, needling the president that perhaps he had not signed the executive order desegregating public housing because his pen was dry. The 'Ink for Jack' campaign was nearly fruitless. Kennedy waited until after the 1962 midterm elections before signing a weak executive order banning such bias. The order applied only to future housing financed by federal loans or grants, which was a small part of the market.

The Freedom Ride forced president Kennedy to confront civil rights issues, however weakly. He sent emissaries to report on racial wrongdoing and negotiate an end to it. And he ordered US marshals to escort the riders. Still, Kennedy faced a stiffer challenge. When a black student applied for admission to an all-white university in Mississippi, would Kennedy send in federal troops as Eisenhower had in Little Rock?

CHAPTER EIGHT

BATTLE OF OLE MISS

In January 1961, Air Force veteran James Meredith sought to transfer from Jackson State College to the University of Mississippi in Oxford. As a Mississippi resident with many college credits, the 28-year-old Meredith was entitled to attend the state's premier university and citadel of white supremacy, but he faced very long odds. Five black men had tried unsuccessfully to integrate higher education in the Magnolia State before Meredith. One was admitted to a mental institution instead while another was sentenced to seven years on a chain gang on a trumped-up charge of stealing chicken feed. Indeed, not a single black student had gone to any white school in Mississippi since *Brown* prohibited segregated education. Despite this record of futility, Meredith believed that his 'divine responsibility' was to crack the color line at Ole Miss by forcing a national crisis. Just days before Meredith made his plans, he learned that Charlayne Hunter and Hamilton Holmes had peacefully ended 175 years of segregation at the University of Georgia.

When Meredith inquired about applying to Ole Miss, he concealed his race. The unaware registrar sent Meredith a letter that said, 'We are very pleased to know of your interest in becoming a member of our student body.' Meredith then revealed that he was an 'American-Mississippi-Negro citizen'. This bombshell stunned university and state officials, who schemed for twenty months to keep Meredith out of Ole Miss. Hotly denying that race was a factor, school officials refused Meredith's application because it was 'late', because Jackson State and Ole Miss operated on different academic calendars, because Jackson State was not accredited by the major accrediting association, and because Meredith did not present letters of recommendation from five Ole Miss alumni. As the duplicitous delays became transparent, Meredith asked the NAACP for help. Although Thurgood Marshall remarked that 'this man has got to be crazy' to challenge Mississippi officials, he assigned the case to Constance Baker Motley when black woman lawyers were rarely seen in a southern courtroom.

When Meredith sued Ole Miss, his case was heard in the South's most unreconstructed federal courtroom. Judge Sidney Mize, a believer in genetically fixed racial differences, added insult to injury by holding a kangaroo court. Sitting in front of a mural of slaves picking cotton, Mize denied Motley's request to depose university personnel, even though the university deposed Meredith. Mize then postponed the trial, claiming the court's docket was too full. When the trial ultimately resumed, Mize hinted that Meredith was morally unfit for Ole Miss because Meredith registered to vote in a county different from his legal residence. (Meredith had lived in both counties and was unsure where to register.) The registrar told the court that Meredith was a 'trouble maker' with 'psychological problems'. Mize agreed with this assessment and issued a dubious finding that Ole Miss had not excluded Meredith because of his race.

A tussle ensued within the federal courts. In June 1962, the Fifth Circuit Court of Appeals reversed Mize's 'never-never land' decision and ordered Ole Miss to admit Meredith that fall. The majority of judges – John Minor Wisdom, Elbert Tuttle, Richard Rives, and John P. Brown – held that Ole Miss had 'engaged in a carefully calculated campaign of delay, harassment, and masterly inactivity' to exclude Meredith for racial reasons. When the order was appealed to the US Supreme Court, justice Hugo Black forbade state officials from blocking Meredith's immediate enrollment into Ole Miss.

Unwilling to surrender, governor Ross Barnett decried Meredith's admission to Ole Miss as 'our greatest crisis since the War Between the States'. Beholden to the Citizens' Council, Barnett held out for six more weeks until Ole Miss erupted in gunfire. The grandstanding governor, whose father was a Confederate veteran, stirred up racial hatred to divert attention from repeated gaffes, a sales tax hike, and a scandal over gold-plated faucets in his mansion. Resurrecting the discredited doctrine of states' rights, Barnett interposed the 'sovereignty' of Mississippi against federal authority over education, vowing that 'No school will be integrated in Mississippi while I am your governor. . . . We will not drink from the cup of genocide.' Appealing to white fears, he claimed that 'there is no case in history where the Caucasian race has survived social integration. We must either submit to the unlawful dictate of the federal government or stand up like men and tell them, "NEVER!"'. The governor's incendiary words encouraged the violence that followed.

Mississippi's defiance of federal court decisions pulled the president into the Meredith matter, even though he did not want to alienate an important region or get backed into a corner by a demagogic governor as Eisenhower had been. Above all, Kennedy wanted to avoid bloodshed between federal troops and white Mississippians, which would revive bitter memories of the Civil War and Reconstruction. To resolve the matter peacefully, the administration kept a low profile, as it had during the Freedom Ride in Alabama. White House officials conferred with senator James Eastland, university professors, and business leaders to lobby Ole Miss trustees to admit Meredith. Secret telephone negotiations with the governor became the centerpiece of the administration's behind-the-doors campaign. That strategy proved fruitless. Counting on his powers of persuasion, the attorney general called the slippery governor twenty times to find a way out of the dilemma. No compromise was possible, the governor observed, for the bottom line was 'whether Mississippi can run its institutions or the federal government is going to run things'. Martin Luther King found this deal-making disturbing, for it 'made Negroes feel like pawns in a white man's political game'. He realized sadly that president Kennedy and governor Barnett were closer to each other than the president was to him.

The campaign against James Meredith escalated on 20 September, the beginning of registration at the University of Mississippi. At midnight, klansmen burned a gigantic cross between two dormitories. Hours later, state legislators rammed through a bill denying university admission to anyone guilty of 'moral turpitude' or any criminal offense. It was a law written only for Meredith. Later that day, when Meredith was sentenced *in absentia* to a year in jail for voter fraud, he was ineligible for Ole Miss. Meredith defied state officials and went to the campus with chief federal marshal James McShane, a tough former New York cop. As the unflappable Meredith faced thousands of students cursing and pelting his car with rocks, he thought, 'What a terrible waste of time and money and energy to iron out some rough spots in our civilization.'

The Fifth Circuit Court of Appeals threatened the university trustees with contempt for denying Meredith's registration. The trustees relented, and federal lawyers obtained a court order that forbade the governor from blocking Meredith's registration. But when Meredith arrived at the Woolfolk State Office Building in Jackson, Barnett stood in the doorway and read another proclamation of interposition denying him admission 'now and forevermore'. A state senator praised the governor's stand as 'the most brilliant piece of statesmanship ever displayed in Mississippi'. That night, the appeals court found Barnett guilty of civil contempt and ordered him to register Meredith within a week or face arrest and a staggering fine of $10,000 per day.

To avoid bankruptcy while protecting his reputation among businessmen who feared a catastrophe, Barnett proposed several deals with the Kennedys. Barnett would allow Meredith to register at Ole Miss if the federal marshals pulled their guns against the state police, a charade that would demonstrate that Mississippi had to surrender to superior force. The bizarre arrangement fell through when Barnett called the attorney general with the frightening news that wild-eyed vigilantes were prowling Oxford's streets, ready to defend the state's color line. After Robert Kennedy failed four times to register Meredith, the president tried to clean up the 'God-damn mess' by calling the 'loony' governor himself. 'I don't know Mr Meredith,' the president began, 'but . . . under the Constitution I have to carry out the orders of the Court. . . . I would like to get your help doing it.' The governor finally promised to preserve order on campus 'as best we can', thereby avoiding jail. Just to hedge their bets, the president, secretary of the Army, and chairman of the Joint Chiefs of Staff met in the war room of the White House to pore over maps of Mississippi.

As the battle became imminent, the governor again stirred the pot of racism. On Saturday night, 29 September, Barnett appeared at an Ole Miss football game where 41,000 fans waved Confederate flags during the national anthem and chanted 'We want Ross!' At the fifty-yard line, Barnett raised a clenched fist in defiance and roared over loudspeakers to the adoring crowd: 'I love Mississippi! I love her people! Our customs! And I love and respect our *heritage*!' The crowd responded with a defiant song:

> Never, Never, Never, Never, No-o-o Never, Never, Never
> We will not yield an inch of any field,
> Fix us another toddy, ain't yieldin' to no-body,
> Ross's standin' like Gibraltar, he shall never falter,
> Ask us what we say, it's to hell with Bobby K,
> Never shall our emblem go from Colonel Reb to Old Black Joe.

In this ugly, Nazi-like scene, segregationists announced their readiness to die for white supremacy.

As the day for Meredith's registration approached again, white defiance deepened. Radio stations played 'Dixie' to rouse resistance. When word spread of plans to arrest Barnett, thousands of whites surrounded the governor's mansion. Outside the state, former major general Edwin Walker from Dallas, Texas, called for an insurrection of 10,000 armed volunteers 'to rally to the cause of freedom' in Oxford. Five years earlier, Walker had overseen the desegregation of Central High School in Little Rock. Since then, he was dismissed from the army for indoctrinating troops with right-wing literature from the John Birch Society. Walker's appeal led many troublemakers from across the South to Ole Miss. Sporting greasy, duck-tail haircuts, these toughs brought along high-powered rifles, shotguns, and squirrel guns. Recognizing serious trouble was in the offing, Mississippi's congressional delegation telegraphed an ominous warning to president Kennedy: 'A HOLOCAUST IS IN THE MAKING.'

At last, the White House discovered a weak point in the governor's façade. When the governor kept stonewalling, Robert Kennedy told a petrified Barnett that he would leak their incriminating taped telephone conversations. The governor, who publicly urged resistance to the federal government, was privately negotiating the state's surrender to it. Realizing the jig was up, Barnett would let Meredith register on Sunday, 30 September, when the campus would be largely deserted. Barnett would not oppose Meredith's registration if he could 'just raise cain' about it to protect his reputation. He could then claim that the Kennedys hoodwinked him and that he had not retreated a single inch on segregation.

Once Meredith was escorted safely to a heavily guarded dorm room, the oak-lined campus became a battleground. For fourteen hours, a frenzied mob of 3,000 roughnecks and Ole Miss students charged federal marshals defending the Lyceum administration building with rocks, Coke bottles, lead pipes, eggs, and smoke bombs. 'Give us the nigger!' the mob screamed. One marshal confessed to being 'more scared in Mississippi' than he was at Pearl Harbor. Having donned protective masks, the marshals fired back tear gas, but the wind blew much of it into the faces of the Klan-dominated state highway patrolmen, who were manning campus roadblocks. As the choking fog spread, the patrolmen withdrew to their cars, allowing the mob to toss Molotov cocktails, chunks of concrete, and acid from the chemistry lab at the marshals. The marshals dug themselves a huge hole because they had no campus maps, bullhorns for crowd control, flak jackets, or first-aid equipment. Before long, the mob fired shotguns, burned vehicles, and drove a bulldozer at the marshals. Many students fled, but some fraternity boys joined the riot, enraged by rumors that a sorority girl was killed. Episcopal priest Duncan Gray, Jr., and Ole Miss chaplain Wofford Smith entered the battlefield to persuade some rioters to surrender their weapons, but the indiscriminate violence lasted through the night, reminding a federal official of the Alamo.

The Battle of Ole Miss was the most serious federal–state confrontation since the Civil War. To stop the mayhem, the president federalized the National Guard – one of whom was Ross Barnett's son – and sent troops from Memphis to Oxford. Several foul-ups ensued, delaying the troops until 2 a.m. All told, 31,000 army troops, US marshals, and National Guardsmen arrived to protect one black student at a cost of $2.7 million. There were three times more US troops in Oxford than in West Berlin. To avoid offending white Mississippi sensibilities, Robert Kennedy agreed to segregate hundreds of black soldiers, sending them to the back of the occupation force, where they washed dishes. By the time all the troops arrived, two were dead and 375 injured, including half of the marshals. French journalist Paul Guilhard had been forced at gunpoint to an abandoned area, where he was executed. His telling last dispatch read: 'The Civil War has never ended.' The murders were never solved, and no rioter was expelled or convicted of the crime he was charged with – insurrection. President Kennedy called the riot 'the worst thing I've seen in forty-five years' and blamed himself for not sending the troops earlier.

Hours after the gunshots ended, an unscathed and stoic Meredith crossed the rubble-strewn campus to register at 8.30 a.m. on 1 October. It was his fifth attempt at registration. 'Was it worth two lives, nigger?' a student yelled at him. Meredith's refusal to drop out led a group called the Rebel Resistance to drive 'the coon from the curriculum'. The Underground slashed tires, threw cherry bombs, smeared excrement in dorm rooms, and made hate calls to Meredith and his 'communist' supporters. In the mail, Meredith received a rope and a poem: 'Roses are red, violets are blue; I've killed one nigger and might as well make it two.' His teenaged sister was nearly killed when buckshot sprayed their father's house. To shield Meredith, five hundred soldiers and marshals – referred to as 'Kennedy's *Koon Keepers*' – stayed with him until he graduated with a political science degree a year later 1963. On the last day of classes, Meredith triumphantly wore a 'Ross is Right!' badge upside-down. Having survived death threats to graduate from Ole Miss, Meredith escaped to Nigeria.

The Battle of Ole Miss cost the state dearly, and most whites hated Kennedy for helping Meredith. Car bumper stickers appeared, reading, 'FEDERALLY OCCUPIED MISSISSIPPI' and 'KENNEDY'S HUNGARY.' Congressman John Bell Williams compared the Kennedys to Hitler and his 'infamous Gestapo', and the state senate expressed its 'complete, entire and utter contempt for the Kennedy administration and its puppet courts'. With Kennedy beyond reach, a grand jury indicted federal marshal McShane for inciting the riot. At Ole Miss, student enrollment dropped, and thirty-seven professors resigned, including most of the chemists and all of the philosophers. James Silver, a transplanted New Yorker who was president of the Southern Historical Association, became 'the most hated white man in Mississippi' for giving a speech that exposed the state for what it was – 'a closed society' in which Jim Crow was king. For his impudence, Silver was run out of the state.

Such sentiment notwithstanding, the bloodshed at Ole Miss helped turn the tide against massive resistance, because violence repelled many white southern clergy, educators, businessmen, labor leaders, and editors. South Carolina governor Ernest Hollings told state legislators to accept school desegregation: 'We have all argued that [*Brown*] is not the law of the land. But everyone must agree that it is the fact of the land. Interposition, sovereignty, legal motions, personal defiance have all been applied – and all attempts have failed.' Mississippi governor-elect Paul Johnson did an ideological about-face, vowing that 'hate or prejudice or ignorance will not lead' the state while he was in charge. He backed up his promise by cutting off state funding to the Citizens' Council and dismantling barriers to black voting. Businessmen in Jackson defied general sentiment to comply with a new civil rights act mandating integrated public facilities.

The Battle of Ole Miss demonstrated again that the federal government had the power to enforce the law, if the president had the will. For two years, Kennedy was a captive of political expediency and his distorted view of American history. Finally, Kennedy sent troops into battle to protect the rights of one black man, the first time since Lincoln had done so. Nevertheless, Martin Luther King would have to push the Kennedy administration further by making a frontal attack on segregation as a moral crime, beginning in Birmingham.

CHAPTER NINE

BOMBINGHAM

After World War II, George Wallace launched his political career in Alabama as a progressive Democrat who protected the poor and avoided race-baiting. But when state attorney general John Patterson bested him for governor with the Klan vote, the former bantamweight boxing champion vowed never to be 'out-nigguhed' again. In his second gubernatorial bid, Wallace underwent a dramatic metamorphosis, pledging to cheering crowds that he would stand in every schoolhouse door in the state to defy desegregation. At his inauguration in 1963, Wallace breathed racial fire: 'In the name of the greatest people that have ever trod this earth, I draw the line in the dust and toss the gauntlet before the feet of tyranny and I say, segregation now, segregation tomorrow, segregation forever!' Martin Luther King regarded Wallace as the 'most dangerous racist in America today. . . . I am not sure that he believes all the poison he preaches, but he is artful enough to convince others that he does.' Within six months, Wallace and his supporters lost two key rounds to the civil rights movement – one in Birmingham, the other in Tuscaloosa.

At first, it appeared that the movement might not get off the ground in Alabama because of a notable failure in Albany, a peanut and pecan community in southwest Georgia. In the fall, 1961, two scruffy SNCC organizers and veteran freedom riders arrived to challenge segregation and job discrimination head on. Charles Sherrod, a young Baptist preacher from Virginia, and his 18-year-old companion, Cordell Reagon of Nashville, aimed at mobilizing the entire black community, especially students at Albany State College and the high school. Pushed by SNCC, the NAACP and other leading groups formed a partnership called the Albany Movement, which was led by William Anderson, an osteopath and drugstore owner, and Slater King, a realtor.

In November, hundreds of eager students were arrested for staging sit-ins at bus and train stations that ignored the ICC's order to desegregate. At their first mass meeting, local blacks heard the testimony of students who survived a wretched jail only to be expelled from college. Afterward, the crowd vented their frustrations through music. Bernice Johnson and Rutha Harris – preachers' daughters with operatic ambition – joined tenor Cordell Reagon in singing such inspirational and adaptable songs as 'This Little Light of Mine', 'Ain't Gonna Let Nobody Turn Me 'Round', 'If You Miss Me at the Back of the Bus', and especially, 'We Shall Overcome'. These powerful songs rocked the churches with thunderous handclapping and foot-stomping and became movement standards. 'Nobody knew what kept the top of the church on its four walls,' one participant recalled. 'It was as if everyone had been lifted up on high.'

Still, the Albany Movement could not force immediate integration any-where. A boycott of white businesses produced a sharp decline in sales, but the city commissioners refused to negotiate. When blacks entered hotels, restaur-ants, and theaters, they were arrested for breach of peace. When the demon-strators kept coming, the wily police chief, Laurie Pritchett, was ready for them. He had studied the Montgomery bus boycott and Freedom Ride and concluded that violence attracted the media like bees to pollen, which then pressured the federal government to intervene. So to prevent any 'nigger organization' from taking over the town, the chief arrested demonstrators with a velvet fist and received glowing press coverage. The beatings took place off-camera. In jail, the authorities broke a white demonstrator's jaw and kicked Slater King's pregnant wife Marion so badly that she miscarried. Most effectively, Pritchett undercut the jail, no bail strategy by sending the demonstrators to rented jails up to thirty miles away. In a war of attrition, the Albany Movement ran out of marchers before Pritchett ran out of jails.

Without consulting SNCC, Anderson asked his old friend, Martin Luther King, to rescue the movement. King expected to make a speech and then leave, but at the end of an emotional rally, Anderson asked King to lead a march on city hall the next day. Boxed in, King could only agree and was jailed. Although King vowed not to accept bond, his attorney hammered out a verbal agreement with the mayor and police chief that would release him and all local activists. In return for an end to the demonstrations, the city promised to comply with the ICC desegregation ruling and initiate biracial negotiations. It was all a 'hoax', King realized later. Different theories account for King's bailing out on Albany: SNCC was jealous of SCLC; city officials were intransigent; Anderson was literally hallucinating; the demonstrators needed to get out; King wanted to get out. Once King was released, federal district judge Robert Elliott – a segregationist appointed by Kennedy – forbade him from leading any more marches, an order King obeyed. Dozens of local blacks marched without him and were arrested. The low point came when blacks rioted to protest against police abuse, prompting sheriff Pritchett to ridicule the movement for 'them non-violent rocks'. Tired of this costly quagmire, King declared the agreement a victory and left segregation intact.

Even in defeat, the Albany campaign profoundly affected the civil rights movement because new techniques were developed to sustain mass militancy. Albany was unusual in its broad membership, its comprehensive attack on Jim Crow, its plan to fill the jails, its use of energizing music, and its alliance of local and outside leaders. The campaign against segregation showed that nonviolence by itself could not exert enough pressure on politicians as opposed to more vulnerable businessmen. An outside power – the federal government – had to take the side of blacks. Because King was humiliated in Albany, he vowed not to dive into future crises. 'I don't want to be a fireman anymore,' he said wearily. He had not won a major civil rights victory in the seven years since Montgomery, and SCLC was flat broke.

Moreover, the civil rights movement was losing ground to restless young blacks, such as heavyweight boxing champion Muhammad Ali, who found black nationalism irresistible. The leading black nationalist organization was Elijah Muhammad's Lost-Found Nation of Islam, a secretive group commonly called the Black Muslims. With thousands of members, largely from the ghetto, the Nation believed that the only antidotes to racism and violence were self-control, self-reliance, self-defense, and complete separation of the races. Malcolm X, a gangly street hustler turned spellbinding Muslim minister, picked up where Marcus Garvey left off. Declaring integration unworkable, Malcolm accused King's middle-class movement of deceiving the black masses into thinking that Christian nonviolent protest would improve their lives. King's plan to love the white man into submission, Malcolm thought, was delusional and dangerous. Malcolm did not want 'to integrate into this corrupt society, but to separate from it, to a land of our own, where we can reform ourselves, lift up our moral standards, and try to be godly'. In the meantime, he urged blacks to protect themselves from white devils 'by any means necessary', suggesting that 'killing is a two-way street'.

The civil rights movement was clearly at a crossroads. Aware of the stakes, King devised a carefully laid, narrowly focused plan called Project Confrontation to desegregate Birmingham. The South's largest industrial city had a history of racial discord because of rising black unemployment, meager public assistance, substandard housing, and police brutality. For years, five Klan groups tormented Birmingham's black section with a steady diet of cross burnings, mutilations, and bombings. Fearful blacks christened their community 'Dynamite Hill' and their city 'Bombingham'. Because of its violent past, King believed that Birmingham could greatly help the civil rights movement. He counted on public safety commissioner Bull Connor, patron saint of the local Klan, 'to commit his brutality openly – in the light of day – with the rest of the world looking on'. Such mindless villainy, King thought, would compel federal intervention. If 'the most segregated city in America' could be integrated through nonviolent direct action, the back of Jim Crow would be broken throughout the South. The plans for Birmingham became more imperative when president Kennedy told King that congressional opposition consigned civil rights to the back burner.

At the forefront of the battle to end such injustice stood the fiery Baptist preacher Fred Shuttlesworth. When Alabama banned the NAACP in 1956 for helping the Montgomery bus boycott, Shuttlesworth founded the Alabama Christian Movement for Human Rights, which became SCLC's strongest affiliate. Before long, ACMHR sought black police officers, challenged bus segregation, and tried to integrate the schools and railroad station. Shuttlesworth paid a heavy price for staring down evil. Klansmen bombed his home and church on Christmas Eve, and the police infiltrated ACMHR meetings, tapped his telephone, and harassed every black person walking down his street. When Shuttlesworth enrolled his children at the white school near his home, a mob stabbed his wife and pummeled him with chains while the police looked on. After years of frustration, Shuttlesworth pleaded with King to come to Birmingham.

Unlike Albany, SCLC would not pressure Birmingham politicians who had nothing to fear from the minuscule black vote. In early 1963, SCLC planned instead to disrupt the city's commerce by urging blacks to boycott selected downtown department stores. Using the Sixteenth Street Baptist Church as the protest headquarters, Wyatt T. Walker meticulously calculated how long it would take demonstrators to walk downtown so that traffic and business could be disrupted constantly even if some of them were arrested. Calypso singer Harry Belafonte raised several hundred thousand dollars for bail money when mass arrests came. Just days before the Easter shopping season in April, King laid down a list of demands that included black jobs and the right of blacks to enter any public place.

Project C almost fell apart when a reform candidate beat Bull Connor for mayor and many blacks wanted to give the new man a chance. King had come too far to stop now, despite the Justice department's plea to postpone the protests. Small groups of demonstrators led by Shuttlesworth and A.D. King, King's younger brother, marched downtown, where they were arrested for demonstrating without a permit. Bull Connor's police tired of such demonstrations and consequently thrashed the protesters with nightsticks and set snarling K-9 dogs on them. The cameras caught the ugly spectacle, provoking hundreds of steel mill workers to join the struggle. As the black community mobilized, officials obtained a state court injunction forbidding further protests.

This moment marked a Rubicon for King. In Albany, he obeyed a similar injunction against demonstrations, which stalled the movement. The Birmingham demonstration seemed doomed as well, with bail money having run out and black businessmen urging King to retreat. If King defied the judge's order, he risked alienating allies in Washington who could outlaw segregation. To obey the order, King recognized, would preserve a 'raw tyranny under the guise of maintaining law and order'. On Good Friday, King had an epiphany to obey an 'injunction from heaven' and transgress immoral man-made laws. Promising to lead demonstrations until 'Pharaoh lets God's people go', King marched to city hall and certain arrest. King thus followed Christian and American traditions that sometimes an evil is so great that a higher law must be obeyed. True to form, Connor put King in solitary confinement until Resurrection Sunday, when the Kennedys intervened to get him better treatment.

After King's arrest, a group of white clergymen criticized Project C in a full-page advertisement in the *Birmingham News*. The clergymen labeled the protest as 'unwise and untimely', the illegal actions of outside professional agitators. Scribbling on the margins of that newspaper, King penned a 'Letter from Birmingham Jail', a classic summary of his nonviolent philosophy [*Doc. 8*]. By turns conciliatory and unyielding, King criticized white moderates and the white church and explained that he was no 'outside agitator' but a dutiful Christian fighting 'injustice'. King warned that if the demonstrators were dismissed as 'rabble rousers', millions of blacks would turn to black nationalism, which would 'lead inevitably to a frightening racial nightmare'.

After a week in jail, King was released on bail, only to discover that the demonstrations had fizzled. A King associate admitted that 'we needed more troops' because 'we had scraped the bottom of the barrel of adults' who would go to jail. That reality led SCLC staffer James Bevel to call for a children's crusade: 'We're doing what we're doing for the next generation, so why shouldn't the kids join the struggle?' He noted that 'a boy from high school has the same effect in terms of being in jail, in terms of putting pressure on the city, as his father, and yet there's no economic threat to the family, because the father is still on the job'. The daring proposal left much of the black community aghast.

As another stalemate loomed, King agreed that desperate circumstances required desperate measures. On 2 May, hundreds of children – some as young as 6 years old – gathered at the Sixteenth Street Baptist Church to receive their 'second baptism'. After watching *The Nashville Story*, an inspirational film of the sit-ins, the children left the sanctuary and joyously marched, sang, and prayed for justice. They were soon herded onto paddy wagons and school buses headed to jail, the southern gateway to freedom. Impressed by the children's bravery and appalled by police brutality, many adults submitted to arrest. This compelling story drew reporters to Birmingham from around the country.

Faced with continuing demonstrations, an exasperated Bull Connor retaliated. He ordered firemen to turn high-pressured hoses against demonstrators who gathered at Kelly Ingram park opposite the Sixteenth Street church. The hoses knocked them over like bowling pins. When Fred Shuttlesworth was hospitalized with severe bruises, Connor remarked, 'I'm sorry I missed it. I wish they'd carried him away in a hearse.' Other demonstrators endured free-swinging policemen and surly German shepherd police dogs. As television broadcast the violence, the country was horrified and the president sickened. 'The civil rights movement', Kennedy quipped, 'should thank God for Bull Connor. He's helped it as much as Abraham Lincoln.' Those who did not escape went to jail, where as many as sixty blacks crowded into a single cell. With 3,000 blacks in custody, the movement filled the jails to overflowing for the first time.

The unrest in Birmingham prodded the Kennedy administration to act, lest third-world nations tilt toward Moscow and the Republicans regain the White House. Robert Kennedy persuaded the UAW to send $160,000 to secure bail bonds for the demonstrators. Meanwhile, Burke Marshall, the administration's chief troubleshooter on race, flew to Birmingham to initiate negotiations between King and the city's merchants. Treasury secretary Douglas Dillon and Defense secretary Robert McNamara called large business contractors, including US Steel's Roger Blough, to lean on Alabama businessmen.

After initially rejecting mediation, the city merchants capitulated. They had had enough of the crippling boycott, negative publicity, and stiff pressure from the White House. On 10 May, the chamber of commerce relented, and King won his demands for desegregated public areas and the hiring of some blacks at downtown stores. Shuttlesworth regarded the deal as entirely premature, but the path-breaking agreement brought invaluable media and presidential attention to the civil rights movement. Calling the settlement 'the most magnificent victory for justice we've seen in the Deep South', King told reporters that 'the city of Birmingham has reached an accord with its conscience'. That summer, fifty cities in the upper South desegregated to avoid the turmoil Birmingham experienced.

Sensing the collapse of their society, Alabama whites from the governor on down scorned the accord as the work of 'gutless traitors'. Before a thousand white-robed klansmen and flaming crosses, imperial wizard Robert Shelton declared that 'Martin Luther King's epitaph, in my opinion, can be written here in Birmingham.' That night, bombs blew up the home of King's brother and the Gaston Motel, where King's entourage and many reporters stayed. Blacks choking with rage demanded Connor's head. 'We'll kill him,' they vowed. When infuriated blacks overturned cars, burned white businesses, and pelted lawmen with bottles, state troopers beat the first blacks they found. At the moment of King's greatest triumph, nonviolence was losing its hold on the civil rights movement.

President Kennedy moved rapidly to quell the Birmingham disorder. The president promised to do 'whatever must be done' to prevent the agreement from being 'sabotaged by a few extremists'. He had learned the lessons of Little Rock and Ole Miss and sent federal troops to Ft. McClellan near Birmingham. Fortunately, federal force was unnecessary because the black community accepted King's call for nonviolence. More important, the mayor and city council complied with the negotiated settlement and went beyond it to desegregate the library, golf courses, and public schools.

The Kennedys congratulated themselves on the Birmingham agreement, but ignored warnings that race relations remained in dire need of repair. Novelist James Baldwin blamed whites for dehumanizing blacks through 'torture, castration, infanticide, rape, death and humiliation'. He thought that white liberals were worse than southern bigots because liberals were hypocrites who talked one way but lived another. In his best-selling work, *The Fire Next Time*, Baldwin forecast imminent racial violence unless 'total liberation' was forthcoming. Such sentiments led attorney general Robert Kennedy to set up a freewheeling meeting in his New York apartment with Baldwin and other black intellectuals and activists, including psychologist Kenneth Clark, playwright Lorraine Hansberry, singers Harry Belafonte and Lena Horne, and freedom rider Jerome Smith. For three hours, the group cursed Kennedy as the devil incarnate. 'What is it you want me to do?' Kennedy kept asking. Inside, the attorney general deeply resented such ingratitude over his brother's record. This was Kennedy's first exposure to the deep sense of black alienation in America, and, as Baldwin hoped, the federal government took a more active role in securing civil rights. The Kennedy administration filed a record 57 voting rights suits, appointed forty blacks to important posts, including Thurgood Marshall to a federal appeals court, and endorsed the 24th amendment that banned poll taxes in federal elections.

While the drama in Birmingham played out, two accomplished black students – Vivian Malone and James Hood – sought admission to the University of Alabama in Tuscaloosa, George Wallace's alma mater and the last all-white state university in America. A federal judge ordered the university to admit them to the 1963 summer session, but Wallace had other ideas. He asked colonel Albert Lingo, the state's public safety director, to dig up enough dirt on Malone and Hood to force them to withdraw their applications. When Lingo came up empty-handed, Wallace arranged a charade to enhance his political standing among white voters, as governors Orval Faubus and Ross Barnett had done. This showdown with Washington ran against the advice of his own attorney general and many of the state's newspaper editors, business executives, and university officials. Fearing the worst, the Kennedy administration pressured Wallace to back down or face jail time. 'Dammit,' the pugnacious governor replied to the state attorney general. 'Send the Justice Department word, I ain't compromising with anybody. I'm gonna [make the federal government] bring troops into this state.'

On the scorching morning of 11 June, deputy attorney general Nicholas Katzenbach confronted the governor at Foster Auditorium while Malone and Hood waited in a government sedan. As the television cameras rolled, the diminutive Wallace raised his hand for the 6'2", 200-pound Katzenbach to halt. A visibly angry Katzenbach read a presidential proclamation commanding the governor to step aside so that the students could enroll. Wallace read his own proclamation, a blistering condemnation of the federal government's 'unwelcomed, unwanted, unwarranted, and force-induced intrusion upon the campus of the University of Alabama'. Katzenbach declared that he was 'not interested in a *show*' and escorted Hood and Malone to their dorm rooms while President Kennedy federalized the Alabama National Guard.

Having scored points with his white constituency, Wallace declined the Klan's offer to storm the university and retreated to Montgomery. He admitted, 'I can't fight bayonets with my bare hands.' It was the last college campus showdown involving a southern governor and the federal government. For standing in the schoolhouse door, Wallace and his wife Lurleen were rewarded with an unequalled four more terms as Alabama's governor. Wallace was now America's top spokesman for segregation. The students that he tried to exclude from the University of Alabama excelled. Malone became the university's first black graduate, and Hood, after first dropping out because of stress, received his doctorate there three decades later.

Although the president was relieved that there was no Ole Miss rerun in Tuscaloosa, he faced increasing pressure to take more action for civil rights. In Cambridge, on the Eastern Shore of Maryland, where 70 per cent of blacks were either unemployed or seasonal workers, Gloria Richardson, a college graduate and a divorced, middle-aged mother of two, led a SNCC campaign against discrimination in hiring, housing, and education, rather than voting rights and segregation alone. Described as a Joan of Arc, the uncompromising Richardson was inspired by Harriet Tubman, the great Underground Railroad conductor who had been born a slave on the Eastern Shore. The Cambridge movement was the first grassroots movement outside the deep South and the first time a woman headed a direct-action campaign. When the demonstrators and police clashed, the National Guard used bayonets and pepper gas to restore order. Kennedy was sobered further by reports that racial clashes in the textile town of Danville, Virginia, sent forty-eight demonstrators to the hospital. That summer, 100,000 protesters demonstrated across the nation against police brutality, lily-white construction sites, and segregated schools, resulting in ten deaths. As the country teetered on the brink of racial warfare, King warned Kennedy that 'the Negro's endurance may be at the breaking point'.

Hours after Wallace buckled in Tuscaloosa, Kennedy finally put the weight of his presidency behind the civil rights movement. Speaking on national television with a rarely seen passion, he characterized segregation as 'a moral crisis' that required federal remedy [*Doc. 9*]. Within days, Kennedy proposed the most comprehensive civil rights bill in American history. The measure guaranteed voting rights and required equal access to public accommodations, schools, and employment. Local agencies that persisted in discrimination would lose federal funds. The bill was far from ideal because it was crafted to attract moderate support across party lines. Individuals had to initiate lawsuits against Jim Crow public accommodations before the Justice department could

Plate 1   In what was an all too common phenomenon, white onlookers watched the lynching of a black man with perverse delight.

Source: Brown Brothers, Sterling, PA 18463

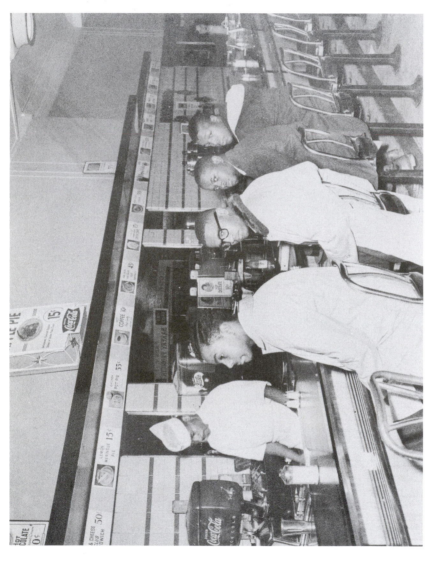

Plate 2 Sit-in protest at the Woolworth's lunch-counter in Greensboro, North Carolina, on the second day, February 2, 1960. Joseph McNeil and Franklin McCain (two of the original protesters) were joined by Billy Smith and Clarence Henderson (*left to right*).

Source: News & Record/Moebes

Plate 3 The Klan firebombed this Freedom Ride bus in Anniston, Alabama, on May 14, 1961.

Source: Associated Press

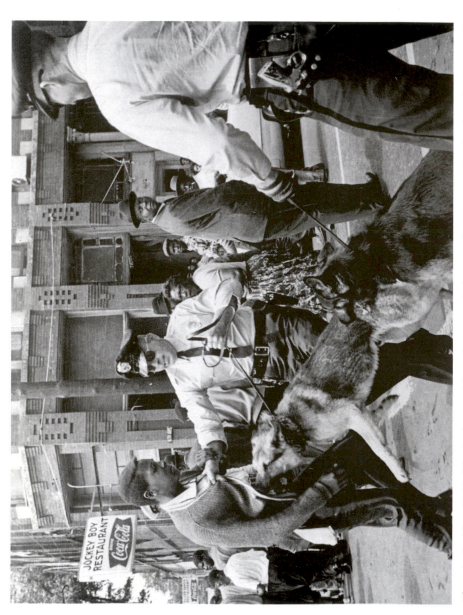

Plate 4 In May 1963, Birmingham public safety commissioner Bull Connor ordered police dogs to attack peaceful demonstrators like William Gadsden.

Source: Associated Press/Bill Hudson

litigate. Additionally, the bill excluded state and local elections from voting rights guarantees, targeted only southern schools that dragged their feet on desegregation, and ignored job discrimination and police brutality altogether. Ever cautious, Kennedy wanted to improve race relations 'without getting us too far out front'. Nonetheless, in breaking with southern Democrats, he staked the country's future, and his own, on civil rights. It amounted to a tectonic shift in American politics.

CHAPTER TEN

MARCH ON WASHINGTON

To win congressional approval of Kennedy's measure, Martin Luther King told aides gravely, 'We are on a breakthrough. We need a mass protest.' The idea of a huge rally in Washington had been advanced by A. Philip Randolph in 1941, and King contacted the 'grand old man' of the movement, to see if all parties could work together. Randolph was glad to cooperate though his focus was different. Black unemployment, he noted, was more than twice the rate for whites, and a typical black family earned about half what an average white family did. Worse, this racial divide in income was widening. America was still one country for whites and another for blacks. Working with Bayard Rustin, the movement's most talented organizer, Randolph suggested that a national gesture for economic reform could prod politicians to double the minimum wage and create a large federal job program. By transforming the civil rights struggle from a regional to a national campaign, the massive demonstration would be the movement's high-water mark.

Other civil rights leaders had reservations about the plan. Roy Wilkins of the influential NAACP opposed a march as too expensive and too in-effectual in influencing legislation. He intimated that any such march would be tainted by Rustin's homosexuality, imprisonment for resisting the draft for the Korean war, and former membership in the Young Communist League. Wilkins overlooked Rustin's twenty-two arrests for human rights, his co-founding of CORE and SCLC, and his international organizing experience. Without the NAACP's money and affiliates, the march might well be doomed. The Urban League's Whitney Young worried that his organization's tax-exempt status would be jeopardized by backing a political event. For SNCC's John Lewis, a march was just the beginning. To challenge a foot-dragging government, he proposed paralyzing Washington with camp-ins on the White House lawn, lie-ins across airport runways, and sit-ins in Congress and the Justice department.

These reservations forced a compromise. All major civil rights leaders, including Wilkins, signed on, provided the purpose was changed to 'Jobs and Freedom' and Randolph was named the march's director. Randolph accepted the draft and named Rustin deputy director. For the first time all major civil rights leaders and organizations set aside their squabbling to collaborate on a national undertaking. But the economic goals Randolph long favored took second place to passing Kennedy's civil rights bill and penalizing states where citizens were disfranchised.

Plans for a large civil rights demonstration repelled FBI director J. Edgar Hoover, who hated blacks in general, despised 'the burrhead' Martin Luther King as a traitor, and resented criticism of the lily-white Bureau's record in race cases. Believing that King was a communist stooge, Hoover convinced attorney general Robert Kennedy, a veteran anti-communist himself, to approve wiretaps on King's home telephone and SCLC office. A spooked Kennedy also might have approved the taps because Hoover could accuse a lax president of being soft on communism and expose the president's serial adultery with women who represented security risks. On his own, Hoover bugged King's hotel bedrooms. When the unauthorized taps revealed that King was a reckless adulterer – though not a communist – Hoover used King's moral failings to try to topple him and destroy the civil rights movement. He passed on the salacious details, including photographs, transcripts, and tapes, to major newspapers, white supremacists, labor leaders, foundation administrators, and the president. In this pre-Watergate era, newspapers refused to publish the damaging information about King's personal life.

In the summer of 1963, Hoover's vendetta against King was useful to the administration, which feared the political costs of continued civil rights agitation. FBI sources alleged that Stanley Levison, King's longtime confidant, was a top communist agent who smuggled gold from Moscow to finance SCLC's operations and roil racial waters in the United States. Armed with this damning allegation, the president's brother and Burke Marshall, the Justice department's top civil rights lawyer, demanded that King drop Levison. Marshall explained that the civil rights bill would make president Kennedy 'put his whole political life on the line', and there could be no communists within King's inner circle. When King laughed off the McCarthyite insinuation, the president himself advised King to purge Levison and fund-raiser Jack O'Dell, declaring flatly that 'they're communists'. He warned King, 'If they shoot you down, they'll shoot *us* down, too.' King reluctantly fired O'Dell, but insisted on communicating with Levison through intermediaries.

When president Kennedy met with the entire civil rights leadership, he attacked the idea of a march in his own backyard because he claimed that his approval rating had dropped from 60 to 47 per cent. Surveys indicated that his civil rights stand would cost him dearly, especially in the key industrial states of Illinois, Michigan, Missouri, and New Jersey. Kennedy insisted that 'a big show at the Capitol' would boomerang, giving congressional opponents 'an excuse to be against us. I didn't want to give any of them a chance to say, "Yes, I'm for the [civil rights] bill, but I'm damned if I will vote for it at the point of a gun."' Randolph responded in a booming bass voice that no one could stop the march because blacks were 'already in the streets'.

Recognizing the march's inevitability, the president endorsed it a month later. Privately, the administration pressured organizers to make drastic changes. 'Well, if we can't stop it, we'll run the damn thing,' Kennedy told his advisers. The rally date was set for a Wednesday to prevent weekend mischief. The site was switched from the Capitol building to the Lincoln Memorial on the Washington Mall in order to cordon off the demonstrators on three sides by water. The organizers were to recruit as many whites as possible from churches and labor unions and to ensure that all demonstrators dressed conservatively. Special trains and buses would drop off marchers in the morning and depart before sunset. Printed programs would tell them where to go, how to behave, and the sequence of events. The 'march' would consist of a short walk from the Washington Monument and end with speeches, not the embarrassing sit-ins that SNCC had proposed. Should the speakers become too inflammatory, the administration would station an aide beneath the platform to play a phonograph record of Mahalia Jackson singing 'He's Got the Whole World in His Hands' over the loudspeaker. From John Lewis's perspective, the Kennedy administration was so determined to cool off the movement that the march was becoming 'a march *in*, not *on* Washington'.

Without knowing how many people would come, Bayard Rustin faced enormous logistical problems that had to be overcome in sixty days. He arranged for hundreds of volunteer marshals to ensure order and stationed white policemen on the periphery so that white extremists would not be arrested by black officers. With the help of Howard University students, Rustin installed dozens of drinking fountains and portable toilets on the Mall. Emergency medical personnel staffed first-aid stations. Bus drivers kept aspirins, suntan oil, Band-Aids, and salt tablets on hand for minor emergencies. Thousands of blankets were available for marchers who arrived in the pre-dawn hours. Volunteers at New York City's Riverside Church worked around-the-clock to make 80,000 cheese sandwiches to be sent overnight to the march. Because this would be the first time that America would witness a black-organized event of such magnitude, Rustin was determined that there be no hitches.

As the march gathered momentum, Rustin and King pulled together a microcosm of the 'Beloved Community', a coalition of blacks, white intellectuals, union leaders, Christians and Jews, social justice radicals from the 1930s, and folk musicians led by Pete Seeger. A hundred civil, labor, and religious organizations climbed aboard, including the ACLU, International Ladies' Garment Workers' Union, and Archdiocese of Washington, DC. These groups helped underwrite the march's cost of $120,000.

As the date for the march approached, nearly everyone feared that it would become a colossal failure. While congressmen worried about so many black protesters in one place, Rustin worried about falling short of the goal of

100,000 marchers. The attorney general worried that a small turnout would make the president look bad. To spread word of the rally, local churches and civil rights chapters made announcements and hired 'freedom' trains and buses. As white churches became involved, the organizers worried that too many whites would show up. To prevent any civil disturbance, city police had their leaves canceled, and the administration put federal troops on standby. Storekeepers hid their goods in warehouses, and the city's liquor stores were shut down for the first time since Prohibition. Area hospitals delayed elective surgery. Government workers were urged to stay home to keep the streets clear for the incoming demonstrators.

These fears proved groundless. Early in the morning of Wednesday, 28 August 1963, 21 special trains, 1,514 buses, and countless car pools brought 250,000 marchers to Washington from places such as Birmingham, Chicago, Cincinnati, Detroit, Gary, Jacksonville, New York, Miami, Philadelphia, Pittsburgh, and St Louis. Many of the excited passengers stayed up all night singing and clapping freedom songs, such as 'Woke up this morning with my mind set on freedom. Hallelu, hallelu, hallelujah!' An 82-year-old rode his bicycle from Dayton, Ohio, and another man roller-skated from Chicago with a red sash reading 'Freedom'. The majority of the marchers were middle-class blacks; a quarter were white; and 15 per cent were students. Clergy from every faith came too. Altogether, they comprised the largest and best-remembered demonstration in American history.

To warm up the crowd at the Washington Monument, Joan Baez, Odetta, Josh White, Peter, Paul and Mary, and SNCC's Freedom Singers from Albany sang movement favorites and Bob Dylan's new hit song, 'Blowin' in the Wind', a paean to the civil rights movement. After two hours of music, the crowd grew impatient in the sweltering heat and followed a drum-and-bugle corps to the Lincoln Memorial ahead of schedule. 'Freedom Now,' the crowd chanted. The civil rights leaders hurried back from lobbying for Kennedy's bill on Capitol Hill to 'lead' the advancing throng, but they never got to the front. Once in place, the leaders locked arms with march co-chairs Walter Reuther of the UAW, Eugene Carson Blake of the National Council of Churches, Mathew Ahmann of the National Catholic Conference for Interracial Justice, and Joachim Prinz of the American Jewish Congress. A galaxy of stage and screen stars followed, including Harry Belafonte, Marlon Brando, Diahann Carroll, Ossie Davis, Sammy Davis, Jr., Ruby Dee, Anthony Franciosa, James Garner, Dick Gregory, Charlton Heston, Dennis Hopper, Lena Horne, Burt Lancaster, Rita Moreno, Paul Newman, Sidney Poitier, Jackie Robinson, Susan Strasberg, and Joanne Woodward. The stars ignored the FBI's insistent telephone calls not to participate because of the potential danger. A sea of humanity walked closely behind the stars, singing 'We Shall Overcome' and carrying approved placards reading, 'WE DEMAND EQUAL RIGHTS NOW!'

The media gave unprecedented coverage to the March on Washington, surpassing Kennedy's inauguration. More than 2,000 journalists reported on the celebrities and the unjust laws that still circumscribed black life. Overseas newspapers, including Moscow's *Izvestia*, made the march their lead news story. The CBS television network canceled lucrative all-white game shows and soap operas to beam the rally into American homes for three hours from 1.30 to 4.30 p.m. The Voice of America, a US government propaganda agency, and Britain's television news carried the march live, and the rest of the world watched the amazing spectacle as it was simulcast by Telstar, the new communications satellite.

The march's carefully laid plans nearly unraveled when word leaked about the apocalyptic speech that SNCC's John Lewis planned to give. After Kennedy's Justice department, not Georgia prosecutors, obtained indictments against nine Albany picketers, Lewis demanded to know 'which side is the federal government on?' To pressure Washington, he threatened a 'march through the South, through the heart of Dixie, the way Sherman did. We shall pursue our own "scorched earth" policy and burn Jim Crow to the ground – nonviolently.' The speech stung too much for the president, who called SNCC 'sons of bitches' and insisted that the incendiary rhetoric be watered down. Catholic archbishop Patrick O'Boyle of Washington threatened to cancel his invocation unless Lewis's language was softened. Reverend Blake, Eisenhower's personal pastor, took umbrage at such radical terms as 'revolution' and 'the masses'. While Rustin stalled for time, Randolph almost cried as he told Lewis, 'I've waited all my life for this opportunity. Please don't ruin it.' Chastened, Lewis revised the speech just before his scheduled appearance, giving the march a veneer of unity.

After Lewis, the parade of speakers and singers continued as the good-natured crowd fanned themselves or soaked their feet in the Lincoln Memorial's reflecting pool. The *New York Times* reported that 'for many the day seemed an adventure, a long outing in the late summer sun – part liberation from home, part Sunday School picnic, part political convention, part fish-fry'. All of the top civil rights leaders spoke, except James Farmer, who was in a Louisiana jail. As an afterthought, Randolph briefly introduced the heroines of the movement, including Rosa Parks, Daisy Bates, Diane Nash, and Gloria Richardson. Marian Anderson returned to the scene of her great triumph and sang 'He's Got the Whole World in His Hands.' Gospel great Mahalia Jackson delivered such a moving rendition of the spiritual, 'I Been 'Buked and I Been Scorned', that well-dressed businessmen and old women alike arose and cheered. In an impassioned speech, UAW president Walter Reuther criticized president Kennedy for being preoccupied with international crises: 'We cannot *defend* freedom in Berlin so long as we *deny* freedom in Birmingham!'

In the culminating address, Martin Luther King, the unofficial 'President of the Negroes' and the conscience of his country, updated Lincoln's Gettysburg

Address. He declared that blacks had come to Washington 'to cash a check' based on the lofty promises of freedom and equality contained in the Declaration of Independence. Because the check was returned for 'insufficient funds', King declared to the enormous throng that 'now is the time' to honor that check. Having deviated from his prepared text, King began speaking extemporaneously and Mahalia Jackson urged him to 'tell 'em about your dream, Martin!' The charismatic King then delivered a spine-tingling peroration that envisioned a color-blind America [*Doc. 10*]. He drew sizeable portions of it from a speech that he had delivered several times. After a momentary stunned silence, people cheered and wept openly. James Baldwin, who despaired of improved race relations, remarked that 'for a moment, it almost seemed that we stood on a height, and could see our inheritance; perhaps we could make the kingdom real, perhaps the beloved community would not forever remain that dream one dreamed in agony'.

The euphoria over King's masterful speech dissipated quickly. The *New York Times* reported a day later that the demonstration 'appeared to have left much of Congress untouched – physically, emotionally, and politically'. Nor did the president have much clout to clear his bill, especially since a poll showed that white southerners strongly disapproved of his tilt toward civil rights. Black militants chastised King for making a conciliatory gesture to white America, similar to Booker T. Washington's Atlanta Compromise. Malcolm X called King 'a traitor to his race' and dismissed the rally as the 'Farce in Washington . . . subsidized by white liberals and stage-managed by President Kennedy'. He asked sarcastically, 'Who ever heard of angry revolutionaries swinging their bare feet together with their oppressor in lily-pad pools, with gospels and guitars and "I have a dream" speeches?' Real revolution, Malcolm insisted, was 'based on bloodshed . . . and destroys everything in its way' [*Doc. 11*].

Nor were Birmingham klansmen swayed by the march, especially when the city's schools had just desegregated. A bomb demolished the home of Arthur Sholes, the black attorney for students now attending the all-white high school. On Sunday morning, 15 September, a dynamite blast ripped through the Sixteenth Street Baptist Church, wounding twenty-one and killing four defenseless black girls – Addie Mae Collins, Denise McNair, Carole Robertson, and Cynthia Wesley – who had just completed a lesson on 'The Love That Forgives'. Cynthia, the Wesleys' only child, had been decapitated. Denise's sobbing grandfather stumbled across her white dress shoe amid the debris, and shouted, 'I'd like to blow the whole town up!' A black woman whose feet were covered with glass screamed, 'In church! My God, you're not even safe in church.' Such pathos left a local white supremacist untouched: 'They're just little niggers . . . and if there's four less niggers tonight, then I say, Good for whoever planted the bomb!'

With roving bands of armed black and white vigilantes, the city was poised for a race war. Hundreds of angry blacks set white businesses afire and threw stones at the police. A policeman fatally shot 16-year-old Johnny Robinson in the back for tossing rocks at a car covered with racial slurs. That same day, Larry Joe Sims, a white Eagle Scout with a straight-A average, attended Sunday school in the morning and a segregationist rally in the afternoon before fatally shooting 13-year-old Virgil Ware, who was perched on his brother's bicycle handlebars. Although Sims confessed to the shooting, he served only a short time in a juvenile detention center before being released on probation.

To solve the church bombing, FBI agents launched the nation's greatest manhunt since gangster John Dillinger was gunned down in 1934. The investigation produced several plausible suspects, including 'Dynamite Bob' Chambliss, a 59-year-old truck driver and klansman whose hit squad had flogged blacks and bombed their homes. FBI director J. Edgar Hoover opposed prosecution because his agents could not nail down an airtight case. The state police made three arrests, including the volatile Chambliss, but the charge was possessing dynamite, a misdemeanor offense. In any event, no indictments ensued. Thanks to a dogged state attorney general, Chambliss was convicted of murder in 1977, and two accomplices were sent to prison almost forty years after the killings.

Not even the sickening Birmingham murders could spring Kennedy's civil rights bill, which faced an uncertain future on Capitol Hill. When president Kennedy was assassinated in November 1963, few assumed that his successor – Lyndon Johnson of Texas – would break the back of segregation. Johnson, after all, opposed Truman's initiatives to end lynching and the poll tax and neutered key provisions of Eisenhower's civil rights bills. Deep down, Johnson considered segregation to be an immoral system that retarded the South's economic advancement. Moreover, he had seen poverty cripple the lives of blacks and Latinos and 'vowed that if I ever had the power I'd make sure every Negro had the same chance as every white man. Now I have it. And I'm going to use it.' Johnson realized that civil rights was the litmus test of his leadership, and without a strong bill, liberals would be gunning for him. 'I'd be dead before I could even begin,' he admitted. In a memorial oration for his slain predecessor, Johnson wholeheartedly embraced the movement: 'We have talked long enough in this country about equal rights. We have talked for 100 years or more. It is time now to write the next chapter – and to write it in the books of law.'

Using his extraordinary horse-trading skills, Johnson strengthened the Kennedy measure and enlisted Joseph Rauh of the ADA and Clarence Mitchell of the NAACP to lobby Capitol Hill. It was all-out political warfare. In the House, Howard W. Smith of Virginia tried to split off liberal white congressmen from the black civil rights bill by adding an amendment for gender equality. In the Senate, Richard Russell of Georgia, Johnson's erstwhile mentor, deployed eighteen southern Democrats to talk the bill to death day after day.

Neither southern strategy worked. As the proceedings moved to a critical stage, the Leadership Conference on Civil Rights and the National Council of Churches sent teams of ministers, priests, rabbis, and nuns to Congress, which nonplussed politicians from the Bible Belt. Brooking no compromise, Johnson and floor leader Hubert Humphrey of Minnesota twisted arms for six months to close debate in the Senate and deflect 115 amendments aimed at gutting the measure. The administration promised federal money to Republican leader Everett Dirksen's home district in Illinois to win his support. In explaining his changed position, Dirksen quoted French playwright Victor Hugo: 'Stronger than all the armies is an idea whose time has come.'

To press for the long-delayed bill, Martin Luther King accepted an invitation from Robert Hayling, a dentist active in the NAACP, to organize a campaign in the picturesque town of St Augustine, Florida. America's oldest city, which King called 'a small Birmingham', was about to celebrate its 400th birthday and still excluded blacks from public life. In the spring of 1964, SCLC's Andrew Young, Fred Shuttlesworth, and C.T. Vivian led wade-ins at the beach and night-time marches to the historic slave market. Angry at this attack on white supremacy, Holstead 'Hoss' Manucy, a pig farmer and bootlegger, led a thousand klansmen to retaliate. They fired on King's rented cottage and descended on the helpless marchers with bats, garbage cans, park benches, and a cement birdbath. When blacks desegregated a motel swimming pool, the owner poured acid into the water as the screaming swimmers dogpaddled to escape. The month-long face-off between the demonstrators and standpatters brought damaging publicity to the tourist town, which lost 40 per cent of its business. As the situation spiraled out of control, the governor promised that a biracial committee would study local problems. This olive branch was enough for King, who gladly retreated from the stalemated campaign, especially when the civil rights measure was assured of passage.

On 2 July, Johnson signed the extraordinary bill and handed souvenir pens to King and other elated black leaders. At this moment of high drama, the president was deflated, telling an aide, 'I think we delivered the South to the Republican Party for your lifetime and mine.' Under the law, which virtually wiped out Jim Crow in a single stroke, blacks no longer had to file their own lawsuits to stop segregation in schools, housing, employment, and public accommodations; that was now the attorney general's responsibility. Any school, business, or program that discriminated against blacks would lose its federal money. Title VII outlawed job discrimination by creating a permanent watchdog federal agency – the Equal Employment Opportunity Commission – that succeeded Franklin Roosevelt's wartime FEPC. A Community Relations Service would mediate racial problems. The law's weakest provision concerned voting rights, a shortcoming that prolonged the civil rights movement.

Having secured this sweeping civil rights law, Johnson challenged America to solve its race problem by breaking the cycle of poverty and welfare dependency. To build a 'great society', Johnson established an Office of Economic Opportunity, headed by president Kennedy's brother-in-law, Sargent Shriver. Under OEO, Shriver established a comprehensive, but under-funded, 'war on poverty' that included programs such as Head Start for disadvantaged pre-schoolers, Job Corps for high school dropouts needing vocational training, Upward Bound for troubled youth, food stamps for the poor, legal aid for those who could not afford an attorney, Medicaid to treat the poor's health problems, and VISTA as a domestic Peace Corps to economically depressed areas. Underlying the Great Society was the cultural assumption that blacks were poor because they had not learned the middle-class value of work. Nothing was done to create new jobs that paid a living wage or to stop blatant discrimination by employers and labor unions. Despite their limitations, Johnson's initiatives improved the quality of life for many Americans.

While one hand of the government helped blacks, the other hand warred on them. When Martin Luther King received the Nobel peace prize in December 1964, an enraged J. Edgar Hoover called him 'the most notorious liar in the country' and plotted his death. The FBI mailed a package to King that contained a lurid recording of King's hotel room, as well as an unsigned note urging him to commit suicide: 'You are done. . . . There is only one thing left for you to do. You know what it is. . . . You better take it before your filthy, abnormal fraudulent self is bared to the nation.' In the hope that King's suicide was likely, the FBI selected King's successor, a conservative black New York City attorney. Hoover did not recognize that the civil rights movement was not the creation of a single leader. The events in Mississippi in the early 1960s proved yet again that the movement relied on many indigenous and imported workers.

PART FOUR

THE MOVEMENT FRACTURES

CHAPTER ELEVEN

FREEDOM SUMMER

'How many bubbles are there in a cake of soap?' a Mississippi registrar teased a black man registering to vote. The would-be voter realized that the situation was hopeless and needled the registrar back: 'Well, I don't want to be an ignorant man all the rest of my life. . . . Tell me how many bubbles are there in a bar of soap?' The registrar grew angry and, as expected, failed the black man in the literacy test [*Doc. 12*]. Other registrars asked bewildered black applicants to translate unfamiliar Latin phrases. By contrast, a white applicant passed who interpreted the section, 'There shall be no imprisonment for debt', as 'I thank that a Neorger should have 2 years in collage before voting because he don't under stand.'

Behind the Magnolia Curtain, registration tricks kept black voter registration extremely low. Only 5.2 per cent of blacks could vote, compared to the South's average of one-third of blacks and two-thirds of whites. In heavily-black Holmes county the registrar disqualified all but 0.02 per cent of blacks and fraudulently enrolled *more than* 100 per cent of whites. In Amite, Tallahatchie, and Walthall counties, not a single black voted. As a result, no Mississippi black had held elective office since Reconstruction ended in 1877. Even if blacks voted, there was no choice but the Democratic party of James Vardaman, Theodore Bilbo, James Eastland, and Ross Barnett, rabid racists all. In campaigning for governor in 1903, Vardaman called for the repeal of the 14th and 15th Amendments and described the Negro as 'a lazy, lustful animal which no conceivable amount of training can transform into a tolerable citizen'. The white man, he averred, 'would be justified in slaughtering every Ethiop on earth to preserve unsullied the honor of one Caucasian home'.

Voting was the least of blacks' problems in Mississippi, the poorest and most racially violent of states. More than 80 per cent of blacks were locked in grinding poverty, in part because chemical fertilizers and mechanical cotton pickers displaced many field hands. When welfare was available, it went to poor whites first. Education for blacks was pitiful, with the state spending three times more on a white student than on a black one. With most black children attending only elementary school and half of their teachers without a high school diploma, 70 per cent of black Mississippians were functionally illiterate. There was one black dentist, five black lawyers, and sixty black doctors in the whole state. With so few doctors, a black baby was twice as likely to die in childbirth as a white baby. Although the state reported 534 lynchings by the early 1950s, including two men roasted to death by blow torches, no white accused of murdering blacks was ever convicted. A half million black Mississippians gave up and migrated to northern cities, especially Chicago. Without the ballot, blacks who remained were powerless to improve their miserable lot.

To stop such misery, three black veterans returned to Mississippi after World War II. Far from welcoming them back, many white Mississippians were enraged by wartime breaches of racial etiquette, particularly magazine pictures of German women sitting on black soldiers' laps. Such rage led to the murder of a black man in the delta each week for months. Medgar Evers, a survivor of the bloody Normandy invasion, saw much of the state's racism. Whites stole his grandparents' farm, lynched a close family friend who offended a white woman, spat on him as he walked to school, and flashed guns to block him and his friends from voting. After the University of Mississippi's law school excluded him, Evers became the state's first NAACP field secretary, tirelessly encouraging blacks to vote, file lawsuits, and join the association. Amzie Moore, a gas station operator in Cleveland, was shocked when he saw a black family of fourteen half-naked children, who had no food, no beds, and no heat in their home. To change sorry situations like this, Moore helped organize the Regional Council of Negro Leadership, a local version of the NAACP. Moore would sing gospel songs at church services and then pleaded with blacks to vote. Angered by the gang rape of two black girls, a pharmacist named Aaron Henry started an NAACP chapter in Clarksdale and soon headed the state's affiliate. Vowing to make jails 'Temples of Freedom', Henry conducted voter-registration drives and boycotts to integrate schools and all public facilities. He was soon convicted of a fabricated morals charge in a town he had never visited; his wife was fired from her teaching job; and the Henry home and drugstore were shot at repeatedly.

As NAACP activists organized, white Mississippi counterattacked. The state established a cloak-and-dagger spy agency, the State Sovereignty Commission, which employed misinformation, espionage, intimidation, and extortion to keep blacks from crossing Jim Crow's lines. The commission funneled $5,000 a month in state tax money to the Citizens' Councils, which was used to bribe black editors and ministers to oppose integration, pay informants to betray the civil rights movement, and spread the gospel of segregation nationwide with a huge speakers bureau. It vilified black activists and their white allies as faggots, lechers, and drug users. This underhand campaign received a powerful boost from two wealthy, extremely powerful brothers, Thomas and Robert Hederman. Their influential newspapers – the only dailies published statewide – printed a steady stream of blatantly racist editorials and slanted stories that reinforced existing prejudice. One reader complained that the Hedermans made Hitler's propagandist 'Joe Goebbels look like an amateur'. When intimidation was ineffective, whites murdered defiant blacks.

The campaign of terror persuaded local NAACP leaders that Mississippi would never change unless they courted the media and invited other civil rights organizations, especially SNCC, into the state. At Amzie Moore's request, young SNCC workers, such as Marion Barry, Ruby Doris Smith, and Charles McDew, reinforced the NAACP's struggle in a state with widespread black apathy and fear. Basing themselves in McComb in 1961, SNCC believed that the only way to change the deep South was to register blacks in remote areas where racial confrontations were likely. The plan required tedious door-to-door canvassing and classes in literacy and citizenship. SNCC counted on reporters to carry word of voting discrimination and mob action to the rest of the country, thereby applying pressure for protection. Ultimately, SNCC expected local leaders like C.C. Bryant, E.W. Steptoe, and Webb Owens to maintain the movement on their own.

SNCC was unique among civil rights groups. Unlike the full-time, middle-class students in Greensboro who politely asked for food at a lunch-counter, SNCC workers were full-time radical activists who organized black communities to secure more of the region's wealth and power through voter registration. Unlike SCLC, SNCC was composed largely of northern, as well as southern, workers, and many of them were non-churchgoers. To appeal to local blacks, SNCC encouraged nonbelievers to attend church services and frowned on alcohol and cohabitation between men and women, though none of these suggestions was widely followed. SNCC activists adopted new organizing techniques, including working with the poor and the young, rather than the middle class that they considered unreliable. Such time-consuming techniques required activists to stay for months in the field, so that terrified blacks would not feel abandoned.

SNCC's ostensible leader in Mississippi was 26-year-old Bob Moses, the antithesis of Martin Luther King. The magnetic King was born to a prominent Atlanta family, attended Morehouse College in his hometown, was inspired by the pacifist teachings of India's Gandhi, and found his vocation serving God. Moses came from a Harlem housing project, attended Hamilton College, an elite, mostly white school in New York, was inspired by French existentialist writer Albert Camus and Chinese philosophers, earned a master's degree from Harvard, and taught high school mathematics. Unlike King, Moses shunned fund-raising and the media spotlight. Unlike King, who wore dark tailored suits, Moses dressed in the working man's bib overalls. Except for his hypnotic eyes, the soft-spoken Moses was uncharismatic and eschewed the cult of personality that sprang up around King. The movement, Moses believed, needed 'a lot of leaders'. As project director of COFO's voter registration campaign, Moses presided loosely over twenty field secretaries in six offices.

Whites beat Moses repeatedly for being the 'nigger who's come to tell the niggers how to register'. Shortly after his arrival in McComb, he took three blacks to the courthouse to complete voter-registration forms. Police promptly jailed him for interfering with their duties. After Moses was released, the sheriff's cousin assaulted him with a hunting knife. Moses brought charges against his assailant – the first time a black man sued a white Mississippian over a beating – but the defendant was found not guilty. Still another time, nightriders fired thirteen bullets into his car.

To withstand this onslaught, Moses advised his cohorts to prepare for a lengthy guerrilla war. SNCC survival tactics included telephoning home base frequently, driving unpredictably, and sometimes carrying .38-caliber handguns. To foil wiretappers, SNCC workers talked with all the water faucets running and the television volume full blast. If anyone failed to check in, a flurry of phone calls were made to hospitals, jails, the police, and then the Justice department – in that order.

The all-out war between white supremacy and racial equality made these guerrilla tactics essential. The Klan bombed churches that hosted voter registration meetings and sprayed gunshots at homes where SNCC workers slept. Blacks who went to the registrar's office were viciously beaten, fired from their jobs, refused medicine, denied credit and government aid, and cut off from their heating fuel. When Hartman Turnbow registered in Mileston, he was denied the ballot, his home was bombed, his family was shot at, and he was arrested for arson. Ten policemen forced SNCC organizer Lawrence Guyot to disrobe and then worked him over for hours until a doctor warned that death was imminent. In broad daylight and in cold blood, state representative E.H. Hurst fatally shot Herbert Lee, a dairy farmer with nine children whom Moses recruited to lead other blacks to vote. An eyewitness was murdered in his driveway by three shotgun blasts. When SNCC workers and black high school students staged a protest march against Lee's murder, a mob went after Bob Zellner, SNCC's first white field secretary. The mob slammed Zellner with a baseball bat, kicked his head, and gouged his eye from its socket. He was hauled off to jail still clutching his Bible. The black students were expelled, and Moses was sent to jail for disturbing the peace. The reign of terror ended SNCC's voter drive in McComb after six blacks had registered.

Moses then moved the Voter Education Project to the impoverished delta. He sent Sam Block, a 23-year-old native Mississippian, to organize Greenwood, near the site where Emmett Till was butchered. Block had no car or place to stay as he canvassed grocery stores, laundromats, and pool halls. Before long, the sheriff cornered Block and spat in his face. 'Nigger,' he demanded to know, 'where you from? . . . I know you ain't from here, 'cause I know every nigger and his mammy.' The sheriff ordered Block to pack his 'goddamn bags' and leave town, an order Block ignored. A few nights later, Block heard noises outside his office. Deathly afraid, he exited through the bathroom window, jumping from rooftop to rooftop before sliding down a television antenna. SNCC sent in reinforcements, only to have most of them serve hard time at the county work farm. County officials punished the entire black community by withdrawing from the federal food surplus program. When emergency shipments of food and clothing arrived from the North, whites burned the supplies. Vigilantes also torched SNCC's headquarters and shot at the remaining activists. By mid-1963, VEP reluctantly cut off funding in Mississippi.

The vulnerable voting-rights workers received no protection from the federal government. Most galling of all, the FBI regularly arrested kidnappers, bank robbers, drug-sellers, and spies, but not violent klansmen. Nor did it enforce Section 242 of Title 18, US Code, which declares that any official depriving a person of his constitutional rights has committed a federal crime. FBI director J. Edgar Hoover only investigated racial crimes, insisting that 'we simply can't wet nurse everybody who goes down to try to reform or re-educate the Negro population of the South'. In one egregious episode, an FBI agent questioned a white activist beaten, kicked, and urinated upon by four Mississippians. 'Well, nigger lover, what seems to be the problem?' SNCC executive secretary James Forman concluded that 'the FBI was a farce. . . . It was all too clear whose side Uncle Sam was on' [*Doc. 13*].

As outside help butted against a stone wall, local black women, such as Unita Blackwell, Annie Devine, Victoria Gray, Fannie Lou Hamer, Winson Hudson, June Johnson, and Laura McGhee, filled important roles. Across the South, women were the indispensable foot soldiers of the movement while men were the officers. Hamer, a heavy-set woman from Ruleville who limped badly from polio, was the twentieth child of illiterate sharecroppers. She learned early on that whites were all-powerful. Her grandmother Liza, an ex-slave, was raped repeatedly by white men. Fannie Lou's mother had gone blind after an accident when she received no medical attention. To help support her family, Fannie Lou started picking cotton when she was 6 and soon dropped out of elementary school. Just as her parents were getting on their feet, a white man poisoned their cows and mules, leaving them perpetually in debt. Upon reaching adulthood, Hamer married a sharecropper and exhausted herself working three jobs. When she went into a hospital for a minor stomach operation, the doctor sterilized her without her consent because she was an indigent. She returned to the cotton fields in despair, thinking 'there must be some way we can change things'.

When SCLC's James Bevel came to her church, Hamer was amazed to hear that 'it was our right as human beings to register and vote'. Hamer and other blacks completed the voter applications and then took the literacy test on the Mississippi state constitution. Unsurprisingly, everyone failed. Hamer admitted that she knew as much about the constitution 'as a horse knows about Christmas Day'. In retaliation, Hamer's landlord forced her off the land she had worked for eighteen years. She fled to a friend's home, which was soon riddled with bullets. She fled again to her niece's home forty miles away. Fed up with the reprisals, Hamer returned to Ruleville and bluntly told the registrar, 'Now, you cain't have me fired 'cause I'm already fired, and I won't have to move now, because I'm not livin' in no white man's house.' Within a month, she passed the test, only to face death threats from armed klansmen who drove by her house every night.

Word of Hamer's courage reached Bob Moses, who made her a SNCC field secretary at $10 a week. At last in a job she loved, the irrepressible Hamer worked 12-hour days for voter registration, spouting Scripture and singing hymns to drive away the fears of registrants. She offered free food and clothing to anyone who would register. Her crusade landed her in jail, where a state highway patrolman told her, 'We are going to beat you until you wish you were dead.' Two designated prisoners pounded her with blackjacks until she was blinded in one eye and sustained permanent kidney damage. Persevering still, 'Mississippi's angriest woman' insisted that 'black people must register and vote'.

Racists tried to shut down the voter drive by eliminating the state's most visible civil rights leader. Not only did Medgar Evers register black voters, he encouraged sit-ins and organized boycotts of the state fair and Jackson's business district. After a read-in at a whites-only library, a spectator pistol-whipped Evers, and the police clubbed him from behind. Anonymous death threats came over the telephone, and his house was bombed. Facing his own mortality, Evers remarked prophetically, 'You can kill a man, but you can't kill an idea.' After a lengthy strategy meeting that ended past midnight on 12 June 1963, the 37-year-old Evers returned to his home. A sniper waited for him, crouching in the honeysuckle bushes behind the brightly lit carport. As Evers got out of his station wagon carrying 'Jim Crow Must Go' T-shirts, he was shot in the back with a deer-hunting rifle. With blood soaking his white shirt, a dying Evers crawled up the stairs where his three children screamed, 'Get up, Daddy, get up!' After 25,000 mourners viewed his remains, Evers was buried with full military honors in Virginia's Arlington National Cemetery.

Thirty years elapsed before justice was done. Byron de la Beckwith, a fertilizer salesman and charter member of the Citizens' Council, was the leading suspect in Evers's murder. While in jail awaiting his first trial, Beckwith was given creature comforts, including a television set and typewriter, and allowed to come and go as he pleased. General Edwin Walker visited Beckwith in jail, and governor Ross Barnett came to the courtroom to shake the defendant's hand. When the jury deadlocked, Beckwith was released and returned home to welcoming banners and a parade. He told a group of klansmen, 'Killing that nigger gave me no more inner discomfort than our wives endure when they give birth to our children. We ask them to do that for us. We should do just as much.' He later ran for lieutenant governor, assuring campaign crowds that he was a 'straight shooter'. Bobby DeLaughter, the indefatigable prosecutor, had to locate the lost police report, trial transcript, even the murder weapon, as well as overcome jury-tampering by the State Sovereignty Commission. His single-minded pursuit of justice led a racially mixed jury in 1994 to hand down a murder conviction and life sentence against Beckwith after three tries.

The escalating violence in the early 1960s led Bob Moses to accept a proposal for a 'Freedom Vote' to permit disfranchised blacks to elect their own representatives. The ingenious idea was suggested by Allard Lowenstein, a peripatetic 34-year-old lawyer who had been NSA president and assistant dean of men at Stanford University. Such a mock election would expose the lie that blacks were politically apathetic and therefore did not deserve suffrage. It would also provide an alternative to white candidates who defended Jim Crow. To organize the vote, Lowenstein recruited dozens of Stanford and Yale students, including Joseph Lieberman, who became a US senator from Connecticut, and Marian Wright, later the first black woman lawyer from Mississippi and president of the Children's Defense Fund.

Although the students were beaten, shot at, and jailed to drive them off, the vote occurred as scheduled in November 1963. About 85,000 blacks – several times the number on the voting rolls – cast 'freedom ballots' at places where they could not be harassed, such as churches, lodges, grocery stores, beauty parlors, streetside tables, and homes. They voted for two 'freedom candidates', Aaron Henry, the state NAACP president, who ran for governor, and his running-mate, Ed King, a young, white Methodist chaplain at the historically black Tougaloo College, whose pray-ins embarrassed segregated churches. One SNCC activist said the election showed that blacks wanted to vote and that politics was 'not just "white folks" business' as it had been since Reconstruction.

The Freedom Vote re-ignited the movement in the Magnolia state. Building on this success, Moses promoted a voter-registration drive called the Mississippi Summer Project, or Freedom Summer, in 1964. The drive's key, but controversial, feature was to import hundreds of northern volunteers – three-quarters of them white college students – to register local blacks and teach their children. The idea for the 'freedom schools' came from Charlie Cobb, a SNCC field secretary and Howard University divinity graduate who wanted to 'challenge the myths of our society'. While some activists, especially those from Mississippi, opposed white involvement for implying black incompetence, undercutting the grassroots movement, and probably antagonizing local sheriffs, most agreed with CORE's Dave Dennis that 'the death of a white college student would bring on more attention to what was going on than for a black college student getting it'. After all, federal officials turned a blind eye to 150 cases of violence against civil rights workers.

A COFO flyer distributed on northern college campuses called for 'A Domestic Freedom Corps' in Mississippi that summer, along the lines of

Kennedy's Peace Corps. The children of prominent Americans signed on to become movement cannon fodder, notably Jerry Brown, the California governor's son who became governor himself; Len Edwards, a California congressman's son; and Harold Ickes, the son of Franklin Roosevelt's Interior secretary. Other volunteers became well known after their stint in Mississippi, including Susan Brownmiller, who became a leading feminist theorist; Barney Frank, a Harvard graduate student who became a Massachusetts congressman; Ed Koch, later the mayor of New York City; and Mario Savio, who initiated the 'free speech' movement that fall at Berkeley. While most came from the North, some were southerners, including Bob Zellner of Alabama and Casey Hayden and Sara Evans of Texas. Many volunteers were the children of Methodist ministers and belonged to such activist groups as SDS and NSA. Some were reared in leftist households, but most came from liberal Democratic families and intended to fight the 'Nazis' of their time. As one put it, 'I'm going because the worst thing after burning churches and murdering children is keeping silent.'

White Mississippians saw the college blitzkrieg as the largest invading army since the Civil War, and the locals intended to preserve segregation at all costs. To send a signal to the volunteers before they came, the 6,000-member White Knights of the Ku Klux Klan committed a rash of arson and murder against the 'satanists' who were 'defiling' Christian civilization. Their leader was imperial wizard Sam Bowers, a navy veteran with a fetish for explosives and swastiskas who ran a vending machine business called Sambo Amusements. The police harassed black and white SNCC workers who were seen in each other's company. One sheriff ordered a white woman out of a car driven by a black man: 'Slut, I know you fuckin' them niggers. Why else would you be down here? Which one is it? If you tell me the truth, I'll let you go.' The state legislature tried to control, if not intimidate, the students by doubling the state police force. In Jackson, the mayor hired more police; stockpiled new shotguns and gas masks; purchased paddy wagons, searchlight trucks, and a 6-ton armored personnel carrier with bulletproof windshields; and turned the fairgrounds into a makeshift prison. The civil rights workers 'won't have a chance', the mayor predicted.

COFO went ahead anyway. The National Council of Churches set up a training center for voter registration and nonviolence tactics at Western College for Women in Oxford, Ohio. For two weeks in June, the volunteers learned how to survive in Mississippi while registering fearful local blacks and teaching in Freedom Schools. Don't travel openly in interracial groups, the volunteers were warned. Don't stand in a lighted window; don't drive down unfamiliar roads; don't take blows to the head. Although white civil rights workers had never been lynched, the volunteers might well be killed because segregationists saw them as traitors. 'Our goals are limited,' Bob Moses explained. 'If we can go and come back alive, then that is something.'

The group grew more somber after a Justice department official admitted that he could do nothing to protect them.

The expected violence came on the first day of Freedom Summer. The White Knights – the Klan's most violent branch – targeted three CORE workers: Michael 'Mickey' Schwerner, a 24-year-old New York social worker who ran the Meridian office in Neshoba county; James Chaney, a 21-year-old black plasterer from Meridian; and Andrew Goodman, a 20-year-old Queens College sophomore. Once the imperial wizard gave the order, Edgar Ray Killen, a Baptist preacher and Klan recruiter, laid a death trap for the bearded Schwerner, explaining that the movement would wither without its leader: 'Goatee is like the queen bee in the beehive. You eliminate the queen bee and all the workers go away.' Killen put the plan in motion when the Klan torched Longdale's Mount Zion Methodist Church, future host of a freedom school. Schwerner and his companions went to investigate the ruins on Sunday, 21 June, only to be arrested by deputy sheriff Cecil Price for allegedly speeding and fire-bombing the church they had just inspected. Price alerted his fellow klansmen about his prized prisoners.

When the activists were released at 10.30 p.m., three carloads of klansmen who had been drinking heavily intercepted the 'heretics' and took them to a deserted dirt road. Wayne Roberts, a 26-year-old salesman and ex-Marine, jerked Schwerner out of the car. 'Are you the nigger lover?' Roberts demanded to know and then shot him him point-blank in the heart. Roberts shot Goodman dead too. Hearing gunshots, Jim Jordan jumped out of his car, shouting, 'Save one for me!' After firing at Chaney's abdomen, Jordan exclaimed, 'Y'all didn't leave me nothing but a nigger, but at least I killed me a nigger.' The victims were then buried beneath thirty feet of Mississippi mud next to a cattle pond. Before dawn, the murderers returned to Philadelphia, where a state official praised them: 'Well, boys, you've done a good job. You've struck a blow for the White Man. Mississippi can be proud of you [for killing] those three sons of bitches tonight.'

As SNCC calculated, a national outcry ensued after the charred car was located in a swamp, and president Johnson called for a massive manhunt. A benumbed Rita Schwerner explained why a manhunt was ordered: 'We all know that this search with two hundred sailors is because Andrew Goodman and my husband are white. If only Chaney was involved, nothing would've been done.' To crack the case code-named 'Mississippi Burning', 258 FBI agents dragged fifty miles of the snake-infested Pearl river, interviewed a thousand people, and compiled a 150,000-page file. The decomposed bodies turned up six weeks later when the FBI offered a $30,000 reward. Nineteen men were implicated, but none stood trial for murder because the state refused to prosecute. Eventually, deputy sheriff Price and six others were convicted of the lesser charge of violating the victims' federal civil rights. It was the first time a Mississippi jury convicted klansmen in connection with the death of a black person. To monitor future terrorist activity as part of its counter-intelligence program (COINTELPRO), the FBI infiltrated all fourteen Klan groups with 2,000 spies.

Despite this dreadful beginning, idealistic volunteers streamed into Mississippi expecting to turn the closed society inside out. Adept at organizational tasks because they were campus leaders, white students wrote press releases, transferred money, answered telephones, and cranked mimeograph machines. At countless meetings, their consciousness was raised, leading them to walk picket lines, teach school, and knock on doors to take blacks to the registrar [*Doc. 14*]. Overall, Freedom Summer proved to be an eye-popping experience for the volunteers, who risked their lives for others and survived by sleeping on bare mattresses and eating beans, peas, and peanut butter and jelly sandwiches. Neil McCarthy described his time in Mississippi as 'the most frightening and rewarding thing I've done in my life . . . the richest part [of the experience] was the bond you felt with everyone in the project. We were really a family' [*Doc. 15*]. Another volunteer admitted that 'Mississippi transformed us more than we transformed Mississippi – much more profoundly.' By sharing meals and their homes with the volunteers, local blacks learned, as Fannie Lou Hamer concluded, that 'white folks are human'.

In wartime conditions, tensions inevitably arose. Inexperienced white students resented how blacks sometimes 'treated us as brusquely as sergeants treat buck privates during the first month of basic training'. Frustration, even bitterness, mounted as whites discovered that most local blacks were more interested in self-preservation than in voting. Blacks resented the Ivy League students for their middle-class background, superior education, and condescending attitudes. Blacks also questioned the commitment of these sunshine soldiers who would retreat to their northern homes at summer's end. Despite SNCC's informal ban, interracial sex was commonplace because it was one of society's greatest taboos. When black men challenged white women to prove their lack of prejudice in bed, some white women succumbed out of liberal guilt. Those who resisted were labeled 'racists' or 'white bitches'. To relieve their stress, many volunteers found solace in drinking alcohol and smoking marijuana, which sometimes produced more trouble.

The endless violence multiplied such tensions. Mississippi literally burned that summer of 1964. Racists beat eighty civil rights workers, shot at thirty-five of them, and killed four. Seventy black homes, businesses, and churches were bombed or burned. The police excused the white Mississippians who perpetrated the crimes and arrested a thousand activists. The emotional strain of dodging white men in pick-up trucks and receiving threatening phone calls prompted Dorie Ladner of the Natchez office to vomit every night after dinner. SNCC leader Cleve Sellers called Freedom Summer 'the longest night-mare of my life'.

Real gains nonetheless came from that nightmare. Three thousand black children attended freedom schools that operated in church basements and abandoned school buildings. The youngsters requested classes in foreign languages, the fine arts, arithmetic, typing, and journalism, none of which was offered regularly in their schools. Historian Staunton Lynd, who had taught at Spelman College in Atlanta, directed forty-one schools in the four 'Rs': reading, 'riting, 'rithmetic, and radicalism. Howard Zinn, Lynd's colleague at Spelman, described the free-form classes, which were a forerunner of the African American studies curricula: 'Nine-year-old Negro children sounded out French words whose English equivalents they had not yet discovered. . . . They learned about Frederick Douglass, wrote letters to the local editor about segregation, and discussed the meaning of civil disobedience.' To nurture a home-grown freedom movement, volunteers built community centres where blacks learned general hygiene and to speak up against injustice. Lawyers from the NAACP, National Lawyers Guild, and American Jewish Committee worked to secure basic rights. To empower blacks directly, the voter registration drive led 17,000 adults to attempt to register as Democrats, though just 1,600 succeeded.

To increase this paltry black registration, COFO organized as the Mississippi Freedom Democratic Party, a grassroots alternative to the state's Jim Crow party. Against all odds, MFDP sought recognition as the state's true delegation to the Democratic party's national convention in Atlantic City, New Jersey. Black demands had escalated from a seat at a lunch-counter to a seat in the legislature. Behind the scenes, former SCLC director Ella Baker pitched MFDP's story to northern Democrats and enlisted Joseph Rauh, a prominent Washington attorney, to serve as the party's legal counsel. At the convention, Aaron Henry and Fannie Lou Hamer headed a delegation of sixty-eight 'Freedom Democrats' who backed Lyndon Johnson and challenged the seating of the state's regular Democratic organization. The regulars not only excluded blacks but rejected Johnson's candidacy and the national party's platform. Many regulars preferred the conservative Republican candidate, senator Barry Goldwater of Arizona, who voted against the new Civil Rights Act. A parade of Freedom party witnesses testified on live television to the state's brutality. The most riveting account came from Hamer, who sobbed as she spoke for Mississippi's disfranchised black majority. 'Is this America?' she asked. 'The land of the free and the home of the brave? Where . . . our lives be threatened daily because we want to live as decent human beings?'

Johnson blew his stack over Hamer's plaintive plea. With blacks backing him, Johnson needed white southerners to win reelection and press his Great Society reforms. Johnson felt heat first from Alabama governor George Wallace, whose maverick campaign for the presidency had done well before collapsing, and then from black rioting in Harlem and elsewhere. He well remembered that Harry Truman's reelection was imperiled when South Carolina governor

Strom Thurmond and other Dixiecrat delegates stormed out of the Democratic convention. Southern governors warned Johnson that if Hamer's group sat with the Mississippi delegation there would be a replay of that 1948 walkout. To divert the cameras from 'that illiterate woman', the president fooled the networks by calling an impromptu press conference to announce the end of a railroad strike. When the networks later showed Hamer's taped testimony during prime time, a deluge of calls and telegrams demanded that MFDP be seated.

Johnson was not through yet. He directed senator Hubert Humphrey, the foremost champion of civil rights in Congress, to resolve the dispute in the Mississippi delegation or forget becoming the party's vice presidential candidate. Humphrey likewise leaned on his protégé, Minnesota attorney general Walter Mondale, who sat on the credentials committee. If Mondale wanted to succeed Humphrey as senator, he would have to hatch a plan acceptable to the convention. J. Edgar Hoover was assigned to tap the telephones of King, SNCC, and MFDP delegates to gain information that would force a compromise. UAW president Walter Reuther was to cut off contributions to SCLC and to dismiss company attorney Joe Rauh unless each accepted a compromise. Johnson barely got his way. The compromise required that Mississippi regulars support the nominees while MFDP would get two token at-large votes chosen by the credentials committee and a promise to ban segregated state delegations at future conventions. Fannie Lou Hamer was blackballed.

The compromise drew a mixed response. All but three Mississippi regulars walked out, as did most of Alabama's. Within MFDP, a fierce debate raged. Bayard Rustin, who believed in pragmatic politics as well as mass action, saw the liberal Johnson as the best hope for black progress. Rustin, joined by Martin Luther King and James Farmer, conceded that the compromise was 'not what any of us wanted, but it's the best we could get'. SNCC and most of the MFDP delegation spurned the deal as an insulting sellout of 400,000 black Mississippians at the hands of their ostensible friends, northern white liberals. The normally cool Moses became livid, shouting at Humphrey, 'You tricked us!' Freedom Democrat Annie Devine rejected the compromise because it 'would let Jim Crow be'. She declared that there 'ain't no Democratic party worth that. We've been treated like beasts in Mississippi. They shot us down like animals. We risked our lives coming here.'

Despite MFDP's repudiation of it, the agreement worked out well on the surface. The convention renominated Johnson by acclamation, adopted a strong civil rights plank, and named Humphrey as Johnson's running-mate. Although Mississippi and four other deep South states went Republican in the 1964 election, Johnson won the greatest landslide in American history, thanks in part to the 94 per cent of blacks who voted Democratic. Mondale replaced Humphrey in the Senate. Subsequently, Johnson rammed more path-breaking civil rights and anti-poverty legislation through Congress. These reforms boosted Mississippi's black voter registration to 62 per cent, a twelve-fold increase. As promised, the Democratic party in 1968 denied party regulars from Mississippi their seats because of racial discrimination, and MFDP took its rightful place. In the long run, however, the white South abandoned the Democratic party, making it problematic for Democrats to win the White House.

The disillusionment over the Democratic convention ruptured the civil rights movement. Henceforth, a demoralized SNCC divided in two with the more militant branch demanding racial separatism and embracing self-defense, which violated cardinal principles of King's crusade. Cleve Sellers explained that 'Never again were we lulled into believing that our task was exposing injustices so that the "good" people of America could eliminate them. . . . After Atlantic City, our struggle was not for civil rights, but for liberation.' Stokely Carmichael believed that whites, including liberals, would never grant blacks justice, so, as SNCC's new chairman, he called for the organization to expel white members, including deeply committed activists like Bob Zellner [*Doc. 16*]. Freedom Summer marked the end of SNCC's efforts to appeal to the nation's conscience and the opening of a more confrontational chapter in the movement.

CHAPTER TWELVE

BLOODY SUNDAY

The crisis over black voting reached a boil in the sleepy town of Selma, once a cotton market on the muddy Alabama river. Bull Connor grew up in Selma, and the state's Citizens' Council first met there. To keep the white monopoly in political power after emancipation, Alabama's state constitutional convention of 1901 instituted a literacy test that excluded nearly all blacks for more than a half century. Although 57 per cent of the voting-age population was black in the surrounding Dallas county, just 1 per cent of them was registered to vote. Elsewhere, intimidation shut the door to black voting entirely. In the adjoining, heavily black counties of Lowndes and Wilcox, not one black had dared to register since Reconstruction. Whites boasted that any black person trying to register would be dead by sundown.

The Dallas county registrar had a bag of tricks to frustrate blacks. The office opened only on the first and third Mondays of the month, and the registrars invariably arrived late, took long lunch breaks, and closed early. When the office was open, perhaps a dozen blacks a day got in, only to confront four-page forms and obscure questions based on the constitution. Registrars had complete discretion to fail applicants. A black person who neglected to cross a 't' on the registration form, could not define words like 'turpitude', or was unable to recite the 14th Amendment verbatim was denied the right to vote. To frighten black applicants, the registrar would ask them, 'Does your employer know you're here?' Blacks with common-law marriages or illegitimate children flunked the 'good character' test. The snail's pace in Dallas county limited black registration to 156, mainly teachers, professionals, and businessmen. At that rate, a century would pass before all eligible blacks could vote. For the foreseeable future, blacks could never outvote the 9,500 whites who were already registered.

Against all odds, SNCC's Bernard LaFayette, a veteran of the Nashville sit-ins and Freedom Ride, and his wife Colia led a campaign in Selma in early 1963 to register intimidated blacks. At first, black leaders denied there were any racial problems. A minister told the LaFayettes, 'We know how to get what we want from white people. You just have to know how to ask.' The

108

LaFayettes explained that only through political action would blacks get their garbage hauled away, streets paved, and schools opened more than three hours a day. Most adults were too frightened to step forward, so the LaFayettes appealed to students and farmers to shame city folk into registering to vote. But the high school principal and president of Selma University threatened to expel any student participating in demonstrations. Slowly the LaFayettes built up trust in the local community, especially after the 22-year-old Bernard was nearly killed by a klansman swinging a gun. Bernard wore his blood-soaked shirt for weeks as a badge of honor.

SNCC's voter-registration drive invariably ended in harassment, dismissals, and beatings after photographs of the applicants appeared in the newspaper. Undeterred, canvassers held a 'Freedom Day' on 7 October, which attracted 350 blacks to the Dallas county courthouse. As federal officials watched impassively, the police clubbed and arrested volunteers who gave sandwiches to those in line. When SNCC organized a boycott of city buses after an impatient driver dragged a pregnant black woman to her death, its office was raided, and several workers were arrested. Selma's boss, circuit court judge James Hare, accused the activists of being 'Communist agitators' and forbade public gatherings of more than three people, an injunction that ended mass marches. Hare was predisposed against blacks, believing they were innately inferior and could not be domesticated 'any more than you can get a zebra to pull a plow, or an Apache to pick cotton'. Such obstacles kept black registration minuscule despite months of civil rights agitation.

As SNCC's voter-registration drive faltered, the Voters League (the reincarnated NAACP) recruited Martin Luther King. The league was led by Frederick Reese, a dynamic young Baptist clergyman and science teacher; Sam Boynton, a US agricultural extension agent, and Amelia Boynton, an insurance agent and past president of the local NAACP; Marie Foster, a dental hygienist who taught citizenship education classes; and J.L. Chestnut, Selma's only black attorney. King accepted their challenge in part because a voter registration drive among the state's 500,000 unregistered blacks would memorialize the four Birmingham girls murdered in their church. King also needed to put SCLC's stalemated campaign in St Augustine behind him. Most important, Selma had a violent sheriff in the Bull Connor mold. The villain this time was the tempestuous Jim Clark, who dressed and acted like general George Patton as he kept local blacks under his thumb. A King aide remarked that 'Bull Connor gave us the civil rights bill, and Jim Clark is going to give us the voting rights bill.'

Selma's new mayor, Joe T. Smitherman, realized that Clark's strong-arm tactics threatened the northern investment he coveted. The mayor was especially interested in the Hammermill paper company of Erie, Pennsylvania, which proposed a $30 million plant with 250 employees. To bring in this new business, Smitherman needed to keep sheriff Clark from escalating civil rights demonstrations into riots. The mayor established a new city position – director of public safety – for a soft-spoken former police captain named Wilson Baker who also disliked Clark's methods. Baker offered the Justice department a tantalizing deal: if Robert Kennedy could keep Martin Luther King out of Selma for a year, local authorities would refrain from excessive force and liberalize voting procedures so that black could vote. Such a deal was impossible, but the attorney general told Baker that 'if you're smart enough, you can beat him at his own game'. When King's plans became public knowledge, Baker followed Albany police chief Laurie Pritchett's successful formula of arresting the demonstrators quickly and quietly, blunting nonviolence with nonviolence.

To provoke violence, King and SNCC's John Lewis led a march to the courthouse on 18 January 1965. Along the way, the marchers confronted George Lincoln Rockwell, the *fuehrer* of the American Nazi party, and Jimmy George Robinson of the National States' Rights party. Sheriff Clark acted out of character, peacefully herding the demonstrators into an alley away from the media, where they stood in the cold for the registrar. The registrar called whites forward but ignored blacks. After the courthouse closed, King and his staff registered at the all-white Hotel Albert, where Robinson punched King in the head and kicked him in the groin. Chief Baker wrestled Robinson away and arrested him. Because this attack occurred off-camera, SCLC worried that the campaign would fall flat if demonstrations did not soon produce media attention. Baker learned of King's possible departure by blackmailing a young, gay civil rights worker.

Egged on by militant possemen, Clark could not keep his cool. The sheriff swore he would arrest 'every goddam one' of the demonstrators who came to the courthouse. He expected that the demonstrations would so anger white Alabamians that he would win the governorship. The next day, fifty demonstrators went to the registrar's office, refusing to stay in the back alley behind the courthouse. When Amelia Boynton did not get back in line fast enough for the sheriff, an enraged Clark shoved her down the street to a squad car. As she reeled, Boynton told Clark that she hoped reporters saw her being manhandled. The sheriff replied, 'Dammit, I hope they do.' The sheriff got his ill-advised wish as Boynton's photograph appeared in the *New York Times*. Clark's misstep was the publicity break for which King had been waiting.

A week after the demonstrations began, the belligerent sheriff lost his cool completely. A tall, sturdy 53-year-old woman named Annie Lee Cooper confronted Clark after he elbowed her roughly back in line. Cooper told Clark defiantly: 'Ain't nobody scared around here.' Then she sent the sheriff sprawling with a right cross. As deputies restrained her, Cooper taunted Clark: 'I wish you would hit me, you scum.' The wild-eyed sheriff obliged, pounding her head with a club until she bled. King was angered, but he held back men who wanted to stop the assault. The beating got invaluable national attention.

King upped the stakes on 1 February, the next day for registration, when he decided to get arrested. King hoped his jailing would draw media attention and bring in celebrities and needed money. From his cell, he penned a letter like the one from Birmingham and published it as an advertisement in the *New York Times*. 'THIS IS SELMA, ALABAMA,' he wrote. 'THERE ARE MORE NEGROES IN JAIL WITH ME THAN THERE ARE ON THE VOTING ROLLS.' Jail conditions were primitive. Prisoners slept on the concrete floor, used a stopped-up toilet with no seat, and subsisted on black-eyed peas and cornbread. Sheriff Clark flooded the floor with water and turned off the heat in the dead of winter, but the drafty jail cell became a sauna as a hundred men sang and clapped feverishly. Reports of the dreadful conditions led a congressional delegation to investigate, but no uproar developed over King's jailing.

Days after King's arrest, the movement got unexpected help. At SNCC's invitation, Malcolm X told a packed audience at Brown AME Chapel that 'the white people should thank Dr King for holding people in check, for there are others who do not believe in these measures'. He urged black Selmians to demand that president Johnson pay them back for helping him win reelection. And if Johnson proved unresponsive, blacks should expose American racism before the United Nations. Malcolm's message alarmed SCLC executive director Andrew Young, who enlisted Coretta Scott King to calm the crowd with a talk on nonviolence. After Coretta's impromptu talk, Malcolm apologized to her: 'I didn't come to Selma to make [your husband's] job difficult,' he insisted. 'I really did come thinking that I could make it easier. If the white people realize what the alternative is, perhaps they will be more willing to hear Dr King.'

In truth, Malcolm's views on race were in flux, especially after a pilgrimage to the Muslim holy city of Mecca. The white man, Malcolm concluded, was not inherently satanic, a heretical view within the Nation of Islam. Malcolm had soured on Elijah Muhammad, the self-proclaimed ascetic divine who fathered illegitimate children and made Malcolm an unthinking 'zombie'. It became clear to Malcolm that the Black Muslims and their racial theories represented a bastardized version of Islam. Malcolm was painfully aware that Muslims spent their energies on condemning racism while Martin Luther King manned the frontlines to end injustice, however ineffectively. Malcolm now reached out to civil rights leaders who still eyed him warily, and endorsed voting, not gunfire, as an important tool to improve black life. Malcolm's evolution was cut short by rival Black Muslims who murdered him days after visiting Selma.

As the Selma demonstrations continued, the police jailed 3,000 protesters. A clueless sheriff Clark never understood that each arrest was an indictment of the police. As the arrests proceeded, Fred Reese, the Voters League president, prodded his fellow teachers to register to vote, lest they set a bad example. A hundred teachers defied school officials to march to the courthouse where Clark shook with anger. The students were thrilled and gave their teachers a standing ovation. Civil rights workers told each other, 'Brother, we got a *move*-ment goin' *on* in *Selma*!' Once the teachers – the traditionally conservative black elite – became involved, other groups, including the undertakers and beauticians, joined the protest.

Weary of electoral shenanigans, a federal judge barred the registrar from using complicated tests or disqualifying applicants for minor mistakes. The registrar had to enroll at least a hundred blacks a day when the office was open. For the first time, local officials would be violating the law if blacks were kept from registering. Responding to the ruling, officials offered an 'appearance book' in which blacks could sign up for registration appointments on a first-come, first-served basis when the office was closed. SCLC leaders smelled a rat, calling the plan just another trick to deny black rights because the appointment book would not speed black registration in any appreciable way. Other changes were needed, SCLC argued, including a six-day schedule for the registrar's office, branch offices for registration, black deputy registrars, and the elimination of all voting requirements except minimum age and local residence.

When the appearance book gambit failed, the sheriff went after 165 high school protesters carrying signs reading, 'JIM CLARK IS A CRACKER.' When the students would not disperse from the courthouse, Clark sent them on a three-mile forced march out of town. To move the panting students faster, the deputies stung them in the groin with electric prods. One deputy shouted, 'March, dammit, march! You want to march so bad, now you can march. Let's go!' Some exhausted teenagers vomited by the roadside. When a 15-year-old reminded a guard that 'God sees you', the guard clubbed the boy in the mouth. Appalled, public safety director Baker retrieved some injured children, explaining, 'I'm human, too.'

The following day, sheriff Clark complained of chest pains stemming from the demonstrations and checked into a hospital. He told a reporter that 'the niggers are givin' me a heart attack'. The demonstrators knelt and prayed in the rain for Clark's full recovery 'in mind as in body', as one sign read. Clark recovered physically, but left the hospital wearing a badge that read, 'NEVER!' Sensing Clark might come mentally unglued, the Reverend C.T. Vivian baited the sheriff by comparing him to Hitler. An apoplectic Clark ordered the cameras turned off or be shot out, prompting his deputies to restrain him, but it was too late. The sheriff broke his finger knocking Vivian down the courthouse steps.

On 18 February, the Selma protest took a decisive turn in the town of Marion, twenty miles away. C.T. Vivian and Albert Turner, a bricklayer and president of the Perry County Civic League, led an emotional rally at Zion's Chapel Methodist Church, before making a dangerous evening march around the courthouse. Local whites sprayed television cameras with black paint and savagely beat NBC news reporter Richard Valeriani. A man stuck his face against Valeriani's and declared coldly, 'We don't have doctors for people like you'. Suddenly, the lights went out, and public safety director Al Lingo and fifty state troopers ran wild against the demonstrators and reporters. One eyewitness said that the troopers 'beat people at random. . . . All you had to do was be black.' As the panicked demonstrators retreated to the church, troopers stormed in after them, stopping only when marchers beat them back with furniture.

The troopers then went after blacks left outside, smashing heads and ribs. Two of the victims were Viola Jackson and her frail father, Cager Lee. Viola's 26-year-old son, Jimmie Lee Jackson, an army veteran, pulpwood cutter, and Baptist deacon who tried to register to vote five times, leaped to their defense and was shot in the stomach. A week later, Jackson succumbed to infection, the first person to die in an SCLC campaign. The sheriff's chief deputy accused SCLC of having 'wanted him to die. They wanted to make a martyr out of him and they did.' Although colonel Lingo knew that a trigger-happy state trooper killed Jackson, no one was ever prosecuted for the death.

The killing enraged local activists. To accuse the governor, they planned to walk 54 miles from Selma to Montgomery and deposit Jackson's corpse on the capitol steps. 'We were going to get killed or we was going to be free,' one leader recalled. An ambitious five-day trek to Montgomery seemed unlikely because George Wallace decided a march was 'not conducive to the orderly flow of traffic and commerce'. With his eye on the presidency, he told an aide: 'I'm not gonna have a bunch of niggers walking along a highway in this state as long as I'm governor.' If the demonstrators stayed in Selma, sheriff Clark, not governor Wallace, would be blamed for the unrest. Meanwhile, King fled to Atlanta because he received more death threats during the Selma campaign than at any other time. Besides, Wallace's press release said the march would be aborted.

The march proceeded without King. On Sunday, 7 March, 1965, SCLC's Hosea Williams and SNCC's John Lewis defied Wallace in leading 525 subdued demonstrators from Brown Chapel to Edmund Pettus Bridge. As the well-dressed marchers passed the hump of the bridge that crossed the river east of town, they saw their way blocked by Wallace's 'storm troopers', brandishing nightsticks and wearing blue uniforms, white helmets, and gas masks. Sheriff Clark's mounted possemen waited out of sight. With bloodshed likely, ambulances and hearses stood at the ready. A scared Williams asked Lewis if he could swim because 'I'm sure we're gonna end up in that river'. Just then, major John Cloud shouted in a bullhorn that the demonstrators had two minutes to 'turn around and go back to your church! You will not be allowed to march any further!'

The troopers and deputies then slammed forward in the most savage police riot of the civil rights era. Black bodies toppled like bowling pins. Lewis suffered a fractured skull, and five women, including Amelia Boynton, were beaten unconscious. After the police blinded the marchers with tear gas, sheriff Clark's possemen rode their horses into the foggy fray and clubbed them. One posseman swung a rubber tube wrapped with barbed wire. Clark fanned the possemen's rage. 'Get those god-damned niggers!' he shouted. 'Please, no!' a terrified marcher cried. 'My God, we're being killed!' Some marchers slid down the riverbank or under cars to escape. Others ran for their lives, as the possemen chased them across open fields all the way to the chapel. All the while, white spectators cheered the lawmen on with bloodcurdling yells. When night fell, fifty-seven blacks were treated for injuries ranging from broken teeth and head gashes to fractured limbs. Hosea Williams, a World War II combat veteran, insisted that 'the Germans never were as inhuman as the state troopers of Alabama'.

The television networks interrupted their programming to flash the savagery of 'Bloody Sunday' across the country. ABC was showing the premiere of Stanley Kubrick's *Judgment at Nuremberg*, a powerful story of Nazi racism. The shocking footage of racism in Alabama produced a tidal wave of indignation. Thousands of white and black Americans flooded the White House with telegrams, signed petitions, and demonstrated in eighty cities to end the violence. Conservative Republican congressmen, including Gerald Ford of Michigan, denounced the police riot and endorsed a voting rights bill for blacks. Hundreds of clergymen accepted King's call to join a 'ministers' march' to Montgomery, even though more violence was clearly in the offing.

King realized that bold action was required, lest the public lose interest. He announced his intention to lead the people across Pettus Bridge on 9 March. To his surprise, federal judge Frank Johnson, whose civil rights record was the best in the South, enjoined the march until the governor could respond. King was caught in a bind between the law, which forbade the march, and the militants and hundreds of out-of-town volunteers who demanded it forthwith. As King deliberated, attorney general Nicholas Katzenbach warned him to stay away from Selma because of a Klan plot against his life. Katzenbach also made clear that a march would embarrass the administration and delay a voting rights bill. When King ignored the warning, the president dispatched former Florida governor Leroy Collins, head of the federal Community Relations Service, to delay the march until it was legal. Collins negotiated a face-saving deal in which Clark and Lingo agreed not to use force if the marchers walked to the bridge and then retreated. Without telling the marchers of the agreement that spared him a contempt citation, King told them he would march regardless of the cost: 'There may be beating, jailings, and tear gas. But I would rather die on the highways of Alabama than make a butchery of my conscience by compromising with evil.'

As agreed, major Cloud stopped 1,000 blacks and 450 whites and, upon King's request, allowed them to pray. A white Methodist bishop compared the marchers to the Israelites fleeing Egypt and asked God to open the Red Sea to let them through. The bishop's prayer was miraculously answered as the troopers wheeled out of the way, leaving the highway unobstructed. Unbeknownst to King, Wallace's press aide hatched a plan to have the troopers step aside as the unprepared demonstrators approached the bridge, making them 'the laughing stock of the nation and win for us a propaganda battle'. Suspecting a trap, King stuck to the agreement and asked his flabbergasted followers to return to Brown Chapel. As the marchers retreated, they sang, 'Ain't Gonna Let Nobody Turn Me 'Round.' Infuriated SNCC leaders labeled King's retreat the 'Tuesday Turnaround'.

A mob unintentionally reenergized the protest that evening. Several whites carrying baseball bats went after three white northern ministers who were lost after dinner in Selma's tough white section. 'You want to know what it's like to be a real nigger?' the toughs snarled, before bludgeoning James Reeb, a 38-year-old Unitarian clergyman from Boston's slums. Two days later, Reeb died of a blood clot in his brain, the second casualty of the Selma campaign. Sheriff Clark circulated rumors that the 'so-called minister' was drunk and had his skull crushed by civil rights workers to create sympathy for the movement. Reeb's assailant – whose rap sheet included twenty-six arrests for assault and battery – was quickly found not guilty, to the cheers of the packed courtroom.

The outcry over the white minister's death far exceeded that for Jimmie Lee Jackson. Thousands of clergymen, teachers, and students headed to 'Hate City, USA' to demand black voting rights, the cause for which Reeb sacrificed his life. Although president Johnson had not intended to push for more civil rights legislation any time soon, this new wave of outrage forced his hand. In a three-hour White House meeting, Johnson at first empathized with Wallace and then scolded the governor for not letting 'the niggers vote'. When Wallace hemmed and hawed, Johnson grew stern: *'Don't you shit me, George Wallace!'* Having easily dispatched the Alabama governor, Johnson gave a stirring address to Congress and 70 million Americans watching by television. In a democracy, he declared with finality, 'It is wrong – deadly wrong – to deny any of your fellow Americans the right to vote in this country.' The president considered the Selma protest a turning point in American history, comparable to the American Revolution and the Civil War. In a Texas drawl, he fully embraced the civil rights movement: 'Their cause must be our cause too. Because it is not just Negroes, but really it is all of us, who must overcome the crippling legacy of bigotry and injustice. And we *shall* overcome.' For the first time, Martin Luther King's aides saw him cry with joy.

Judge Frank Johnson soon allowed the Selma-to-Montgomery march to proceed. The judge recognized that the march might impede traffic, but the 'enormous' wrongs suffered by the demonstrators entitled them to march to the capital. Governor Wallace called his old college friend a 'low-down, carpetbaggin', scalawaggin'; race-mixin' liar'. When Wallace complained that the march was too costly, president Johnson federalized the Alabama National Guard to protect the marchers as they headed down Highway 80. He also sent 2,000 army troops, FBI agents, US marshals, and a dozen planes and helicopters to neutralize snipers and bombers. Pentagon generals would follow the march minute-by-minute via a hot-line telephone hook-up.

On 21 March, two weeks after Bloody Sunday, 3,200 black and white marchers set out for a third time on what John Lewis called 'a holy crusade, like Gandhi's march to the sea'. King led the march, bedecked with flowers, and was joined by A. Philip Randolph, Roy Wilkins, Whitney Young, Nobel peace prize winner Ralph Bunche, labor leader Walter Reuther, actor Gary Merrill, rabbi Abraham Heschel of the Jewish Theological Seminary, and several eminent historians, including John Hope Franklin, C. Vann Woodward, and Richard Hofstadter, who recognized history-in-the-making. Lewis walked every mile, but on doctor's orders he was driven back to Selma each night to sleep in a bed. Ordinary folks, students, and children accounted for most of the marchers. Cager Lee, Jimmie Lee Jackson's 82-year-old grandfather, was there. Jim Letherer, a one-legged, husky white laborer from Saginaw, Michigan, trudged the entire way on crutches.

Although most whites stared at the marchers as they passed by, other whites revealed ugly prejudice. As the marchers left town, a record store's loudspeaker blared, 'Bye, Bye, Blackbird.' On the first day, a 'Confederate Air Force' plane dumped hate leaflets on the highway. Along the route, hecklers waved Confederate flags, gestured obscenely, and held up signs reading, 'FAKE CLERGY & BEATNIKS GO HOME!' They cursed the marchers, chanting, 'Go back to Africa where you belong, you black jigaboos.' A car cruised by with painted signs on its doors: 'CHEAP AMMO HERE' and 'OPEN SEASON ON NIGGERS.'

When the highway narrowed to two lanes on the second day, judge Johnson required the band to shrink to three hundred and walk two abreast facing traffic. As troops surrounded the marchers and a convoy of army vehicles, utility trucks, and ambulances trailed behind, the marchers walked up to sixteen miles a day, singing and handclapping as they passed freshly plowed red fields, oak trees draped with Spanish moss, and snake-filled swamps. The palpable enthusiasm kept most going as the miles passed. One tired woman could hardly lift her feet in the evening. She rubbed alcohol on them and prayed that God would give her the strength to go on the next morning. She awoke refreshed, and marched onward. Not even torrential rain could dampen the marchers' spirits. Each night, the shivering marchers camped out on black-owned pastures along the route. The encampment, a reporter thought, 'resembled a cross between a "Grapes of Wrath" migrant labor camp and the

Continental Army bivouac at Valley Forge'. Incredibly, the state legislature accused the weary marchers of conducting lurid sex orgies in the freezing cold. Amazed, John Lewis responded, 'All these segregationists can think of is fornication, and that's why there are so many shades of Negroes.'

On the last night, celebrities showed up for a jamboree organized by Harry Belafonte. A local black funeral home loaned coffins to make a stage for Joan Baez, James Baldwin, Tony Bennett, Leonard Bernstein, Bobby Darin, Ossie Davis, Sammy Davis, Jr., Ruby Dee, Billy Eckstein, Ella Fitzgerald, Mahalia Jackson, Alan King, Johnny Mathis, the Chad Mitchell Trio, Paul Newman, Odetta, Floyd Patterson, Anthony Perkins, Sidney Poitier, Nipsey Russell, Pete Seeger, and Shelley Winters. Dick Gregory told jokes about segregation. Peter, Paul and Mary sang Bob Dylan songs, including, 'The Times They Are a-Changin'.' This extraordinary assemblage was a powerful endorsement of black civil rights. When a reporter asked screenwriter Elaine May if the sudden appearance of the stars turned the march into a circus, she snapped, 'The only real circus is the state of Alabama and George Wallace.'

As the demonstrators approached the tense capital city on 25 March, word spread that snipers were gunning for King. SCLC organizers camouflaged him by moving fifteen black men dressed in the same blue suit King wore to the front. They hoped that a white assassin could not tell black men apart and would give up. Masking their fears, the marchers sang, 'Keep your eyes on the prize, hold on', and carried signs reading 'WALLACE, IT'S ALL OVER.' The return to Montgomery represented a triumphant homecoming for King, Rosa Parks, and Ralph Abernathy, for it was there that the modern civil rights movement began.

With governor Wallace peering from behind his closed blinds, King gave the climactic address to 25,000 people, the largest civil rights gathering in southern history. Speaking eloquently from the very spot where Jefferson Davis became president of the Confederacy, King knew the marchers wanted to know 'How long will it take?' He answered his own question in rhythmic repetition: 'How long? Not long, because no lie can live forever. How long? Not long, because you will reap what you sow. How long? Not long. Because the arm of the moral universe is long but it bends toward justice.' Although Wallace's troopers refused the marchers' voting rights petition, the Selma march was the capstone of the civil rights movement. 'We Have Overcome Today', the joyous crowd sang.

Tragedy struck hours after King's speech, eliminating any doubt that a voting rights law was needed. Birmingham klansmen chased down Viola Liuzzo, a red-haired mother of five who was married to a Detroit union official. As an NAACP member, she volunteered to use her sedan to shuttle civil rights workers through 'Bloody Lowndes' county between Selma and Montgomery. The klansmen were enraged that Liuzzo violated a southern taboo by letting a young black male, Leroy Moton, ride with her. Traveling at

90 m.p.h., the klansmen pulled their red-and-white Chevrolet alongside Liuzzo's Oldsmobile and shot her in the face. Her car kept rolling for awhile, but the killer assured another klansman: 'Baby Brother, don't worry about it. That bitch and that bastard are dead and in hell. I don't miss.' Liuzzo was indeed dead while a blood-splattered Moton survived by pretending to be dead.

In an especially shameful episode, it was the dead woman and the movement she died for that were put on trial. One of the klansmen in the car was FBI informant Tommy Rowe, who forewarned of violence the very day Liuzzo died but had not tried to stop the murder. An embarrassed FBI covered its incompetence by branding the victim as an adulterer, criminal, and drug addict. J. Edgar Hoover told president Johnson that Liuzzo sat 'very, very close to the Negro' in the car, giving 'all the appearances of a necking party'. Sheriff Clark contacted the Michigan police to undertake a background check on Liuzzo. Clark passed along the gossip that surfaced to the Alabama Klan. State officials commissioned a hack writer and a Dallas film company to prepare lurid exposés of the alleged debaucheries committed on the Selma march. In court, the Klan's attorney called Liuzzo 'a white nigger' who 'turned her car over to a black nigger' for the purpose of 'haulin' niggers and Communists back and forth'. The real culprit, he alleged, was Moton, who shot Liuzzo to steal her purse. Despite Rowe's eyewitness testimony, a state jury acquitted the murderers. Only in federal court were the killers found guilty, not of murder but of violating Liuzzo's civil rights, and given a maximum 10-year jail sentence.

The Selma march pressured both political parties to approve a Voting Rights Act that would enforce the 15th Amendment. President Johnson worried that his health care bill might be derailed if he kept dismantling Jim Crow, but he pressed hard for black voting rights when public opinion polls showed 75 per cent of Americans supported it. Even senator Harry Byrd of Virginia – the guiding force behind Massive Resistance – conceded. 'You can't stop this bill,' he told an aide. 'We can't deny the Negroes a basic constitutional right to vote.' The administration finally shut off the debate, and Johnson signed the measure in the same place that Lincoln signed the Emancipation Proclamation. At a private meeting that day, the president implored SNCC's John Lewis to get other blacks to vote: 'You've got to go back and get those boys by the *balls*. Just like a bull gets on top of a cow. You've got to get 'em by the balls and you've got to *squeeze*, squeeze 'em till they *hurt*.'

The Voting Rights Act of 1965 confirmed that blacks were fully American citizens and rewrote the rules of southern politics that had prevailed since Reconstruction. In states and counties where less than half the population voted in the 1964 election, the law automatically suspended literacy and understanding tests. If too few blacks registered after the tests were suspended, the executive branch could dispatch federal registrars to enroll the disfranchised. This triggering mechanism brought Alabama, Georgia, Louisiana, Mississippi,

South Carolina, Virginia, and parts of North Carolina under federal supervision. Because the law circumvented local courts, which ignored black voting rights, the measure had an immediate impact. Within a month of the bill's enactment, over 60 per cent of Selma blacks registered, including Cager Lee, whose grandson was killed by the police. One of the first political casualties was none other than sheriff Jim Clark. To stave off the inevitable, he hosted a barbecue for blacks, but lost anyway to his former deputy, Wilson Baker.

In some places, whites lashed back with deadly violence. In a Lowndes county, Alabama, grocery store, a fortnight after the Voting Rights Act passed, a highway department worker and part-time deputy sheriff killed Episcopalian seminarian Jonathan Daniels of New Hampshire. The bullet was meant for a black teenager who wanted a soft drink, but Daniels shoved her out of danger. Despite eyewitness testimony, the deputy sheriff was acquitted, and one of the jurors jovially greeted the freed defendant: 'We gonna be able to make that dove shoot now, ain't we?' In January 1966, voting-rights organizer Sammy Younge, Jr., a Tuskegee Institute student, asked to use a gas station bathroom, and was shot in the head by the attendant. An all-white jury ruled that the attendant acted in self-defense. Days later, Vernon Dahmer, a respected 58-year-old Mississippi merchant and head of Hattiesburg's NAACP, was murdered by klansmen. The same day that Dahmer announced over the radio that blacks could pay their poll taxes in his grocery store, the White Knights tossed Molotov cocktails into his home. Dahmer fired at the assailants as his family escaped, but he died of smoke inhalation. The murder's mastermind, imperial wizard Sam Bowers, boasted that 'a jury would never convict a white man for killing a nigger in Mississippi'. He was partly right, thanks to jury tampering. Bowers had ordered nine murders and hundreds of bombings, assaults, and arsons, before a fifth trial resulted in a life sentence in 1998.

Such isolated violence did not stop blacks from going to the polls in the same proportion as whites. Three years after the Voting Rights Act, a majority of blacks in Alabama and Mississippi could vote. Through VEP's renewed efforts, 2 million more blacks voted within ten years, producing a phenomenon not seen in a century – black officials. Within twenty years, the number of black officials nationwide rose from 103 to 3,503. In 1967, Cleveland's Carl Stokes became the first black mayor of a major American city, leading the way for black mayors in other northern cities, including Chicago, Detroit, Los Angeles, New York, and Philadelphia. Within Dixie, Atlanta, Birmingham, New Orleans, and eventually Selma voted in black mayors too. SNCC veterans John Lewis, Marion Barry, and Charles Sherrod won election as Atlanta's congressman, Washington's mayor, and Albany's city councilman, respectively. With a large pool of black voters in his camp, Jesse Jackson made the first serious black campaigns for the presidency. In 1989, Douglas Wilder of Virginia became the first elected black governor.

Black voting strength became so significant that even George Wallace and Strom Thurmond kissed black babies, hired black assistants, and funneled government aid to black areas. Wallace acknowledged that his racist rhetoric was wrong and crowned a black homecoming queen at the University of Alabama ten years after he had stood in the doorway to keep blacks out. He received an honorary degree from Tuskegee University for his political conversion.

Selma taught powerful lessons to all involved. With black voting realized, white liberals moved on to other causes, not recognizing that racial justice was far from achieved. Having lost so badly, racists avoided similar confrontations, lest the federal government help blacks further. The breach between young SNCC activists and King's SCLC widened to an unbridgeable chasm. SNCC regarded King's refusal to violate federal court injunctions as a betrayal of the movement's basic philosophy. Moreover, SNCC resented King's 'juggernaut' for taking over areas that SNCC cultivated for years. In a rebuke of SCLC's here-today-gone-tomorrow tactics, Stokely Carmichael promoted a third party in Alabama – the Lowndes County Freedom Organization – to encourage indigenous, poor, and uneducated people to escape racism on their own. With a snarling panther as its emblem, the Black Panther party sought to seize political power with an all-black slate of candidates, which lost as a result of wholesale election fraud. The nonviolent civil rights movement for equality and integration was largely over. It did little, if anything, for blacks north of Dixie, and their impatience erupted in deadly riots.

CHAPTER THIRTEEN

BLACK POWER

The civil rights movement cleansed the country of a great moral evil. But major problems in the ghettoes remained because racism was often more intractable in the North than the South. Unlike white immigrants who clawed their way to the suburbs, native-born blacks remained stuck in the ghetto. A combination of interests kept northern neighborhoods segregated. Realtors steered most black homebuyers to black neighborhoods. On occasion, realtors moved a black family into a white neighborhood and then profited by spreading rumors that more blacks were coming. Panicked whites sold their homes at fire sale prices to brokers, who then sold them to middle-class blacks at higher prices. As the cities became blacker, whites fled the centre on new federal highways, leaving urban areas destitute. Low-income people could not help themselves because banks and insurers refused them assistance, a practice called redlining. The result was that more blacks sank into poverty. Politicians responded to the urban crisis by erecting public housing projects to warehouse blacks. Blacks understandably concluded that 'urban renewal equals Negro removal'.

Blacks in the seething ghetto had almost no chance of success. In these hellholes, blacks battled rat-infested apartments, an unemployment rate twice that of whites, prying welfare officials, soaring drug use, rampant gang violence, police harassment, inadequate mass transit, and condescending teachers in second-rate schools. Economic opportunity was an illusion, as manufacturing firms relocated to the suburbs and craft unions excluded blacks from apprenticeships in good-paying positions. Many unemployed black men abandoned their families. Blacks with jobs worked in dead-end positions that were hidden from the eyes of the white public, such as dishwasher and janitor. Television advertisements of consumer goods heightened the frustrations of impoverished young blacks. Merchandise in the ghetto was often inferior but expensive. Short on cash, blacks bought goods on credit for which they paid exorbitant rates. Estranged from their surroundings, many northern blacks struggled without strong family, church, or community ties.

When their anger could no longer be capped, blacks rioted in cities across America in the worst period of unrest since the Civil War. In August 1965, the squalid Los Angeles ghetto of Watts exploded in the wake of stories that white policemen had savagely beaten a young pregnant woman. An estimated 35,000 enraged blacks chanted, 'burn, baby, burn!' as they ransacked white-owned stores that charged excessive prices. Far from being apologetic, the rioters trumpeted their actions as a political statement, viewing the riot as a black Bunker Hill. A teenager excoriated the law: 'These fucking cops have been pushin' me 'round all my life. . . . Whitey ain't no good. He talked 'bout law and order. It's his law and his order, it ain't mine'. When Martin Luther King arrived in the still-smoldering ghetto, teenagers heckled him as an 'Uncle Tom' and told him to 'go back where you came from.' Order was restored five days later after thousands of police and National Guardsmen arrived. The riot's toll stood at 34 deaths, 1,000 injured, 4,000 arrests, and $40 million in property damage, not to mention the evaporating goodwill of white liberals.

Although the Watts riot bewildered liberals and alienated the white middle class, it was not mindless mayhem. California's general prosperity did not trickle down to black neighborhoods. Median income in Watts was declining, in part because the male unemployment rate was a staggering 34 per cent, six times that for the entire city. Overcrowding from a land give-away to the Los Angeles Dodgers baseball team forced blacks and Latinos to compete for scarce jobs and housing. The sprawling metropolis had inadequate public transportation, which limited access to better-paying jobs in suburbia. A quarter of the residents were on welfare, but Sam Yorty, the conservative mayor, blocked federal funds to depressed urban areas. White-owned businesses in Watts exploited blacks twice over, paying black workers low wages and charging black customers inflated prices. Schools were inferior, and 13 per cent of the residents were illiterate. Garbage collection was irregular, and the sewers stank in summer because there was not enough water pressure to flush toilets. In an area where health was often precarious, there was no hospital at all. The mostly white police force encouraged one another to 'LSMFT', meaning 'let's shoot a motherfucker tonight'. The police did exactly that to sixty-five people in Los Angeles in thirty months before the riot. Watts foreshadowed the racial violence that erupted every summer thereafter. Between 1965 and 1968, a half million blacks participated in three hundred similar street battles in northern cities like Detroit and Newark, resulting in 250 deaths (mostly blacks), 10,000 injured, 60,000 arrests, and billions of dollars in property damage.

Authorities responded in different ways to the riots. President Johnson appointed Illinois governor Otto Kerner to investigate the causes of the disorders. The Kerner Commission delivered a scathing indictment of an American society that was on the verge of becoming two nations, one black and poor and the other white and rich [*Doc. 17*]. The controversial report blamed this division on institutional racism and maintained that only a long-term national commitment larger than Johnson's Great Society could reverse the 'deepening racial trend'. Although Johnson was insulted by the report, he had abandoned domestic reforms to run what he termed 'that bitch of a war' in Vietnam. Some cities attempted to ameliorate the miserable conditions that produced such chaotic violence. Slum clearance, job training, recreational facilities, and civilian review boards of police actions provided a kind of 'riot insurance' for local governments. In case social programs proved ineffective, mayors trained their police in riot control and bought them powerful weapons. California governor Ronald Reagan dismissed social programs as unnecessary since he guessed that just 2 per cent of ghetto dwellers – 'mad dogs', he called them – were involved.

Martin Luther King gambled that his nonviolent formula would work in the explosive ghetto, which he called 'a system of internal colonialism'. He now believed that blacks were just as oppressed by low-wage jobs, inadequate housing, and inferior schools as by racist laws. Al Raby, a young teacher who presided over the Coordinating Council of Community Organizations, invited King to address these thorny problems in Chicago, infamous for its high-rise housing projects on the South Side. In 1966, King put together a grassroots coalition called the Chicago Freedom Movement and moved with his family into a urine-stenched tenement.

Focusing on open housing, King persuaded some tenants to withhold their rents, but he was overwhelmed by the 'monster of racism' in the nation's second-largest city. The local black leadership was largely unsupportive mainly because the Tammany-style political machine employed minorities. When King led a march through a white ethnic neighborhood, he was nearly stoned to death by screaming Poles, Italians, and Irish wearing Nazi insignia and waving Confederate flags. King admitted that he had 'never seen, even in Mississippi, mobs as hostile and as hate-filled'. Chicago's boss – Democratic mayor Richard Daley – kept the police in line and killed the movement with soothing words and empty promises, a far cry from Birmingham's fire hoses. Because of Daley's influence as a kingmaker, the national Democratic party had no interest in pressuring him as it had southern governors. Never again did the civil rights movement make a serious effort to change the North, where the commitment to racial equality was more abstract than real. All that was left in Chicago was Operation Breadbasket, an SCLC program headed by Jesse Jackson that boycotted businesses with few, if any, black workers.

In the South, King found his vision and tactics questioned as never before. In June 1966, James Meredith, the first black graduate of Ole Miss, began a perilous three-week, 220-mile March Against Fear from Memphis, Tennessee, to Jackson, Mississippi. He insisted that 'the old order was passing', which permitted blacks to 'stand up as men' and vote. Armed with a Bible, a plastic helmet, and an African walking stick, Meredith hoped to inspire other blacks by walking alone through the nation's most racially violent state. After just ten miles, a 40-year-old unemployed white man from Memphis ambushed a unarmed Meredith with painful birdshot, causing him to crumple to the highway and cry out in pain. Civil rights leaders gathered at Meredith's hospital bed, determined to finish his march. It was the last time that the leaders of SCLC, CORE, and SNCC would march together.

Old frustrations within the movement bubbled to the surface. SNCC's Stokely Carmichael rejected King's approach altogether as cringingly deferential to whites. After Carmichael shouted, 'The Negro is going to take what he deserves from the white man', the mood shifted dramatically. Marchers vowed, 'White blood will flow', and Mississippi blacks chanted, 'Hey! Hey! Whattaya know? White folks must go – must go!' In Greenwood, Carmichael was arrested for trespassing on public property. He posted bail, jumped onto a flatbed truck, raised his arm in a clenched-fist salute, and wailed to an angry crowd: 'This is the 27th time I have been arrested, and I ain't going to jail no more! . . . We been saying freedom for six years and we ain't got nothin'. What we gonna start saying now is "Black Power!"' Though the term was not new, Carmichael's mantra electrified the crowd, and they screamed back, 'Black Power! Black Power!! Black Power!!!' After this outburst, a shaken King had to accept a paramilitary escort from Louisiana, the Deacons for Defense and Justice. Near the end of the march, even the escort was helpless against policemen who fired tear gas, swung rifle butts, and kicked women on the ground. It was a police riot like the one in Selma.

As the march proceeded, a Klan offshoot in Natchez plotted the murder of an innocent black man as a way of setting up King. Anticipating that King would investigate such a murder, the Cottonmouth Moccasin Gang offered an unsuspecting, elderly handyman named Ben Chester White $2 and a strawberry soda to help 'find' a lost dog. White, a barely literate church deacon, was known as a quiet, humble man with a gold tooth, who had never tried to vote. The gang picked White at random and drove him to a national forest, where he was pumped full of gunshot and dumped into a creek bed. The sordid plot failed because King had returned to Chicago to give a scheduled speech. Some good did come out of the march, as activists knocked on doors in every town they passed and helped to register a record 4,000 blacks.

After the Meredith march, the calls for 'Black Power' helped define black America, especially in the North. Because government policy did not materially uplift blacks, it seemed far less important than group identity and independence. Following Malcolm X's call to 'unbrainwash' themselves, many blacks emphasized their ethnic heritage by adopting African names, donning African clothing, letting their hair grow unstraightened in an 'Afro' style, learning phrases in the east African language of Swahili, and converting to Islam. Increasing numbers of blacks observed the end-of-the-year festival of Kwanzaa, which was devised from African antecedents by Maulana Karenga, a black studies professor who founded the culturally-assertive group called Organization US. Education was a particular target of criticism. Writer Amiri

Baraka, a leader in the Black Arts movement, insisted that all academic subjects be presented from an Afrocentric perspective. Black college students convinced some white administrators to admit more black students, hire more black professors, establish black studies programs, serve 'soul food', and set aside black dormitories. Perhaps the most dramatic display of racial pride came when two track stars at the 1968 Mexico City Olympics raised their fists in a Black Power salute transmitted the world over by television. James Brown, 'the godfather of soul', captured this cultural spirit in his classic song, 'Say It Loud, I'm Black and I'm Proud.'

To change the larger society, black nationalists took different approaches after the mid-1960s. Many black nationalists drew their vision from Frantz Fanon, a Caribbean revolutionary. Fanon's seminal book, *The Wretched of the Earth*, praised anti-imperialist struggles in the Third World, including Algeria, where he died a martyr's death. Robert Williams, who fled to Cuba to escape a bogus kidnapping charge, formed the Revolutionary Action Movement to wage guerrilla warfare in American cities and thereby spark a black insurrection. Former SNCC leader James Forman insisted that white churches and synagogues pay $500 million in reparations for exploiting black America. The reparations would permit blacks to own land, run publishing companies, receive specialized education, and establish a labor strike fund. Forman also resurrected the nineteenth-century idea that blacks were a nation, not a minority, and should aim for an autonomous republic within the United States. New SNCC national director H. 'Rap' Brown had no patience with the movement's nonviolent appeal to the white man. He threatened to assassinate the First Lady and condemned Israel's conquest of Palestinian land, prompting angry American Jews to cut off valuable donations. He incited a crowd in Cambridge, Maryland, to 'burn this town down. . . . When you tear down the white man, brother, you are hitting him in the money. . . . Don't love him to death. Shoot him to death.' That night, young blacks rioted in downtown Cambridge. The call for violence repelled most blacks and mobilized the authorities, thus rendering militant groups impotent.

The most visible militant group was led by Huey Newton and Bobby Seale, who met at a junior college in Oakland, California. As marxists, they believed that American blacks were political prisoners not unlike their African brothers. Inspired by SNCC's militant campaign in Lowndes county, Alabama, Newton and Seale founded the Black Panthers for Self-Defense in October 1966 to demand a better life by resisting the 'racist-capitalist police state' [*Doc. 18*]. They were joined by an ex-convict named Eldridge Cleaver, who characterized rape as an insurrectionary act against white society. These street toughs openly carried loaded Remington rifles and wore black commando garb while patrolling neighborhoods for police misconduct. Simultaneously, women Panthers ran popular bootstrap operations such as community schools, and provided free shoes, legal clinics, ambulance service, breakfasts for ghetto children, testing for sickle cell anemia, and trips to visit imprisoned relatives. These programs were in line with the Panther slogan, 'Power to the People.' In two years, the party attracted a few thousand members in twenty cities.

Whites were horrified by these revolutionary cells, which also engaged in killings, robbery, prostitution, and drug-trafficking. Accordingly, J. Edgar Hoover expanded his war on black America by declaring that the Panthers were 'the greatest threat to the internal security of the country', an exaggerated claim given the group's small size and amateurish methods. To destabilize the Black Panther party, the FBI and police infiltrated the group, arrested 750 Panthers, and killed 28 members in shootouts and ambushes. Newton was in and out of jail on fraud and murder charges until 1989, when he was killed in a drug deal. Hoover's war cut Panthers membership by half. Likewise, RAM dissolved after the FBI arrested members for conspiring to poison police officers and assassinate NAACP leaders.

Civil rights leaders despaired of this new separatist ideology, which commanded considerable press coverage but fed a strong white backlash. Roy Wilkins of the NAACP called Black Power 'the father of hatred and the mother of violence' and compared it to Hitlerism. A. Philip Randolph termed it 'a menace to racial peace and prosperity. No Negro who is fighting for civil rights can support black power, which is opposed to civil rights and integration.' Bayard Rustin declared that 'Black power was born in bitterness and frustration – has left us with a legacy of polarization, division and political nonsense.' While King understood the motivation for it, the slogan was impractical in his view, if not dangerous. With blacks comprising only 10 per cent of Americans, 'the American Negro has no alternative to nonviolence', King concluded. Such criticism notwithstanding, the radicals made civil rights reformers more palatable to white politicians, as Malcolm X had contended.

At the same time, King adopted a leftist critique of American society for leaving so many people of all colors behind. Having defeated legal segregation, he decided that capitalism itself was the enemy. King saw racism and poverty as two branches of the same problem – the exploitation of people to maximize profits. The Vietnam war, he argued, showed how skewed America's priorities were. He observed that the United States spent $500,000 to kill an enemy soldier in Asia but only $35 a year to help a poor American. His denunciation of the war alienated the Johnson administration, white supporters of the civil rights movement, and conservative black leaders. To redistribute America's wealth and power, King began a quixotic Poor People's Campaign to the nation's capital. He planned to fill the jails, boycott major industries, and occupy factories until Congress enacted a $30 billion Marshall Plan to salvage depressed areas. He proposed an array of socialist measures, including full employment, universal health insurance, a guaranteed annual income, and 300,000 low-cost housing units each year. Only then could the dispossessed sit at the welcome table.

On the way to Washington, King honored a request from his longtime ally, Methodist minister James Lawson, to assist a strike in Memphis. Black sanitation workers rebelled against filthy working conditions, inadequate compensation, and the city's anti-union actions. The last straw came when only black workers were sent home without pay due to bad weather. Such disrespect led the workers to adopt the slogan, 'I Am a Man'. To pressure city hall, King led a large demonstration that turned violent when an uninvited group of young blacks smashed windows and looted businesses. The police, in full riot gear, rampaged through the black community, shooting Mace as they went. Sixty blacks were injured and one killed by police gunfire. An exhausted, depressed King told the strikers, 'I've been to the mountaintop. . . . I've seen the promised land. I may not get there with you. But I want you to know tonight, that we, as a people, will get to the promised land.' America's greatest moral leader was murdered the next day.

On 4 April 1968, a career criminal and Hitler admirer named James Earl Ray shot the 39-year-old King on the balcony of the Lorraine Motel to collect a $50,000 reward. Andrew Young felt King's silent pulse and exclaimed, 'Oh, my God, my God, it's all over.' In a macabre scene, Jesse Jackson dipped his palms in the blood and wiped them on his shirt, thus laying a claim to being the dead prophet's heir. Riots, arson, and gunfire erupted across the country, a twisted tribute to a follower of Gandhi. In more than a hundred cities, there were 46 killed, 3,500 injured, and 27,000 arrested.

In the wake of King's murder, Congress passed a weak Civil Rights Act, which prohibited discrimination in renting or buying houses and the intimidation, injury, or death of those exercising their civil rights. To appease conservatives, rioting was made a federal crime. In Memphis, officials recognized the AFSCME union that the sanitation workers supported, touching off a wave of union-organizing by black southern employees. King's closest associate, Ralph Abernathy, carried on their Poor People's Campaign in Washington, erecting a shantytown called Resurrection City near the Lincoln Memorial. Torrential rain, poor leadership, ethnic divisions, and rock-throwing teenagers turned King's largest dream into a fiasco from which SCLC never recovered.

After Martin Luther King's death, the civil rights movement dissipated further. Many were the causes of its decline. The movement achieved its primary goals of ending legal segregation and disfranchisement, resulting in confusion over future goals and methods. King's murder robbed the movement of its most effective voice. The movement preceded King and would have been successful without him, but his charisma and courage appeared indispensable. Several civil rights groups became impotent by embracing black nationalism and characterizing Jewish allies as ghetto bloodsuckers. The NAACP and Urban League lost membership as their legal and educational initiatives produced few striking results. The movement's *bêtes noires* – James Eastland, George Wallace, and Strom Thurmond – either repented of their racism, grudgingly

accepted the new reality, or died, removing convenient targets. Most disturbing, the urban riots of the 1960s convinced many whites that blacks were an
ungrateful people to be feared rather than helped further.

With the Democrats saddled with race riots and the Vietnam war, Richard
Nixon became president in 1968 in part by promising to restore 'law and
order', a code phrase to end racial unrest. Although the Nixon administration
increased subsidies for minority businesses, threatened to cut off federal funding of segregated public schools, proposed a guaranteed annual income for
all Americans, and devised the Philadelphia Plan that required unions with
federal contracts to set targets and timetables for hiring minorities, these
initiatives encountered stiff conservative headwind and were quickly jettisoned.
Nixon's top domestic adviser Daniel Patrick Moynihan, a prime mover of
Johnson's war on poverty, convinced the new president that racial demands
should be treated with 'benign neglect'.

Despite the growing conservatism in Washington, some civil rights gains
were made. The Voting Rights Act was renewed. The US Supreme Court tired
of southern subterfuges that kept public schools segregated. In *Alexander* v.
Holmes (1969), the Court ordered Mississippi's schools to desegregate 'now'.
In *Swann* v. *Charlotte-Mecklenberg Board of Education* (1971), the Court
authorized citywide busing to achieve racially integrated schools in Charlotte,
North Carolina. Attorney Morris Dees of the Southern Poverty Law Center
bankrupted Klan groups through lawsuits. The murderers of Medgar Evers, the
four black girls in Birmingham, Vernon Dahmer, and Ben Chester White were
brought to justice recently. In a symbolic gesture, the state of Mississippi voted
in 1995 to ratify the 13th Amendment abolishing slavery. That same year, the
Southern Baptist Convention apologized for defending slavery and resisting
racial justice. In 2003, the Georgia state legislature finally removed the Confederate symbol from its flag, Ole Miss banished its Johnny Reb mascot from
football games, and the Supreme Court upheld the principle of affirmative
action.

Increasingly, however, the tide has run against the civil rights movement.
When the federal government undertook affirmative action and anti-poverty
programs for minorities, white America blanched, especially blue-collar workers
who had recently moved out of poverty. Many whites saw such efforts to
redress a long history of racial discrimination as unfair reverse discrimination against the majority. Since the milestone *Bakke* case of 1978, the Supreme
Court has walked a fine line between allowing schools, businesses, and
government bodies to set recruitment goals and forbidding them to establish
minority quotas. Upon becoming president in 1981, Ronald Reagan and the
Republicans took dead aim against the movement. Reagan used a meat cleaver
on Johnson's Great Society, neutralized EEOC and the Civil Rights Commission, restored tax exemptions for segregated private schools, challenged
court-ordered school busing, and proposed diluting the Voting Rights Act.

By reducing federal assistance to the poor and using tax policies to favor the wealthy, Reaganomics contributed to a black poverty rate of 34 per cent, a rate triple that of whites. Reagan's successor, George H.W. Bush, replaced Supreme Court justice Thurgood Marshall, a civil rights hero, with Clarence Thomas, a black conservative who condemned liberal reform that had benefited him. Reading the political tea leaves, president Bill Clinton agreed to cap welfare benefits. In the same vein, black nationalist leader Louis Farrakhan organized a Million Man March on Washington in 1995 to refocus attention away from government solutions to personal responsibility, but little of consequence resulted. The civil rights movement has been dead in the water for years now.

Like other mass movements, the civil rights movement produced a mixed record. By almost any measure, blacks as a whole are better off now than at any time since slavery ended. The most obvious successes were to end systematic racial terror and the most degrading features of Jim Crow in the South. Blacks are legally entitled to live, eat, shop, and sit on buses where they wish. The old tricks that disfranchised black voters have disappeared, resulting in black legislators, mayors, and sheriffs. Local officials increased black home ownership, provided better services, including indoor plumbing and paved streets, and hired and promoted blacks in police and fire departments. Thanks to government jobs and corporate investment, black income is the highest in history, and a majority of blacks have now reached the middle class [*Doc. 19*]. American culture, especially sports, music, and television, is thoroughly integrated, though blacks are seldom hired as top administrators. Even the greatest taboo – interracial sex – has been broken as marriages between blacks and whites have soared in recent years. The movement also helped white southerners escape the closed society they had designed and encouraged black northerners to return to the South in a reversal of the Great Migration. With race relations improved, blacks and whites engineered the South's robust economy. The movement also spurred women, Latinos, Indians, Asians, gays, the elderly, and the disabled to use the philosophy and tactics of nonviolence to seek justice for themselves. And Congress scrapped its 40-year-old immigration policy in order to welcome all peoples, regardless of national origin.

Despite this progress, America still does not have a color-blind society, and a large underclass has been left behind. City officials – black and white – are bedeviled by insuperable problems, including the demise of heavy industry, falling revenues, woeful public school education, toxic waste dumps in minority neighborhoods, and policemen who employ racial profiling and assault blacks with impunity. At least twice as many blacks are unemployed as whites, and many blacks have given up looking for work altogether as companies have abandoned the inner city. Schemes to bus children across racial lines backfired as white enrollment plummeted. Schools are largely resegregated, including the one attended by Ruby Bridges. Even in integrated schools, blacks are often put in remedial coursework. Without jobs, resources, or adequate social services, inner cities have degenerated into urban cesspools with endemic violence, casual sex, drug addiction, and spiraling AIDS rates. Black men are six times more likely than white men to be murdered and one in three black men will end up in jail, on parole, or on probation. A sense of hopelessness hasled too many young black men to fantasize about becoming one of the few millionaire athletes. Middle-class blacks are only too glad to run from failing cities to the suburbs. As they did so, black-owned businesses have collapsed. While Martin Luther King's dream for a just America seems far less remote than when he died, president Kennedy's words echo through the decades: America 'can do better'.

PART SIX   DOCUMENTS

Before Confederate states could return to the Union, they were required to approve the 14th Amendment to the US Constitution, which guaranteed blacks full citizenship rights and equal protection of the laws.

Sec. 1 All persons born or naturalized in the United States, and subject to the jurisdiction thereof, are citizens of the United States and of the State wherein they reside. No State shall make or enforce any law which shall abridge the privileges or immunities of citizens of the United States; nor shall any State deprive any person of life, liberty, or property, without due process of law; nor deny to any person within its jurisdiction the equal protection of the laws.

With this classic decision, Supreme Court chief justice Earl Warren rejected the separate-but-equal doctrine that justified apartheid for over a half century.

The plaintiffs contend that segregated public schools are not 'equal' and cannot be made 'equal,' and that hence they are deprived of the equal protection of the laws. . . .

In approaching this problem, we cannot turn the clock back to 1868 when the [Fourteenth] Amendment was adopted, or even to 1896 when *Plessy* v. *Ferguson* was written. We must consider public education in the light of its full development and its present place in American life throughout the Nation. Only in this way can it be determined if segregation in public schools deprives these plaintiffs of the equal protection of the laws. . . .

In these days, it is doubtful that any child may reasonably be expected to succeed in life if he is denied the opportunity of an education. Such an opportunity, where the state has undertaken to provide it, is a right which must be made available to all on equal terms.

We come then to the question presented: Does segregation of children in public schools solely on the basis of race, even though the physical facilities and other 'tangible' factors may be equal, deprive the children of the minority group of equal educational opportunities? We believe that it does.

To separate [black children] from others of similar age and qualifications solely because of their race generates a feeling of inferiority as to their status in the community that may affect their hearts and minds in a way unlikely ever to be undone. . . .

We conclude that in the field of public education the doctrine of 'separate but equal' has no place. Separate educational facilities are inherently unequal. Therefore, we hold that the plaintiffs and others similarly situated for whom the actions have been brought are, by reason of the segregation complained of, deprived of the equal protection of the laws guaranteed by the Fourteenth Amendment. . . .

Brown v. Board of Education of Topeka, Kansas 347 US 483 (1954)

DOCUMENT 3   **DECLARATION OF CONSTITUTIONAL PRINCIPLES:
THE SOUTHERN MANIFESTO, 12 MARCH 1956**

Although the Southern Manifesto's sentiment for nullification was hardly new, the document did record the opposition of 101 southern representatives and senators to Brown, *and legitimated additional resistance.*

. . . This unwarranted exercise of power by the Court, contrary to the Constitution, is creating chaos and confusion in the States principally affected. It is destroying the amicable relations between the white and Negro races that have been created through 90 years of patient effort by the good people of both races. It has planted hatred and suspicion where there has been heretofore friendship and understanding.

Without regard to the consent of the governed, outside agitators are threatening immediate and revolutionary changes in our public-school systems. If done, this is certain to destroy the system of public education in some of the States.

With the gravest concern for the explosive and dangerous condition created by this decision and inflamed by outside meddlers:

We reaffirm our reliance on the Constitution as the fundamental law of the land.

We decry the Supreme Court's encroachments on rights reserved to the States and to the people, contrary to established law, and to the Constitution.

We commend the motives of those States which have declared the intention to resist forced integration by any lawful means.

We appeal to the States and people who are not directly affected by these decisions to consider the constitutional principles involved against the time when they too, on issues vital to them, may be the victims of judicial encroachment.

Even though we constitute a minority in the present Congress, we have full faith that a majority of the American people believe in the dual system of government which has enabled us to achieve our greatness and will in time demand that the reserved rights of the States and of the people be made secure against judicial usurpation.

We pledge ourselves to use all lawful means to bring about a reversal of this decision which is contrary to the Constitution and to prevent the use of force in its implementation. . . .

'Declaration of Constitutional Principles', *Congressional Record*, 84th Congress,
2nd sess., vol. 102, pt. 4, 12 March 1956, p. 4460.

DOCUMENT 4   **HERBLOCK, 'TSK TSK – SOMEBODY SHOULD DO SOMETHING ABOUT THAT', 3 APRIL 1956**

Herblock, an editorial cartoonist for the Washington Post, *criticized president Dwight Eisenhower for standing on the sidelines after the* Brown *decision as racial troubles threatened to burn out of control.*

"Tsk Tsk — Somebody Should Do Something About That"

Washington Post, 3 April 1956.
From *Herblock: A Cartoonist's Life* (Times Books, 1998).
Reprinted by permission of The Herb Block Foundation.

DOCUMENT 5   JAMES FARMER, 'SEPARATION OR INTEGRATION? A DEBATE AT CORNELL UNIVERSITY', 7 MARCH 1962

James Farmer, a pioneer of the sit-in tactic, defended students who wanted immediate change in society's racial rules. The tactic, as he notes, was readily employed by anyone and was powerfully effective.

The masses of Negroes are through putting up with segregation; they are tired of it. They are tired of being pushed around in a democracy which fails to practice what it preaches. The Negro students of the South who have read the Constitution, and studied it, have read the amendments to the Constitution, and know the rights that are supposed to be theirs – they are coming to the point where they themselves want to do something about achieving these rights, not [to] depend on somebody else. The time has passed when we can look for pie in the sky, when we can depend upon someone else on high to solve the problem for us. The Negro students want to solve the problem themselves. Masses of older Negroes want to join them in that. We can't wait for the law. The Supreme Court decision in 1954 banning segregated schools has had almost eight years of existence, yet less than 8 percent of the Negro kids are in integrated schools. That is far too slow. Now the people themselves want to get involved, and they are. I was talking with one of the student leaders of the South only last week; he said, 'I myself desegregated a lunch counter, not somebody else, not some big man, some powerful man, but me, little me. I walked the picket line and I sat in and the walls of segregation toppled. Now all people can eat there'. . . . So that's what's happening; you see, we are going to do something about freedom now, we are not waiting for other people to do it. The student sit-ins have shown it; we are winning. As a result of one year of the student sit-ins, the lunch counters were desegregated in more than 150 cities. The walls are tumbling down.

Haig and Hamida Bosmajian, *The Rhetoric of the Civil-Rights Movement* (New York: Random House, 1969), pp. 64–5.

DOCUMENT 6   'WE SHALL OVERCOME' (NEW WORDS AND MUSIC ARRANGEMENT BY ZILPHIA HORTON, FRANK HAMILTON, GUY CARAWAN, AND PETE SEEGER)

This old spiritual became the majestic anthem of the civil rights movement.

Chorus	We are not afraid. . . .
We shall overcome,	We are not alone (today). . . .
We shall overcome,	The truth will make us free. . . .
We shall overcome someday	We'll walk hand in hand. . . .

Oh, deep in my heart (I know that)	The Lord will see us through. . . .
I do believe (oh — —)	Black and white together (now). . . .
We shall overcome someday.	We shall all be free. . . .

Guy and Candie Carawan, *Sing for Freedom: The Story of the Civil Rights Movement Through Its Songs* (Bethlehem, PA: A Sing Out Publication, 1990), p. 15.

DOCUMENT 7 TELEPHONE CALLS TO AND FROM ATTORNEY GENERAL ROBERT KENNEDY DURING THE FREEDOM RIDE, 22 MAY 1961

The attorney general used the telephone frequently to orchestrate the Kennedy administration's civil rights strategy. In one day, he made eleven calls trying to ease tensions involving CORE's Freedom Ride.

Time	Caller	Place	Called
1.10 a.m.	Robert Kennedy	Montgomery, Alabama	Martin Luther King Fred Shuttlesworth James McShane
1.30 a.m.	Robert Kennedy	Montgomery, Alabama	John Patterson
1.30 a.m.	Robert Kennedy	Montgomery, Alabama	Martin Luther King
9.25 a.m.	J. Edgar Hoover	Washington, DC	Robert Kennedy
11.25 a.m.	Senator Lister Hill	Washington, DC	Robert Kennedy
3.35 p.m.	Robert Kennedy	Washington, DC	Gen. Shoup
5.10 p.m.	Mayor Earl James	Montgomery, Alabama	Robert Kennedy
5.25 p.m.	ex-Gov. James Folsom	Cullman, Alabama	Robert Kennedy
5.50 p.m.	John F. Kennedy	Washington, DC	Robert Kennedy
6.02 p.m.	Senator James Eastland	Washington, DC	Robert Kennedy
6.10 p.m.	ex-Gov. James Folsom	Cullman, Alabama	Robert Kennedy

Michal Belknap, *Civil Rights, The White House, and the Justice Department, 1945–1968*. Vol. 8, 'Desegregation of Public Transportation, Facilities, and Programs' (New York: Garland Publishing, 1991), pp. 17–18.

DOCUMENT 8 MARTIN LUTHER KING'S 'LETTER FROM BIRMINGHAM JAIL', 16 APRIL 1963

While King was in jail after his Good Friday arrest, eight white Birmingham clergymen criticized the demonstrations in an open letter that appeared in the Birmingham News. King's response – 'Letter from Birmingham Jail'- became a classic of protest literature.

My Dear Fellow Clergymen:

While confined here in the Birmingham city jail, I came across your recent statement calling my present activities 'unwise and untimely.' . . . Since I feel that you are men of genuine good will . . . I want to try to answer your statement in what I hope will be patient and reasonable terms. . . .

I cannot sit idly by in Atlanta and not be concerned about what happens in Birmingham. Injustice anywhere is a threat to justice everywhere. We are caught in an inescapable network of mutuality tied in a single garment of destiny. Whatever affects one directly, affects all indirectly. . . .

We know through painful experience that freedom is never voluntarily given by the oppressor; it must be demanded by the oppressed. Frankly, I have yet to engage in a direct-action campaign that was 'well timed' in the view of those who have not suffered unduly from the disease of segregation. For years now I have heard the word 'Wait!' It rings in the ear of every Negro with piercing familiarity. This 'Wait' has almost always meant 'Never.' We must come to see, with one of our distinguished jurists, that 'justice too long delayed is justice denied.'

We have waited for more than 340 years for our constitutional and God-given rights. The nations of Asia and Africa are moving with jetlike speed toward gaining political independence, but we still creep at horse-and-buggy pace toward gaining a cup of coffee at a lunch counter. Perhaps it is easy for those who have never felt the stinging darts of segregation to say, 'Wait.' But when you have seen vicious mobs lynch your mothers and fathers at will and drown your sisters and brothers at whim; when you have seen hate-filled policemen curse, kick and even kill your black brothers and sisters; when you see the vast majority of your twenty million Negro brothers smothering in an airtight cage of poverty in the midst of an affluent society; when you suddenly find your tongue twisted and your speech stammering as you seek to explain to your six-year-old daughter why she can't go to the public amusement park that has just been advertised on television . . . then you will understand why we find it difficult to wait. There comes a time when the cup of endurance runs over, and men are no longer willing to be plunged into the abyss of despair. . . .

You express a great deal of anxiety over our willingness to break laws. This is certainly a legitimate concern. Since we so diligently urge people to obey the Supreme Court's decision of 1954 outlawing segregation in the public schools, at first glance it may seem rather paradoxical for us consciously to break laws. One may well ask: 'How can you advocate breaking some laws and obeying others?' The answer lies in the fact that there are two types of laws: just and unjust. I would be the first to advocate obeying just laws. One has not only a legal but a moral responsibility to obey just laws. Conversely, one has a moral responsibility to disobey unjust laws. I would agree with Saint Augustine that 'an unjust law is no law at all.' . . .

We should never forget that everything Adolf Hitler did in Germany was 'legal' and everything the Hungarian freedom fighters did in Hungary was 'illegal.' . . .

I have almost reached the regrettable conclusion that the Negro's great stumbling block in his stride toward freedom is not the White Citizen's Counciler or the Ku Klux Klanner, but the white moderate, who is more devoted to 'order' than to justice; who prefers a negative peace which is the absence of tension to a positive peace which is the presence of justice; who constantly says: 'I agree with you in the goal you seek, but I cannot agree with your methods of direct action'; who paternalistically believes he can set the timetable for another man's freedom; who lives by a mythical concept of time and who constantly advises the Negro to wait for a 'more convenient season.' Shallow understanding from people of good will is more frustrating than absolute misunderstanding from people of ill will. . . .

In your statement you assert that our actions, even though peaceful, must be condemned because they precipitate violence. But is this a logical assertion? Isn't this like condemning a robbed man because his possession of money precipitated the evil act of robbery? . . .

You speak of our activity in Birmingham as extreme. . . . Was not Jesus an extremist for love. . . . Was not Martin Luther an extremist. . . . And Abraham Lincoln. . . . And Thomas Jefferson. . . . So the question is not whether we will be extremists, but what kind of extremists will we be. Will we be extremists for hate or for love? . . .

DOCUMENT 9 JOHN F. KENNEDY'S RADIO AND TELEVISION REPORT TO THE AMERICAN PEOPLE ON CIVIL RIGHTS, 11 JUNE 1963

Following racial turmoil in Birmingham and governor George Wallace's unsuccessful attempt to obstruct black students from entering the University of Alabama, president Kennedy called on Congress to legislate equal rights.

We are confronted primarily with a moral issue. It is as old as the Scriptures and is as clear as the American Constitution. The heart of the question is whether all Americans are to be afforded equal rights and equal opportunities; whether we are going to treat our fellow Americans as we want to be treated.

If an American, because his skin is dark, cannot eat lunch in a restaurant open to the public; if he cannot send his children to the best public schools available; if he cannot vote for the public officials who represent him; if, in short, he cannot enjoy the full and free life which all of us want, then who among us would be content to have the color of his skin changed and stand in his place?

Who among us would then be content with the counsels of patience and delay? One hundred years of delay have passed since President Lincoln freed the slaves, yet their heirs, their grandsons, are not fully free. They are not yet freed from the bonds of injustice; they are not yet freed from social and economic oppression.

And this nation, for all its hopes and all its boasts, will not be fully free until all its citizens are free. . . .

The fires of frustration and discord are burning in every city, North and South. Where legal remedies are not at hand, redress is sought in the streets in demonstrations, parades and protests, which create tensions and threaten violence – and threaten lives. . . .

I am, therefore, asking the Congress to enact legislation giving all Americans the right to be served in facilities which are open to the public – hotels, restaurants and theaters, retail stores and similar establishments. This seems to me to be an elementary right. . . .

Public Papers of the Presidents of the United States: John F. Kennedy, 1963
(Washington: US Government Printing Office, 1964), pp. 468–71.

DOCUMENT 10   MARTIN LUTHER KING'S 'I HAVE A DREAM' SPEECH, 28 AUGUST 1963

In a fitting climax to the March on Washington, Martin Luther King, Jr., delivered a moving address that envisioned true equality in America.

I have a dream that one day this nation will rise up and live out the true meaning of its creed: 'We hold these truths to be self-evident; that all men are created equal.'

I have a dream that one day on the red hills of Georgia the sons of former slaves and the sons of former slaveowners will be able to sit down together at the table of brotherhood.

I have a dream that one day even the state of Mississippi, a desert state sweltering with the heat of injustice and oppression, will be transformed into an oasis of freedom and justice.

I have a dream that my four children will one day . . . not be judged by the color of their skin but by the content of their character.

I have a dream today.

I have a dream that one day the state of Alabama, whose governor's lips are presently dripping with the words of interposition and nullification, will be transformed into a situation where little black boys and black girls will be able to join hands with little white boys and white girls and walk together as sisters and brothers. . . .

So let freedom ring from the prodigious hilltops of New Hampshire. Let freedom ring from the mighty mountains of New York. Let freedom ring from the heightening Alleghenies of Pennsylvania! . . .

But not only that; let freedom ring from Stone Mountain of Georgia! Let freedom ring from Lookout Mountain, Tennessee! Let freedom ring from every hill and mole hill of Mississippi. From every mountainside, let freedom ring.

When we let freedom ring . . . we will be able to speed up that day when all of God's children, black men and white men, Jews and Gentiles, Protestants and Catholics, will be able to join hands and sing in the words of the old Negro spiritual, 'Free at last! Free at last! Thank God almighty, we are free at last!'

DOCUMENT 11   MALCOLM X'S SPEECH IN CLEVELAND, APRIL 1964

Malcolm's powerful speech is typical of his negative views of the mainstream civil rights movement.

Everything that came out of Europe, every blue-eyed thing is already American. And as long as you and I have been over here, we aren't Americans yet. . . . No, I'm not an American. I'm one of the 22 million black people who are the victims of Americanism. . . . So, I'm not standing here speaking to you as an American, or a patriot, or a flag-saluter, or a flag-waver – no, not I. I'm speaking as a victim of this American system. And I see America through the eyes of the victim. I don't see any American dream; I see an American nightmare. . . .

Black people are fed up with the dillydallying, pussyfooting, compromising approach that we've been using toward getting our freedom. We want freedom now, but we're not going to get it saying 'We Shall Overcome.' We've got to fight until we overcome. . . .

It's time for you and me to stop sitting in this country, letting some cracker senators, Northern crackers and Southern crackers, sit there in Washington, D.C., and come to a conclusion in their mind that you and I are supposed to have civil rights. There's no white man going to tell me anything about my rights. Brothers and sisters, always remember, if it doesn't take senators and congressmen and presidential proclamations to give freedom to the white man, it is not necessary for legislation or proclamation or Supreme Court decisions to give freedom to the black man. You let that white man know, if this is a country of freedom, let it be a country of freedom; and if it's not a country of freedom, change it.

We will work with anybody, anywhere, at any time, who is genuinely interested in tackling the problem head-on, nonviolently as long as the enemy is nonviolent, but violent when the enemy gets violent.

George Breitman, ed., *Malcolm X Speaks*
(New York: Grove Weidenfeld Press, 1965), pp. 23–44.

DOCUMENT 12   MISSISSIPPI VOTER REGISTRATION FORM,
EARLY 1960s

This voter registration form was a principal means by which the state of Mississippi disqualified blacks.

(By reason of the provisions of Section 244 of the Constitution of Mississippi and House Bill No. 95, approved March 24, 1955, the applicant for registration if not physically disabled, is required to fill in this form in his own handwriting in the presence of the registrar and without assistance or suggestion of any other person or memorandum)

1. Write the date of this application: _____
2. What is your full name? _____
3. State your age and date of birth: _____
4. What is your occupation? _____
5. Where is your business carried on? _____
6. By whom are you employed? _____
7. Are you a citizen of the United States and an inhabitant of Mississippi? _____
8. For how long have you resided in Mississippi? _____
9. Where is your place of residence in the district? _____
10. Specify the date when such residence began: _____
11. State your prior place of residence, if any: _____
12. Check which oath you desire to take: (1) General _____ (2) Minister's _____ (3) Minister's Wife _____ (4) If under 21 years at present, but 21 years by date of general election _____
13. If there is more than one person of your same name in the precinct, by what name do you wish to be called? _____
14. Have you ever been convicted of any of the following crimes: bribery, theft, arson, obtaining money or goods under false pretenses, perjury, forgery, embezzlement, or bigamy? _____
15. If your answer to Question 14 is 'Yes', name the crime or crimes of which you have been convicted, and the date and place of such conviction or convictions: _____
16. Are you a minister of the gospel in charge of an organized church, or the wife of such a minister? _____
17. If your answer to Question 16 is 'Yes', state the length of your residence in the election district _____
18. Write and copy in the space below, Section _____ of the Constitution of Mississippi.

(Instruction to Registrar: You will designate the section of the Constitution and point out same to applicant)

19. Write in the space below a reasonable interpretation (the meaning) of the section of the Constitution of Mississippi which you have just copied:

20. Write in the space below a statement setting forth your understanding of the duties and obligations of citizenship under a constitutional form of government.

21. Sign and attach hereto the oath or affirmation named in Question 12.

_____

The applicant will sign his name here.

STATE OF MISSISSIPPI,
COUNTY OF _____
Sworn to and subscribed before me by the within named _____
on this the _____ day of _____ 19_____.

_____

COUNTY REGISTRAR

Waldo Martin, Jr., *Brown* v. *Board of Education: A Brief History with Documents*
(Boston: Bedford/St Martin's, 1998), pp. 124–6.

DOCUMENT 13   *STUDENT VOICE* **EDITORIAL CARTOON ON THE FBI, 25 NOVEMBER 1964**

This SNCC cartoon lambasts the FBI for its indifference toward the violence experienced by civil rights workers in the deep South.

From *Student Voice*, 25 November 1964, p. 2. Ruth Koenig Collection, Archives Center, National Museum of American History, Behring Center, Smithsonian Institution.

DOCUMENT 14   SNCC HANDBILL ON THE USEFULNESS OF POLITICS IN MISSISSIPPI, 1964

To explain to blacks in the Mississippi delta why they should risk their lives and homes to register to vote, civil rights organizers distributed copies of the Sunflower County Political Handbook.

> Politics is about <u>our lives</u>.
> It is about whether the roads are any good.
> It is about what our kids learn in school.
> It is about what the sheriff does.
> It is about whether we have work to do.

Politics is about <u>who</u> has <u>power</u>.

> The President listens to people who have power.
> So does the Sheriff.

<u>Power</u> is <u>votes</u> to elect people, or not to elect them.

<u>Power</u> is <u>money</u> to pay for election ads.

The people with power get what they want.

Now just a few people have <u>power</u>.

> They get control of government money.
> They get government contracts for their factories.
> They get the tax assessor to list their land at a low value.

We do not have money.

Our power must come from <u>ourselves</u>. From our numbers.

> From us being together.

We must have power for <u>us</u>.

So <u>we</u> control Sunflower County.

So the President listens to us.

So that we get what <u>we</u> need.

This is a book about how things work. It is a book about how <u>power</u> is used to keep us <u>down</u>.

> And how we can use power to lift ourselves <u>up</u>.

Constance Curry, *Silver Rights* (Chapel Hill, NC: Algonquin Books, 1995), p. 62.

DOCUMENT 15   WHITE VOLUNTEERS IN MISSISSIPPI FREEDOM SUMMER, 1964

White college students volunteering in the Summer Project found Mississippi a world apart from their privileged lives in the North.

Dear John and Cleo,

Our hostesses are brave women. And their fear is not at all mixed with resentment of us, but that makes it none the easier for them. The other morning a local newscaster said that someone was reported to have offered someone else $400 to bomb all the houses where volunteers are staying. I'm not convinced that that particular story has any basis, but it touched off the terror that must lie latent always in our sisters' hearts. I overheard one of them on the telephone: 'My guhls probly think I'm out of mah head; I been singin' all mornin, every song I knows – I just has to.' And she had been, moaning 'Lord have musee' in between the songs. I talked with her a little bit. She told me she knows people have suffered and died too long and that we must take risks now so it won't go on forever. But that doesn't make the risk any less painful to bear. She sleeps with a hatchet under her bed. She told me she used to have a gun under her pillow until one night when she almost accidentally shot a neighbor boy. . . .

Jo

Elizabeth Sutherland Martinez, ed., *Letters from Mississippi*
(Brookline, MA: Zephyr Press, 2002), p. 53.

DOCUMENT 16   **SNCC POSITION PAPER, 5 AUGUST 1966**

By the mid-1960s, SNCC had become deeply disillusioned by the interracial civil rights movement championed by Martin Luther King and insisted that white involvement prevented real social change.

In an attempt to find a solution to our dilemma, we propose that our organization should be black-staffed, black-controlled, and black-financed. We do not want to fall into a similar dilemma that other civil rights organizations have fallen. If we continue to rely upon white financial support we will find ourselves entwined in the tentacles of the white power complex that controls this country. It is important that a black organization (devoid of cultism) be projected to our people so that it can be demonstrated that such organizations are viable.

More and more we see black people in this country being used as a tool of the white liberal establishment. Liberal whites have not begun to address themselves to the real problem of black people in this country; witness their bewilderment, fear, and anxiety when nationalism is mentioned concerning black people. . . . Whites can only subvert our true search and struggle for self-determination, self-identification, and liberation in this country. Re-evaluation of the white and black roles must now take place so that white people no longer designate roles that black people play but rather black people define white people's roles. . . .

If we are to proceed toward true liberation, we must cut ourselves off from white people. We must form our own institutions, credit unions, co-ops, political parties, write our own histories.

These facts do not mean that whites cannot help. They can participate on a voluntary basis. We can contract work out to them, but in no way can they participate on a policy-making level.

The charge may be made that we are 'racists,' but whites who are sensitive to our problems will realize that we must determine our own destiny.

Stokely Carmichael, 'What We Want', *New York Review of Books*
(22 September 1966), pp. 5–8.

DOCUMENT 17 REPORT OF THE NATIONAL ADVISORY COMMISSION ON CIVIL DISORDERS, MARCH 1968

The 'Report of the National Advisory Commission on Civil Disorders' was established by President Lyndon Johnson following the bloody race riots of the 1960s. The commission, which was headed by Illinois governor Otto Kerner, concluded that America was dividing into two separate societies, one white and one black, and that white racism was largely responsible for the riots.

The summer of 1967 again brought racial disorders to American cities, and with them shock, fear and bewilderment to the nation. . . .

On July 28, 1967, the President of the United States established this Commission and directed us to answer three basic questions: What happened? Why did it happen? What can be done to prevent it from happening again? . . .

This is our basic conclusion: *Our nation is moving toward two societies, one black, one white – separate and unequal. . . .*

To pursue the present course will involve the continuing polarization of the American community and, ultimately, the destruction of basic democratic values. The alternative is not blind repression or capitulation to lawlessness. It is the realization of common opportunities for all within a single society.

This alternative will require a commitment to national action – compassionate, massive and sustained, backed by the resources of the most powerful and the richest nation on this earth. From every American it will require new attitudes, new understanding, and, above all, new will.

The vital needs of the nation must be met; hard choices must be made, and, if necessary, new taxes enacted.

Violence cannot build a better society. Disruption and disorder nourish repression, not justice. They strike at the freedom of every citizen. The community cannot – it will not – tolerate coercion and mob rule. Violence and destruction must be ended – in the streets of the ghetto and in the lives of people.

Segregation and poverty have created in the racial ghetto a destructive environment totally unknown to most white Americans.

What white Americans have never fully understood – but what the Negro can never forget – is that the white society is deeply implicated in the ghetto. White institutions created it, white institutions maintain it, and white society condones it. . . .

It is time to make good the promises of American democracy to all citizens – urban and rural, black and white, Spanish-surname, American Indian, and every minority group. . . .

Report of the National Advisory Commission on Civil Disorders, March 1, 1968
(Washington, DC: Government Printing Office, 1968), pp. 1–2, 5, 225–6.

DOCUMENT 18   BLACK PANTHERS' FOUNDING DOCUMENT, OCTOBER 1966

Huey Newton and Bobby Seale founded the Black Panther Party as a militant community-based organization to deal with the problems in northern ghettoes.

We had seen Watts rise up the previous year. We had seen how the police attacked the Watts community after causing the trouble in the first place. We had seen Martin Luther King come to Watts in an effort to calm the people, and we had seen his philosophy of nonviolence rejected. Black people had been taught nonviolence; it was deep in us. What good, however, was nonviolence when the police were determined to rule by force? . . . We had seen all this, and we recognized that the rising consciousness of Black people was almost at the point of explosion. . . .

Out of this need sprang the Black Panther Party. Bobby [Seale] and I finally had no choice but to form an organization that would involve the lower-class brothers. . . .

1. We want freedom. We want power to determine the destiny of our Black Community. . . .
2. We want full employment for our people. . . .
3. We want an end to the robbery by the capitalists of our Black Community. . . .
4. We want decent housing, fit for shelter of human beings. . . .
5. We want education for our people that exposes the true nature of this decadent American Society. We want education that teaches us our true history and our role in present-day society. . . .
6. We want all Black men to be exempt from military service. . . .
7. We want an immediate end to POLICE BRUTALITY and MURDER of Black people. . . .
8. We want freedom for all Black men held in federal, state, county and city prisons and jails. . . .
9. We want all Black people when brought to trial to be tried in court by a jury of their peer group or people from their Black communities, as defined by the Constitution of the United States. . . .

10. We want land, bread, housing, education, clothing, justice, and peace. And as our major political objective, a United Nations-supervised plebiscite to be held throughout the Black colony in which only Black colonial subjects will be allowed to participate, for the purpose of determining the will of Black people as to their national destiny.

Black Panther, 5 July 1969.

DOCUMENT 19   GRAPH OF POVERTY STATUS BY RACE, 1939–1994

This graph shows the dramatic decline in the percentage of blacks below the poverty line, a decline that coincided with the migration of blacks to the industrial North, the implementation of federal assistance programs, and the rise of the civil rights movement.

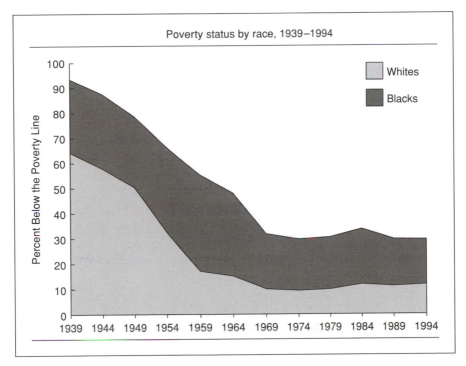

Sources: Reprinted with permission from Jaynes, G.D. and Williams, R.M., Jr. (eds) *A Common Destiny: Blacks and American Society*, Figure 6.1, © 1990 by the National Academy of Sciences, courtesy of the National Academies Press, Washington, D.C. Data from 1959 to 1994 from US Bureau of the Census (1993) 'Poverty Status of Persons, by Family, Relationship, Race and Hispanic Origin: 1959 to 1993', http://www.census.gov/hhes/income/ incpov93/povtab2.html and US Census Bureau (1996) 'Age, Sex, Household Relationship, Race and Hispanic Origin – Poverty Status of Persons in 1994', pub. 18 November, http://ferret.bls.census.gov/macro/03/995/pov/1_001.htm.

CHRONOLOGY

1865
Fall   Southern state legislatures enact Black Codes.
18 Dec.   13th Amendment outlaws slavery.
24 Dec.   KKK organizes.

1866
9 Apr.   First Civil Rights Act becomes law.

1868
28 July   14th Amendment provides 'equal protection of the laws' to all citizens.

1870
30 Mar.   15th Amendment grants black male suffrage.

1875
1 Mar.   Civil Rights Act becomes law.

1881
7 Apr.   Tennessee enacts the South's first permanent Jim Crow law.

1883
15 Oct.   *Civil Rights Cases* nullify congressional power to protect the freedmen.

1890
1 Nov.   Mississippi becomes the first state after Reconstruction to disfranchise blacks.

1895
18 Sept.   Booker T. Washington delivers his Atlanta Compromise speech.

1896
6 May   *Plessy* v. *Ferguson* permits 'separate but equal' treatment of the races.

1898
25 Apr.   *Williams* v. *Mississippi* permits poll taxes and literacy requirements for voting.

1909

1 June   NAACP organizes.

1915

21 June   *Guinn* v. *US* strikes down the grandfather clause.

1919

9 Apr.   CIC organizes.

Summer   Race riots erupt across the country.

1929   Charles Houston creates a law laboratory in civil rights at Howard
              University.

1930

1 Nov.   Association of Southern Women for the Prevention of Lynching organizes.

1931   'Jobs for Negroes' movement begins.

1933   'Don't Buy Where You Can't Work' movement begins.

1938

12 Dec.   *Missouri ex rel. Gaines* v. *Canada* requires that black schools must be
              equal to white schools.

Nov.   SCHW organizes.

1941

18 Apr.   Adam Clayton Powell, Jr., organizes a boycott that forces New York
              City bus companies to hire black drivers.

25 June   After A. Philip Randolph threatens a mass march on Washington,
              Franklin D. Roosevelt bans discrimination in war industries and
              establishes a temporary FEPC.

1942

Apr.   CORE organizes.

1944

26 Jan.   Gunnar Myrdal publishes *An American Dilemma*.

16 Feb.   SRC organizes.

3 Apr.   *Smith* v. *Allwright* invalidates all-white primary elections.

25 Apr.   United Negro College Fund is established.

1946

25 Jan.   SCEF organizes.

3 June   *Morgan* v. *Virginia* bans segregated seating on interstate buses.

1947

9 Apr.   CORE's Journey of Reconciliation challenges segregated bus seating.

10 Apr.   Jackie Robinson breaks baseball's color barrier.

1948

3 May   *Shelley* v. *Kraemer* invalidates restrictive housing covenants.

26 July   President Harry Truman bars discrimination in federal employment and the armed forces.

1950

15 Jan.   Leadership Conference on Civil Rights organizes.

5 June   *Sweatt* v. *Painter, McLaurin* v. *Oklahoma,* and *Henderson* v. *US* prohibit segregation in graduate education and in railroad dining cars that travel across state lines.

1954

17 May   *Brown* v. *Board of Education* invalidates *Plessy*'s 'separate but equal' decree.

11 July   First Citizens' Council organizes.

1955

31 May   *Brown II* orders school desegregation 'with all deliberate speed'.

28 Aug.   Emmett Till is murdered.

25 Nov.   ICC outlaws segregation in interstate transport.

1 Dec.   Rosa Parks's arrest sparks the Montgomery bus boycott.

1956

5 Feb.   Autherine Lucy becomes the first black to enter the University of Alabama.

12 Mar.   Southern Manifesto denounces *Brown.*

1 June   ACMHR organizes.

1957

14 Feb.   SCLC organizes.

17 May   Prayer Pilgrimage to Washington supports *Brown.*

9 Sept.   Civil Rights Act becomes law.

24 Sept.   President Dwight Eisenhower sends federal troops to Little Rock, Arkansas, to compel school desegregation.

1960

1 Feb.   Sit-in movement begins in Greensboro, North Carolina.

15 April   SNCC organizes.

6 May   Civil Rights Act becomes law.

11 Nov.	*Gomillion* v. *Lightfoot* invalidates Alabama's gerrymandering law.
5 Dec.	*Boynton* v. *Virginia* outlaws segregated facilities in interstate travel.

1961

6 Mar.	John Kennedy establishes the President's Committee on Equal Employment Opportunity and initiates the first federal requirement for affirmative action in employment.
4 May	Freedom Ride begins.
July	SNCC establishes a voter education drive in Mississippi.
Sept.	VEP finances voter registration drives in southern states.
1 Nov.	ICC forbids segregated interstate bus terminals.
Nov.–Dec.	Albany Movement begins.

1962

Feb.	COFO coordinates voter registration drives in Mississippi.
Apr.	CCCO organizes.
Summer	CORE's Freedom Highways campaign targets segregated motels and restaurants.
1 Oct.	James Meredith integrates the University of Mississippi.
20 Nov.	Kennedy orders the integration of federally-financed housing.
Sept.	Operation Breadbasket begins.

1963

Mar.–May	SCLC's Project Confrontation aims to desegregate Birmingham.
Apr.–July	Civil rights demonstrations lead to martial law in Cambridge, Maryland.
11 June	Governor George Wallace fails to keep the University of Alabama segregated.
11 June	Kennedy calls civil rights a 'moral issue'.
12 June	Medgar Evers is murdered.
22 June	Kennedy ends job discrimination in federally-financed construction contracts.
28 Aug.	Martin Luther King, Jr., gives his 'I Have a Dream' speech at the March on Washington.
15 Sept.	Four black girls are murdered in their Birmingham church.
23 Oct.	FBI launches a 'Communist infiltration' (COMINFIL) investigation into SCLC.

1964

23 Jan.	24th Amendment bars poll taxes in federal elections.
Mar.–June	SCLC organizes demonstrations in St Augustine, Florida.
26 Apr.	MFDP organizes.

25 May	*Griffin* v. *Prince Edward County School Board* forbids schools from closing to circumvent a desegregation order.
21 June	Michael Schwerner, James Chaney, and Andrew Goodman are murdered at the start of Freedom Summer.
2 July	Civil Rights Act becomes law.
2 Sept.	FBI uses COINTELPRO to neutralize the KKK.
10 Dec.	Martin Luther King receives the Nobel peace prize.
14 Dec.	*Atlanta Motel* v. *US* requires public accommodations to admit all customers.

1965

18 Feb.	The killing of Jimmie Lee Jackson leads to the Selma March.
21 Feb.	Malcolm X is assassinated.
21 Mar.	Selma–Montgomery march begins, resulting in the murders of James Reeb and Viola Liuzzo.
6 Aug.	Voting Rights Act becomes law.
11 Aug.	Race riots erupt in the Watts section of Los Angeles.

1966

13 Jan.	Robert Weaver becomes the first black named to a cabinet post.
24 Mar.	*Harper* v. *Virginia Board of Education* bars poll taxes in state elections.
6 June	James Meredith is shot during his 'March Against Fear'.
10 June	Stokely Carmichael advocates 'black power'.
10 July	Chicago Freedom Movement begins.
1 Oct.	Black Panther Party for Self-Defense organizes.
8 Nov.	Edward Brooke of Massachusetts is elected the first black US senator since Reconstruction.

1967

12 June	*Loving* v. *Virginia* invalidates state laws against interracial marriage.
July	Worst wave of urban rioting in US history.
1 Sept.	Thurgood Marshall becomes the first black US Supreme Court justice.
7 Nov.	Carl Stokes of Cleveland becomes the first elected black mayor of a major city.

1968

8 Feb.	Orangeburg, South Carolina, massacre occurs, in which patrolmen kill three and wound 27 students who protested against a segregated bowling alley.
1 Mar.	Kerner Report appears.
28 Mar.	Martin Luther King leads a march for striking Memphis sanitation workers.
4 Apr.	Martin Luther King is assassinated.

11 Apr.	Fair Housing Act becomes law.
11 May	Poor People's Campaign gets underway in Washington, DC.
27 May	*Green* v. *County School Board* invalidates 'freedom of choice' plans.

1969

27 June	President Richard Nixon requires federal agencies to establish equal opportunity and affirmative action policies (Philadelphia Plan).
29 Oct.	*Alexander* v. *Holmes* requires Mississippi to desegregate its schools at once.

1971

20 Apr.	*Swann* v. *Charlotte-Mecklenburg Board of Education* approves busing to achieve school desegregation.
18 Dec.	PUSH organizes.

1972

8 Mar.	Equal Employment Opportunity Act becomes law.

1974

25 July	*Milliken* v. *Bradley* bars school busing across district lines without proof that the lines were drawn in a racially discriminatory manner.

1978

28 June	*Regents of the University of California* v. *Bakke* rejects racial quotas.

1984

Fall	Jesse Jackson makes the first serious presidential race by a black candidate.

1986

15 Jan.	Martin Luther King, Jr.'s birthday is observed as a national holiday for the first time.

1989

7 Nov.	L. Douglas Wilder becomes the first elected black governor.

1995

16 Oct.	Louis Farrakhan organizes the Million Man March on Washington.

1996

5 Nov.	California voters pass Proposition 209, prohibiting affirmative action in public hiring, contracting, and college admissions.

2003

25 June	*Grutter v. Bollinger* permits universities to use race to diversify their student bodies.

GLOSSARY

Affirmative Action   Government and private programs designed to overcome the legacy of discrimination against minorities, especially in education and employment.

Afrocentricity   The idea that there are definitive African perspectives on knowledge and values that those of African descent should adopt.

Alabama Christian Movement for Human Rights   This organization replaced Birmingham's NAACP, which was outlawed in 1956.

Albany Movement   SNCC's stalemated campaign in Albany, Georgia.

An American Dilemma   Swedish sociologist Gunnar Myrdal's 1944 study that concluded that racism prevented blacks from participating fully in American society.

Americans for Democratic Action   The leading liberal lobbying organization during the Cold War.

Association of Southern Women to Prevent Lynching   A regional organization founded in 1930 to stop lynching at the local level.

Battle of Ole Miss   James Meredith's integration of the University of Mississippi in 1962.

The Birth of a Nation   A 1915 silent film that portrayed newly freed blacks as buffoons and rapists and thereby justified the KKK's vigilantism.

Black Arts Movement   The artistic sister of the Black Power movement.

Black Codes   Southern state laws enacted after the Civil War that greatly restricted black mobility, economic opportunity, and political expression.

Black Muslims   A reference to members of the Nation of Islam.

Black Nationalism   The political ideology that espouses solidarity among blacks the world over and total control of black culture and institutions.

Black Panthers   A radical group founded in 1966 by Huey Newton and Bobby Seale that armed itself against the police and demanded decent housing and education.

Black Power   A slogan that rejected the civil rights movement's goals of nonviolence and integration in favor of self-defense and self-determination.

Boycott   An organized campaign to promote civil rights by refusing to buy goods or services.

Brown v. Board of Education (1954)   Crucial Supreme Court decision that invalidated 'separate-but-equal' public schools.

Busing   An unpopular judicial remedy that transported black and white children to achieve school desegregation.

Buy Black Campaign   The Depression-era strategy for blacks to keep their money within the black community.

Chicago Freedom Movement   An ill-fated attempt by Martin Luther King to move the civil rights movement to the North.

Citizens' Council   A white supremacist organization formed after the *Brown* desegregation decision.

Civil Rights Act of 1866   This first civil rights law declared that all native-born Americans were citizens of the United States, regardless of their race, color, or previous condition.

Civil Rights Act of 1875   Granted all Americans access to public accommodations and transportation, and made them eligible for jury service.

Civil Rights Act of 1957   This first civil rights law since Reconstruction established the Justice department's Civil Rights Division and a federal Civil Rights Commission.

Civil Rights Act of 1960   Authorized federal judges to appoint referees to help blacks register to vote and provided criminal penalties for violence that obstructs school desegregation.

Civil Rights Act of 1964   Sweeping legislation that prohibited discrimination in public accommodations and in hiring, allowed government agencies to withhold federal funds from any program permitting discrimination, authorized the attorney general to file suit to desegregate schools and recreational facilities, and exempted anyone with a 6th grade education from literacy tests for voting.

Civil Rights Act of 1968   Prohibited discrimination in the rental or sale of housing, and provided criminal penalties for interfering with one's civil rights and for inciting riots.

Civil Rights Act of 1991   Banned intentional workplace discrimination by employers.

Commission on Interracial Cooperation   Formed after World War I, this Atlanta-based organization opposed lynching and restrictions on black voting and cautiously promoted socioeconomic opportunities for black southerners.

Congress of Racial Equality   An interracial civil rights group founded by James Farmer in 1942.

Coordinating Council of Community Organizations   The group formed in 1962 to integrate Chicago's housing and schools.

Council of Federated Organizations   An umbrella organization that coordinated civil rights groups during Mississippi Freedom Summer.

Curse of Ham   A biblical passage used to justify black slavery.

Debt Peonage   A practice by white southerners to retain black farm workers who owed them money.

Desegregation   The elimination of laws and customs that separate the races in schools, public accommodations, and neighborhoods.

Disfranchisement   The various means, such as the poll tax and white primaries, to prevent blacks from voting.

Don't Buy Where You Can't Work   Urban protests during the Great Depression against businesses that did not hire black workers.

Equal Employment Opportunity Commission   A federal agency established in 1964 to investigate claims of job discrimination.

Fair Employment Practice Committee   Under pressure from A. Philip Randolph, Franklin D. Roosevelt established this temporary federal agency in 1942 to prevent hiring discrimination by war industries.

Federal Bureau of Investigation   The chief federal law enforcement agency that observed but did not prosecute crimes against civil rights workers.

Fellowship of Reconciliation   Christian pacifist organization that backed racial integration.

Fifteenth Amendment   This 1870 constitutional amendment prohibited racial discrimination in voting.

Fifth Circuit Court of Appeals   This federal court strongly endorsed racial justice in the deep South.

Fourteenth Amendment   This 1868 constitutional amendment made blacks citizens and guaranteed them 'equal protection of the laws'.

Freedom Ride   CORE's 1961 demonstration to test whether interstate transportation facilities were desegregated, as the Supreme Court required.

Freedom Summer   A massive 1964 project by SNCC and CORE to recruit northern college students to register Mississippi blacks to vote.

Gerrymandering   The rearrangement of voting districts to give unfair advantage to one party or race in elections.

Grandfather Clause   A legal provision in southern states that exempted whites from voting restrictions aimed at blacks.

Great Migration   The movement of millions of blacks from the South to the North for a century after the Civil War, transforming society and politics and setting the stage for the civil rights movement.

Great Society   President Lyndon Johnson's plan to end racism and poverty by enacting civil rights laws and establishing federal assistance programs.

Highlander Folk School   An influential labor and civil rights training centre in Tennessee.

Jail, No Bail   The strategy of filling up jail cells so that segregation would collapse.

Jim Crow   A nineteenth-century minstrel character whose caricature of black culture became identified with segregationist practices in the South.

Journey of Reconciliation   A 1947 CORE bus ride through the upper South, which was a prototype for the more famous Freedom Ride.

Kerner Commission   This federal commission blamed white racism for the rioting of the 1960s and urged massive federal funding to prevent future riots.

Ku Klux Klan   A white terrorist organization against integration.

Leadership Conference on Civil Rights   A broad-based coalition that pressed successfully for civil rights laws.

Leftist   A radical view of politics, often supporting socialism and condemning discrimination.

Letter from Birmingham Jail   Martin Luther King's response to white clergymen who thought the civil rights movement was ill-timed.

Literacy Tests   A device used by southern registrars to disqualify blacks from voting.

Lynching   The murder of 3,500 blacks by angry whites, often by hanging from trees.

March Against Fear   James Meredith's ill-fated attempt in 1966 to defy white violence by walking alone through Mississippi.

March on Washington   This demonstration for black jobs and freedom on 28 August 1963 was the largest yet in US history.

Marxism   A political philosophy that opposes racism and favors socialism to prevent worker exploitation.

Massive Resistance   The white South's refusal to comply with *Brown*'s desegregation mandate.

Miscegenation   Marriage or cohabitation between men and women of different races.

Mississippi Freedom Democratic Party   At the 1964 national Democratic convention, this mainly black contingent challenged the legitimacy of the all-white state delegation.

Mississippi Plan   The violent restoration of southern white governments after Reconstruction.

Molotov Cocktail   A homemade bomb used by the KKK against black activists.

Montgomery Bus Boycott   The first large-scale protest of the modern civil rights movement.

Montgomery Improvement Association   The organization that coordinated the Montgomery bus boycott.

Nashville Student Movement   The largest, best-organized group to conduct non-violent sit-ins in 1960.

National Association for the Advancement of Colored People   The oldest, largest, and best-known civil rights organization whose legal and political efforts resulted in major successes in desegregating American society.

Nonviolent Resistance   The major civil rights strategy of achieving social change, mainly by employing boycotts, sit-ins, and civil disobedience.

Operation Breadbasket   SCLC's selective buying campaign to force white businesses to hire black workers.

People United to Save Humanity   A Chicago-based group that boycotted large corporations discriminating against blacks.

Plessy v. Ferguson (1896)   The Supreme Court decision that permitted racial segregation.

Poll Tax   A tax levied by southern states to disfranchise blacks and poor whites.

Poor People's Campaign   Martin Luther King's unsuccessful last protest to force Americans to recognize that racism impoverished millions.

Project Confrontation   The code name for the 1963 civil rights demonstrations in Birmingham.

Racism   The practice of discriminating against ethnic groups different from one's own.

Reconstruction   The federal government's attempts after the Civil War to restore the defeated Confederate states to the Union and to assist the former slaves.

Restrictive Covenant   A binding agreement to exclude minorities in the sale or rental of housing.

Revolutionary Action Movement   A radical underground group whose demands anticipated the Black Panthers.

Sambo   A black person compelled to act deferentially toward whites.

Segregation   The enforced separation of the races.

Selma to Montgomery March   A 1965 march across Alabama led by Martin Luther King to dramatize the need for a federal voter registration law.

Sit-ins   This tactic, borrowed from the labor movement, was designed to compel change by blocking business as usual.

Southern Christian Leadership Conference   This nonviolent, direct-action organization was founded by Martin Luther King in 1957.

Southern Conference Educational Fund   Continued SCHW's support of the civil rights movement through publicity and fund-raising.

Southern Conference for Human Welfare   An organization of New Deal liberals committed to ending poverty and racism in the South.

Southern Manifesto   A defiant statement against the *Brown* desegregation decision signed by almost all southerners in Congress.

Southern Regional Council   An interracial organization formed in 1944 that opposed segregation and promoted black voter registration.

Standing in the Door   The vow of Alabama governor George Wallace to block black students from enrolling at the University of Alabama in 1963.

State Sovereignty Commission   A southern state agency that aimed at disrupting the civil rights movement.

States' Rights   The constitutional claim that states are entitled to operate without the federal government's interference in education and voting.

Student Nonviolent Coordinating Committee   This student-run organization was formed after the 1960 sit-ins to organize a community-based movement in the deep South.

Thirteenth Amendment   This 1865 constitutional amendment abolished slavery in the United States.

To Secure These Rights   President Harry Truman's 1947 report that strongly supported black civil rights.

Twenty-fourth Amendment   This 1964 constitutional amendment outlawed poll taxes in federal elections.

Uncle Tom   A derogatory description of a black person who tries to satisfy whites.

United Auto Workers   An influential labor union that sponsored civil rights activism.

US Civil Rights Commission   Established by the Civil Rights Act of 1957, this federal, bipartisan panel collects and disseminates information on civil rights.

University of California Regents v. *Bakke (1978)* A landmark case in which the Supreme Court struck down the use of quotas for college admission as reverse discrimination.

Urban League Founded in 1910 to promote economic progress for blacks.

Voter Education Project A voter-registration campaign in the deep South supported by the Kennedy administration and funded by northern foundations.

Voting Rights Act of 1965 This federal law banned literacy tests and intimidation at the polls, and dispatched federal registrars to locales where voting totals fell below 50 per cent of those eligible.

Watts Riot A devastating 1965 race riot in south Los Angeles that disillusioned many whites about the civil rights movement.

'We Shall Overcome' The philosophy and anthem of the civil rights movement.

White Primary A device used by southern states to exclude blacks from the Democratic primary, the only election that mattered.

WHO'S WHO

Abernathy, Ralph (1926–90)   Martin Luther King's trusted lieutenant.

Baker, Ella (1903–86)   NAACP activist and SCLC's first executive director who urged the founding of SNCC.

Baldwin, James (1924–87)   Expatriate writer who warned of racial conflagration if the civil rights movement failed.

Barnett, Ross (1898–1987)   Mississippi governor who temporarily blocked James Meredith from entering the University of Mississippi.

Bates, Daisy (1914–99)   Arkansas NAACP president who helped black students desegregate Central High School in Little Rock.

Beckwith, Byron de la (1920–2001)   Murdered Mississippi NAACP leader Medgar Evers.

Belafonte, Harry (1927–)   Calypso singer and civil rights fund-raiser.

Bevel, James (1936–)   Nashville sit-in demonstrator and SCLC organizer of the Birmingham and Selma demonstrations.

Bond, Julian (1940–)   SNCC co-founder and communications director.

Bowers, Sam (1924–)   Mississippi KKK leader who ordered the murder of blacks.

Boynton, Amelia (1910–)   Local leader of the Selma campaign.

Bridges, Ruby (1955–)   Integrated New Orleans public schools.

Brown, H. 'Rap' (1943–)   SNCC national director who coined the phrase 'burn, baby, burn' when race riots erupted in the mid-1960s.

Byrd, Harry, Sr. (1887–1966)   US senator from Virginia who urged Massive Resistance to *Brown*.

Carmichael, Stokely (1941–98)   Organizer of voter registration projects in Mississippi and Lowndes county, Alabama; charismatic SNCC chairman who popularized the term 'black power'.

Chambliss, Bob (1904–85)   Birmingham klansman who murdered four black girls in their church.

Chaney, James (1943–64)   CORE worker murdered by Mississippi klansmen at the start of Freedom Summer.

Clark, James, Jr. (1922–)   Dallas county sheriff whose violence swelled the Selma demonstrations.

Clark, Kenneth (1914–)   Psychologist whose research on black child development helped the NAACP to win the *Brown* desegregation case.

Clark, Septima (1898–1987) Highlander Folk School teacher and Citizenship School organizer who trained many civil rights workers and prepared unlettered rural blacks to vote.

Connor, Bull (1897–1973) Birmingham's public safety commissioner who ordered dogs, nightsticks, and pressure hoses against civil rights demonstrators.

Douglass, Frederick (1817–1995) An ex-slave and abolitionist known as the 'father of the civil rights movement'.

Du Bois, W.E.B. (1868–1963) Harvard-trained intellectual and NAACP co-founder who believed that the black elite should lead the race in demanding equality.

Durr, Virginia (1903–99) Alabama civil rights activist against Jim Crow and the poll tax.

Eastland, James (1905–86) Powerful Senate Judiciary chairman from Mississippi who blocked civil rights legislation.

Eisenhower, Dwight (1890–1969) US president who appointed Earl Warren as Supreme Court chief justice and sent troops to integrate Central High School, Little Rock, Arkansas.

Evers, Medgar (1925–63) Murdered Mississippi NAACP field secretary.

Farmer, James (1920–99) CORE co-founder who pioneered the sit-in technique, organized the Freedom Ride, and pushed voter registration.

Faubus, Orval (1910–94) Arkansas governor who blocked the Little Rock Nine from Central High School.

Forman, James (1928–) Former SNCC executive secretary who demanded reparations for slavery.

Gandhi, Mohandas (1887–1940) Nonviolent philosopher from India who inspired American civil rights leaders, especially Martin Luther King, Jr.

Garvey, Marcus (1887–1940) Black nationalist from Jamaica whose UNIA promoted a 'Back to Africa' movement.

Gomillion, Charles (1900–95) Educator who successfully challenged the gerrymandering of black voters in Tuskegee, Alabama.

Gray, Fred (1930–) Civil rights attorney who won desegregation cases against the Montgomery bus company and University of Alabama.

Green, Ernest (1941–) First black graduate of Central High School, Little Rock, Arkansas.

Hamer, Fannie Lou (1917–77) Dynamic Mississippi SNCC organizer and MFDP co-founder.

Henry, Aaron (1922–97) Pharmacist who headed Mississippi's NAACP, COFO, and MFDP.

Hoover, J. Edgar (1895–1972) FBI director who warred on the civil rights movement and black nationalism.

Houston, Charles (1895–1950) Howard University law dean and architect of the NAACP's legal strategy to defeat Jim Crow.

Jackson, Jesse (1941–) Headed Operation Breadbasket and PUSH and sought the presidency in the 1980s.

Jackson, Jimmie Lee (1938–65)   Civil rights activist whose killing inspired the Selma-to-Montgomery voting-rights march.

Johnson, Frank, Jr. (1918–99)   Federal judge who supported civil rights in Alabama.

Johnson, Lyndon (1908–73)   US President who waged a war on poverty and secured the epic civil rights acts of 1964 and 1965.

Kennedy, John F. (1917–63)   US president who called civil rights 'a moral issue', asked for comprehensive civil rights legislation, and desegregated the universities of Mississippi and Alabama.

Kennedy, Robert (1925–68)   US attorney general who enforced federal court orders to desegregate the universities of Mississippi and Alabama.

King, Martin Luther, Jr. (1929–68)   Charismatic Southern Baptist minister who was America's most prominent nonviolent civil rights champion until his murder.

Lawson, James, Jr. (1928–)   Clergyman who led the sit-in movement in Nashville, helped found SNCC, joined the Freedom Ride, and conducted workshops for FOR and SCLC.

Lewis, John (1940–)   Participated in the Nashville sit-ins, Freedom Ride, and Selma march; SNCC co-founder and chairman who spoke at the March on Washington; VEP director.

Liuzzo, Viola (1925–65)   White Detroit mother murdered by klansmen for helping the Selma march.

Lucy, Autherine (1929–)   Graduate student who was expelled by the University of Alabama when mob violence erupted.

McCain, Franklin (1942–)   One of the four original Greensboro sit-in participants.

McKissick, Floyd (1922–91)   CORE attorney who organized North Carolina sit-ins and later preached black power.

Malcolm X (1925–65)   Fiery Nation of Islam minister who mocked the civil rights movement before being murdered.

Malone, Vivian (1942–)   Desegregated the University of Alabama.

Marshall, Burke (1922–2003)   US assistant attorney general who handled the Kennedy administration's response to civil rights demonstrations.

Marshall, Thurgood (1908–93)   NAACP chief counsel nicknamed 'Mr Civil Rights' for his many legal victories over discrimination, especially *Brown*.

Meredith, James (1933–)   First black to enroll at the University of Mississippi; shot during his March Against Fear.

Moore, Amzie (1911–82)   Businessman and NAACP activist who invited SNCC to transform Mississippi.

Moses, Robert (1935–)   Low-key organizer of SNCC's Freedom Summer project.

Nash, Diane (1938–)   A leader of the Nashville student movement who rescued the Freedom Ride.

Newton, Huey (1942–89)   Co-founder of the Black Panther Party.

Nixon, E.D. (1899–1987)   Union leader, president of Alabama's NAACP, and organizer of the Montgomery bus boycott.

Parks, Rosa (1913–)   'The mother of the civil rights movement' who sparked the Montgomery bus boycott.

Patillo, Melba (1941–)   One of the Little Rock Nine who desegregated Central High School, Little Rock, Arkansas.

Powell, Adam Clayton, Jr. (1908–72)   Harlem clergyman and congressman who pushed for black jobs and antipoverty programs.

Pritchett, Laurie (1926–2000)   Police chief who stifled the Albany Movement by using restraint.

Randolph, A. Philip (1889–1979)   Union leader and architect of MOWM.

Rauh, Joseph, Jr. (1911–92)   Attorney who lobbied for civil rights legislation and represented the ADA, UAW, Brotherhood of Sleeping Car Porters, LCCR, and MFDP.

Reagon, Bernice Johnson (1942–)   Albany protester and founder of Sweet Honey in the Rock, a choral group that sings civil rights standards.

Reeb, James (1927–65)   White clergyman beaten to death in Selma.

Reuther, Walter (1907–70)   UAW president and financial backer of civil rights campaigns.

Richardson, Gloria (1922–)   Led an SNCC affiliate in Maryland called the Cambridge Nonviolent Action Committee.

Robinson, Jackie (1919–72)   Broke baseball's color bar in 1947, opening the door to integrating other sports.

Robinson, Jo Ann (1912–)   Alabama State College professor who helped organize the Mongomery bus boycott.

Rowe, Gary Thomas (1934–98)   An Alabama klansman and FBI informant.

Rustin, Bayard (1910–87)   A leading activist who organized the March on Washington.

Schwerner, Michael (1939–64)   White CORE worker murdered by Mississippi klansmen at the start of Freedom Summer.

Seale, Bobby (1937–)   Co-founder of the Black Panther Party.

Sellers, Cleveland (1944–)   SNCC program director and black power advocate.

Sherrod, Charles (1939–)   SNCC organizer of the Albany Movement.

Shuttlesworth, Fred (1922–)   Co-founder of ACMHR and SCLC and a principal organizer of Project Confrontation in Birmingham.

Till, Emmett (1941–55)   Chicago teenager murdered in Mississippi for flirting with a white woman.

Truman, Harry (1884–1972)   US president who opposed segregated schools, neighborhoods, and the military.

Wallace, George (1919–98)   Alabama governor who symbolized the segregationist cause in the South.

Warren, Earl (1891–1974)   US Supreme Court chief justice who wrote the *Brown* decision.

Washington, Booker T. (1856–1915)   Ex-slave who founded Tuskegee Institute to promote his belief that blacks should seek economic self-reliance first, not political equality.

Wells-Barnett, Ida B. (1862–1931)   Crusader against lynching and NAACP co-founder.

White, Walter (1893–1955)   NAACP executive secretary who fought against lynching.

Wilkins, Roy (1901–81)   Lobbied for civil rights as head of the NAACP.

Williams, Hosea (1926–2000)   Fiery SCLC organizer of demonstrations in Savannah, Georgia; St Augustine, Florida; and Selma, Alabama.

Wisdom, John Minor (1905–99)   Fifth US Circuit Court judge who helped dismantle Jim Crow.

Young, Andrew (1932–)   SCLC executive director who played a major role in the Birmingham and Selma demonstrations.

Young, Whitney (1921–71)   Urban League executive secretary who was nicknamed the movement's 'chairman of the board' for his mediating skills.

The civil rights movement is one of the most studied aspects of American history, and the sources that follow are hardly exhaustive. The earliest writings came from journalists and nonhistorian scholars, including attorneys, political scientists, and sociologists. Many activists have penned revealing, sometimes riveting, accounts of their harrowing experiences. When historians first turned their attention to the subject, they believed that the movement was a political reform best studied from the vantage point of public policy in Washington. They focused on national black leadership and organizations that pressed presidents, Congress, and federal judges to act. In the late 1970s, scholars redirected their attention to communities and regions such as Greensboro, Birmingham, and the Mississippi delta, where local activists organized on their own. Scholars have also incorporated the roles of women and organized labor, and analyzed the topics of education and religion. Collective biographies of several figures, such as black women, white women, and southern clergymen, have been particularly illuminating. More recent studies have stressed the Cold War in shaping America's response to racism at home and its foreign policy in less developed countries. Most recently, scholars have suggested that national concern for civil rights began in the Great Depression and continued into Richard Nixon's administration. An excellent overview of civil rights historiography can be found in Charles Eagles, 'Toward New Histories of the Civil Rights Era', *Journal of Southern History* 66 (November 2000), pp. 815–48.

Origins of Racism

Convincing works on the connection between slavery and racism are Bernard Lewis, *Race and Color in Islam* (1971), Ronald Segal, *Islam's Black Slaves* (2001), Robin Blackburn, *The Making of New World Slavery* (1997), Winthrop Jordan, *White Over Black* (1968), Scott Malcomson, *One Drop of Blood* (2000), Bruce Dain, *A Hideous Monster of the Mind* (2002), and George Frederickson, *The Arrogance of Race* (1988). David Brion Davis, *In the Image of God* (2001), provides an invaluable overview of the ongoing debate as to how racism reached the Western Hemisphere.

Jim Crow South

The most influential account of segregation's beginnings is C. Vann Woodward, *The Strange Career of Jim Crow* (1974). In *Trouble in Mind* (1998), Leon Litwack portrays black southerners in the Jim Crow era. Grace Hale, *Making Whiteness* (1998), shows how southern attitudes on race crystallized after the Civil War. Joel Williamson, *The Crucible of Race* (1984), examines the rage that white southerners felt toward the freedmen. James Allen, *Without Sanctuary* (2000), and Philip Dray, *At the Hands of Persons Unknown* (2002), examine the sordid lynching phenomenon. Stephen Kantrowitz, *Ben Tillman and the Reconstruction of White Supremacy* (2000), looks at a leading racist. J. Morgan Kousser, *The Shaping of Southern Politics* (1974), details the political tricks that kept blacks out of politics. Pete Daniel's *The Shadow of Slavery* (1972) explores the pernicious practice of peonage. See Louis Harlan's *Booker T. Washington* (1972, 1983), for a biography of a black leader who urged temporary acceptance of white dominance.

Movement Overviews

The most valuable history of the civil rights movement is the multi-volume account rendered by Taylor Branch, *Parting the Waters* (1988) and *Pillar of Fire* (1998). Shorter, but still valuable, accounts include Adam Fairclough, *Better Day Coming* (2001), Robert Weisbrot, *Freedom Bound* (1990), Harvard Sitkoff, *The Struggle for Black Equality* (1993), Steven Lawson, *Black Ballots* (1976), Robert Cook, *Sweet Land of Liberty?* (1998), Manning Marable, *Race, Reform, and Rebellion* (1984), David Goldfield, Jr., *Black, White, and Southern* (1990), William Riches, *The Civil Rights Movement* (1997), Vincent Harding *et al.*, *We Changed the World* (1997), Kevern Verney, *Black Civil Rights in America* (2000), and Lois Blumberg, *Civil Rights* (1984). Juan Williams, *Eyes on the Prize* (1987), is the companion volume to the acclaimed PBS television documentary.

Useful edited collections of documents are Joanne Grant, *Black Protest* (1968), Peter Levy, *Let Freedom Ring* (1992), and Manning Marable and Leith Mullings, *Let Nobody Turn Us Around* (1999).

The best collections of interviews are Howell Raines, *My Soul Is Rested* (1977), Clayborne Carson *et al.*, *Eyes on the Prize Civil Rights Reader* (1991), Henry Hampton and Steve Fayer, *Voices of Freedom* (1990), and Bud Schultz and Ruth Schultz, *The Price of Dissent* (2001).

The most useful periodicals are *Freedomways, Race Relations Law Reporter*, and *The Civil Rights Digest*. See also these black newspapers for insights into race relations and the movement: *Amsterdam News, Arkansas State Press, Atlanta Daily World, Baltimore Afro-American, Birmingham World, Chicago Defender, Louisville Defender, Norfolk Journal & Guide*, and *Pittsburgh Courier. Reporting Civil Rights* (2003) is a splendid collection of journalistic accounts of the movement.

Harry Ashmore, *Civil Rights and Wrongs* (1994), Pat Watters, *Down to Now* (1971) and Pat Watters and Reese Cleghorn, *Climbing Jacob's Ladder* (1967), Fred Powledge, *Free at Last?* (1991), and Michael Dorman, *We Shall Overcome* (1964), provide accounts by white journalists of changing race relations in the South. Carl Rowan's *Go South to Sorrow* (1957) is a black reporter's assessment of race relations.

Martin Luther King, Jr., the movement's chief spokesman, is the subject of several competent biographies, including David Levering Lewis, *King* (1970), Stephen Oates, *Let the Trumpet Sound* (1982), and Marshall Frady, *Martin Luther King, Jr.* (2002). Michael Eric Dyson, *I May Not Get There With You* (2000), recovers King in his radical guise. Clayborne Carson has edited a synthetic *Autobiography of Martin Luther King, Jr.* (1998). A careful delineation of Martin Luther King's theological debts is presented in Keith Miller, *Voice of Deliverance* (1992). Gerald Posner, *Killing the Dream* (1998), confirms that James Earl Ray gunned down Martin Luther King. King's closest associates – Ralph Abernathy, *And the Walls Came Tumbling Down* (1989), Andrew

Young, *An Easy Burden* (1996), Coretta Scott King, *My Life with Martin Luther King, Jr.* (1969), and John Lewis, *Walking with the Wind* (1998) – have written memoirs of the movement.

Perceptive state and local studies that examine race relations and reform include Robert Norrell, *Reaping the Whirlwind* (1985), J. Mills Thornton, *Divided Lines* (2002), David Colburn, *Racial Change and Community Crisis* (1985), Ronald Bayor, *Race and the Shaping of Twentieth-Century Atlanta* (1996), Adam Fairclough, *Race and Democracy* (1995), Jack Davis, *Race Against Time* (2001), and Stephen Tuck, *Beyond Atlanta* (2001). Elizabeth Jacoway and David Colburn, *Southern Businessmen and Desegregation* (1982), examine how fourteen southern cities accepted desegregation.

Milton Viorst, *Fire in the Streets* (1960), profiles key movement activists. David Chappell, *Inside Agitators* (1994), and Morton Sosna, *In Search of the Silent South* (1977), study a forgotten minority – white southerners who supported the civil rights movement. Carol Polsgrove, *Divided Minds* (2001), chronicles the ambivalent reaction of intellectuals to the movement.

Jack Mendelsohn, *The Martyrs* (1966) commemorates sixteen heroes who were killed.

Weary Feet, Rested Souls (1998), by Townsend Davis, is a superb guidebook to civil rights sites.

Movement Beginnings

Catherine Barnes, *Journey from Jim Crow* (1983), traces the origins and demise of segregated transit. In *The Souls of Black Folk* (1903), W.E.B. Du Bois condemned Booker T. Washington's accommodationist strategy. David Levering Lewis, *W.E.B. Du Bois* (1993, 2000), has written the definitive biography of the NAACP's leading voice. E. David Cronon, *Black Moses* (1969), is a biography of black nationalist Marcus Garvey.

The interwar period has been a fertile area for historical investigation. Gunnar Myrdal's *An American Dilemma* (1944) is a seminal examination of black life. John Dollard, *Caste and Class in a Southern Town* (1937), Raymond Wolters, *Negroes and the Great Depression* (1970), Harvard Sitkoff, *A New Deal for Blacks* (1978), and Patricia Sullivan, *Days of Hope* (1996), examine black southern life and civil rights in the Great Depression. Charles Hamilton, *Adam Clayton Powell, Jr.* (1991) traces the rise and fall of a flamboyant Harlem congressman. Paula Pfeffer, *A. Philip Randolph* (1990), describes the life of MOWM's leader. Herbert Garfinkel, *When Negroes March* (1969), studies Randolph's threatened march. John Egerton, *Speak Now Against the Day* (1994), discusses white southerners who were active on civil rights issues in the 1930s and 1940s.

A wide range of black experiences during and right after World War II are covered in Neil Wynn, *The Afro-American and the Second World War* (1976), Richard Dalfiume, *Desegregation of the United States Armed Forces* (1969), Louis Ruchames, *Race, Jobs, Politics* (1948), Lee Finkle, *Forum for Protest* (1975), and Robert Shogan and Tom Craig, *Detroit Race Riot* (1964). Darlene Clark Hine, *Black Victory* (1979), looks at the end of the white primary in Texas. Sudarshan Kapur, *Raising Up a Prophet* (2001), traces the appeal of Gandhi to activists before Martin Luther King. Jules Tygiel, *Baseball's Great Experiment* (1984), examines that storied season when Jackie Robinson crossed the most sacred colour line in sports. Truman's path-breaking report on race relations is *To Secure These Rights* (1947). Septima Clark, *Echo in My Soul* (1962), tells of her citizenship classes that helped blacks register to vote. Ben Green, *Before His Time* (1999), recounts the activism and murder of Florida's Harry Moore.

Kari Frederickson, *The Dixiecrat Revolt and the End of the Solid South* (2001), looks at the defection of southern Democrats after Truman endorsed civil rights initiatives.

Emmett Till's grisly murder is examined in William Bradford Huie, *Wolf Whistle* (1959), Stephen Whitfield, *A Death in the Delta* (1988), and Christopher Metress, *The Lynching of Emmett Till* (2002).

The international dimension of the civil rights movement is discussed in Thomas Borstelmann, *The Cold War and the Color Line* (2001), Mary Dudziak, *Cold War, Civil Rights* (2000), and Azza Salama Layton, *International Politics and Civil Rights Policies in the United States* (2000).

Education

In the field of school desegregation, one must begin with Richard Kluger's magisterial work, *Simple Justice* (1975). Mark Tushnet, *The NAACP's Legal Strategy Against Segregated Education* (1987), is a study before *Brown*. Charles Houston, the brains behind the NAACP's school desegregation strategy, is the subject of Genna McNeil's *Groundwork* (1983). Howard Ball, *A Defiant Life* (1998), is a fine biography of Houston's protégé, Thurgood Marshall. Mark Tushnet, *Making Civil Rights Law* (1994), and Jack Greenberg, *Crusaders in the Courts* (1994), recount the NAACP's exhaustive crusade against Jim Crow. Psychologist Kenneth Clark reports on his findings in *Prejudice and Your Child* (1955). Ed Cray, *Chief Justice* (1997), studies the pivotal leadership of Earl Warren. Examinations of *Brown*'s debatable effects on public education include Gary Orfield, *Dismantling Desegregation* (1996), and Peter Irons, *Jim Crow's Children* (2002).

Segregation is defended in Theodore Bilbo, *Take Your Choice* (1947), Tom Brady, *Black Monday* (1955), Herman Talmadge, *You and Segregation* (1955), and James J. Kilpatrick, *The Southern Case for School Segregation* (1962). I.A. Newby, *Challenge to the Court* (1967), notes that segregationists used scientific racism to refute *Brown*. Liberal rejoinders are Harry Ashmore's *Epitaph for Dixie* (1958), and John Martin, *The Deep South Says 'Never'* (1957).

Virginia's futile attempts to block school desegregation are chronicled in James Ely, Jr., *The Crisis of Conservative Virginia* (1976), Francis Wilhoit, *The Politics of Massive Resistance* (1973), Matthew Lassiter and Andrew Lewis, *The Moderates' Dilemma* (1998), Benjamin Muse, *Virginia's Massive Resistance* (1961), Bob Smith, *They Closed Their Schools* (1965), and Robert Pratt's *The Color of Their Skin* (1992).

The political and social impact of the *Brown* decision is examined by James Patterson, *Brown v. Board of Education* (2001), Numan Bartley, *The Rise of Massive Resistance* (1969), and Pete Daniel, *Lost Revolutions* (2000). The desegregation of schools in Louisiana is recounted in Ruby Bridges, *Through My Eyes* (1999), and Liva Baker, *The Second Battle of New Orleans* (1996). Charlayne Hunter-Gault, *In My Place* (1992), and Robert Pratt, *We Shall Not Be Moved* (2002), look at the desegregation of the University of Georgia (2002). Constance Curry, *Silver Rights* (1995), is a compelling story of a black Mississippi family that desegregated a white school in the Mississippi delta. Ronald Formisano, *Boston Against Busing* (1991), and J. Anthony Lukas, *Common Ground* (1985), look at the crisis involving school busing.

Little Rock Crisis

Daisy Bates, head of the Arkansas NAACP, presents her moving story in *The Long Shadow of Little Rock* (1962). Orval Faubus, the demagogic Arkansas governor, has collected editorial cartoons and columns in *Down from the Hills* (1980), and is the subject of Roy Reed's convincing biography, *Faubus* (1997). Virgil Blossom, *It Has Happened Here* (1959), explains the whirlwind that the school superintendent found himself in. The student perspective comes from Melba Patillo Beals, *Warriors Don't Cry* (1994). Vice principal Elizabeth Huckaby, *Crisis at Central High* (1980), highlights the tense actions within the school. As US attorney general, Herbert Brownell, *Advising Ike* (1993), explains how the president reacted to civil rights issues. A frustrated parent, Sara Alderman Murphy, traces her fight to reopen the schools in *Breaking the Silence* (1997). Brooks Hays, *A Southern Moderate Speaks* (1959), looks at the crisis that cost him his congressional seat. Elizabeth Jacoway and C. Fred Williams, *Understanding the Little Rock Crisis* (1999), and Irving Spitzberg, *Racial Politics in Little Rock* (1987), provide useful overviews. John Kirk, *Redefining the Color Line* (2002), looks at local black activism in Little Rock.

Montgomery Bus Boycott

Two women who started the Montgomery bus boycott have written memoirs: Rosa Parks, *My Story* (1992), and Jo Ann Gibson Robinson, *The Montgomery Bus Boycott and the Women Who Started It* (1987). Douglas Brinkley's biography, *Rosa Parks* (2000), is the best introduction to this heroine. Martin Luther King, *Stride toward Freedom* (1958) provides the story and philosophy of the boycott's leader. Fred Gray examines the legal challenges in *Bus Ride to Justice* (1994). Stewart Burns, *Daybreak of Freedom* (1997), provides firsthand material related to the boycott. Jack Bass, *Taming the Storm* (1993), is a biography of federal judge Frank Johnson of Alabama.

Sit-ins

The Greensboro demonstration that set off the movement's sit-in phase is covered by Miles Wolff, *Lunch at the 5 & 10* (1970), and William Chafe, *Civilities and Civil Rights* (1980). David Halberstam, *The Children* (1998), has written a sympathetic account of the Nashville students he covered as a reporter.

Freedom Ride

In *Lay Bare the Heart* (1985), James Farmer writes movingly about the Freedom Ride he organized. James Peck, *Freedom Ride* (1962), is a memoir of a white rider. Dorothy Kaufman, *The First Freedom Ride* (1989), describes the brutality suffered by Walter Bergman. Attorney William Kunstler, *Deep in My Heart* (1966), relates his defense of the riders, the first of many such courtroom battles.

Battle of Ole Miss

James Meredith, *Three Years in Mississippi* (1966), tells of his daunting quest to desegregate the University of Mississippi. Two university professors recount the trouble over Meredith's admission: James Silver, *Mississippi: The Closed Society* (1964), and

Russell Barrett, *Integration at Ole Miss* (1965). Erle Johnston, *I Rolled with Ross* (1980), defends the governor who blocked Meredith. Constance Baker Motley, *Equal Justice Under Law* (1998), reveals the career of an NAACP attorney and the first black woman appointed to the federal bench. William Doyle, *An American Insurrection* (2001), is a sprightly narrative of the bloodshed at Ole Miss. Nadine Cohodas, *The Band Played Dixie* (1997), places the traumatic event within the long-range history of the university. Paul Hendrickson, *Sons of Mississippi* (2003), looks at how racism infected Mississippi lawmen and their progeny.

Albany

There is no book-length treatment of the Albany Movement, though this episode is treated in several surveys, including Howard Zinn, *The Southern Mystique* (1964).

Bombingham

William Nunnelley, *Bull Connor* (1991), and Andrew Manis, *A Fire You Can't Put Out: The Civil Rights Life of Birmingham's Reverend Fred Shuttleworth* (1999), are biographies of two key Birmingham men on opposite sides of civil rights. Martin Luther King, Jr., *Why We Can't Wait* (1964), is a classic summary of nonviolence. Diane McWhorter's *Carry Me Home* (2001), tells of her white middle-class family as protests erupt. Glenn Eskew, *But for Birmingham* (1997), studies the intersections of local and national organizations. Charles Morgan, Jr., *A Time To Speak* (1964), accuses his fellow white Birminghamians of complicity in the city's poisoned race relations. Bill Jones, *The Wallace Story* (1966), defends his boss. Gary Rowe, *My Undercover Years with the Ku Klux Klan* (1976), details the seamy side of being an FBI informant. S. Jonathan Bass, *Blessed Are the Peacemakers* (2001), looks at the white clergymen who rebuked King, as well as his famous rejoinder. Elizabeth Cobbs, *Long Time Coming* (1994), identifies her uncle as the mastermind of the Birmingham church bombing. Frank Sikora, *Until Justice Rolls Down* (1991), narrates the dastardly Birmingham church bombing.

Tuscaloosa

E. Culpepper Clark's *The Schoolhouse Door* (1993) provides a thorough account of the standoff at the University of Alabama between George Wallace and the federal government. Dan Carter, *The Politics of Rage* (1995), is a critical portrait of Wallace's career and political impact.

March on Washington

The most comprehensive account is Thomas Gentile, *March on Washington* (1983). Patrik Bass, *Like a Mighty Stream* (2002), presents an overview. Lucy Barber, *Marching on Washington* (2002), looks at several memorable demonstrations to the nation's capital. Daniel Levine's *Bayard Rustin and the Civil Rights Movement* (2000) recounts the extraordinary life of the movement's man-behind-the-scenes. In *The Dream* (2003), Drew Hansen closely analyzes Martin Luther King's inspirational speech.

Freedom Summer

Len Holt, *The Summer That Didn't End* (1965) is a compelling overview of that exciting, yet dreadful, time in Mississippi. Anne Moody, *Coming of Age in Mississippi* (1968), Charles Evers, *Have No Fear* (1996), Myrlie Evers, *For Us, the Living* (1967), Aaron Henry, *Aaron Henry* (2000), Winson Hudson and Constance Curry, *Mississippi Harmony* (2000), and Dick Gregory, '*Nigger*' (1964), are memoirs of activists. John Dittmer, *Local People* (1994), and Charles Payne, *I've Got the Light of Freedom* (1995), examine the activism of lesser-known figures in the Magnolia state. Medgar Evers's death is the subject of Adam Nossiter, *Of Long Memory* (1994), Reed Massengill's *Portrait of a Racist* (1994), and Maryanne Vollers, *Ghosts of Mississippi* (1995). Eric Burner, *And Gently He Shall Lead Them* (1994), powerfully portrays SNCC leader Bob Moses. William Chafe, *Never Stop Running* (1998), is a biography of Allard Lowenstein, who prodded white students to get involved. The high price for getting involved is narrated by William Bradford Huie, *Three Lives for Mississippi* (1965), Florence Mars, *Witness in Philadelphia* (1977), and Seth Cagin and Philip Dray, *We Are Not Afraid* (1988). Mary Aickin Rothchild, *A Case of Black and White* (1982), and Doug McAdam, *Freedom Summer* (1988), are in-depth studies of the young volunteers who went to Mississippi in 1964. Sally Belfrage's *Freedom Summer* (1965), Tracy Sugarman, *Stranger at the Gates*, and Nicholas Von Hoffman, *Mississippi Notebook* (1964), are revealing firsthand accounts. Elizabeth Sutherland has collected poignant letters from volunteers in *Letters from Mississippi* (1965). Charles Marsh, *God's Long Summer* (1997), brilliantly contrasts the religious motivations of Mississippi activists, klansmen, and bystanders.

Selma

David Garrow, *Protest at Selma* (1978), examines black activists who precipitated violence to elicit white support and federal government intervention. Amelia Platts Boynton, *Bridge Across Jordan* (1979), J.L. Chestnut, Jr., *Black in Selma* (1990), Sheyann Webb and Rachel West Nelson, *Selma, Lord, Selma* (1980), are memoirs of activists. Three martyrs of the Selma campaign are chronicled in Duncan Howlett, *No Greater Love* (1966), Mary Stanton, *From Selma to Sorrow* (1998), and Charles Eagles, *Outside Agitator* (1993). The notorious sheriff James Clark, Jr., *The Jim Clark Story – 'I Saw Selma Raped'* (1966), denounces the voting rights crusade while Charles Fager, *Selma 1965* (1974), defends it. James Forman, *Sammy Younge, Jr.* (1968), recounts the death of a Tuskegee student activist.

Chicago

Two perspectives on the Chicago Freedom Movement are provided in Alan Anderson and George Pickering, *Confronting the Color Line* (1986), and James Ralph, *Northern Protest* (1993). Stephen Meyer, *As Long As They Don't Move Next Door* (2000), examines the problem of segregated housing in Chicago and other northern cities.

Poor People's Campaign

Charles Fager, *Uncertain Resurrection* (1969), and Gerald McKnight, *Last Crusade* (1998), describe the events of King's ill-fated attempt to address poverty.

Courts

Don Fehrenbacher, *The Dred Scott Case* (1978), and Charles Lofgren, *The Plessy Case* (1987), analyze two fateful cases. John Howard, *The Shifting Wind* (1999), traces the winding path on race taken by the US Supreme Court between Reconstruction and *Brown*. J. Harvie Wilkinson, III, *From Brown to Bakke* (1979), follows the Court's changing attitudes on school desegregation. Tinsley Yarbrough has written an excellent biography of a foresighted federal judge in South Carolina, *A Passion for Justice: J. Waties Waring and Civil Rights* (1987). Jack Peltason, *Fifty-Eight Lonely Men* (1961), and Jack Bass, *Unlikely Heroes* (1981), report on the role of federal judges in desegregating southern schools. In *Federal Law and Southern Order* (1987), Michal Belknap observes that before 1964 Washington generally gave the South a free hand concerning racial violence. Tony Freyer, *The Little Rock Crisis* (1984), argues that constitutional questions overshadowed moral concerns. Paul Moreno, *From Direct Action to Affirmative Action* (1997), traces race-conscious employment remedies to the Great Depression era. Donald Nieman, *Promises to Keep* (1991), looks at the ambivalent relationship that blacks have had with the Constitution. Gail Williams O'Brien, *The Color of the Law* (1999) dissects the legal system's failure to mete out justice after a 1946 race riot in Tennessee.

Politics

Kenneth O'Reilly, *Nixon's Piano* (1995), explores racial politics from Washington to Clinton. Paul Burstein, *Discrimination, Jobs, and Politics* (1985), treats equal employment law since FDR. Truman's civil rights record is discussed in Donald McCoy and Richard Ruetten, *Quest and Response* (1973), and Michael Gardner, *Harry Truman and Civil Rights* (2002). Dwight Eisenhower's record is considered in J.W. Anderson, *Eisenhower, Brownell, and Congress* (1964), and Robert Burk, *The Eisenhower Administration and Black Civil Rights* (1984). Hanes Walton, Jr., *When the Marching Stopped* (1988), examines the workings of new civil rights regulatory agencies. The Kennedy administration's evolution on civil rights is presented in Carl Brauer, *John F. Kennedy and the Second Reconstruction* (1977), James Giglio, *The Presidency of John F. Kennedy* (1991), Harris Wofford, *Of Kennedys and Kings* (1980), Edwin Guthman, *We Band of Brothers* (1971), Arthur Schlesinger, *A Thousand Days* (1965), Theodore Sorensen, *Kennedy* (1965), Victor Navasky, *Kennedy Justice* (1971), and Evan Thomas, *Robert Kennedy* (2000). Lyndon Johnson's civil rights record is detailed in James Harvey, *Black Civil Rights during the Johnson Administration* (1973), and Robert Dallek, *Lone Star Rising* (1991) and *Flawed Giant* (1998). The limits of Johnson's antipoverty reforms are discussed in Allan Matusow, *The Unraveling of America* (1984). Hugh Davis Graham, *The Civil Rights Era* (1990), dissects federal civil rights policy from Kennedy to Nixon. Doug McAdam, *Political Process and the Development of Black Insurgency* (1999), demonstrates that the northern black political power pushed the federal government to guarantee basic civil rights. Jack Bloom, *Class, Race and the Civil Rights Movement* (1987), points to the declining clout of the plantation aristocracy to explain why black civil rights could advance. Hubert Humphrey's indispensable role in pushing for civil rights legislation is told in Timothy Thurber, *The Politics of Equality: Hubert H. Humphrey and the African American Freedom Struggle* (1999). The enactment of the epic 1964 Civil Rights Act is explored in Charles Whalen and Barbara Whalen, *The Longest Debate* (1985), and Robert Mann, *The Walls of Jericho*

(1996). Bruce Dierenfield, *Keeper of the Rules* (1987), studies how the conservative coalition obstructed civil rights measures in Congress. In *Nixon's Civil Rights* (2001), Dean Kotlowski argues that Nixon emphasized economic improvement, rather than integration, to address racial problems. Earl Black, *Southern Governors and Civil Rights* (1976), examines the impact of segregation on southern elections.

Women

Barbara Ransby, *Ella Barker and the Black Freedom Movement* (2003), is a biography of a civil rights activist who midwifed SNCC. Septima Clark, a key figure in the voting-rights campaign, is remembered in Cynthia Stokes Brown's *Ready from Within* (1986). Anne Braden, *The Wall Between* (1958), Sarah Patton Boyle, *The Desegregated Heart* (1962), and Virginia Durr, *Outside the Magic Circle* (1985), are autobiographies of white southern women who took the lead in fighting for civil rights. Chana Kai Lee's *For Freedom's Sake* (1999) is a biography of the unforgettable Fannie Lou Hamer. Cynthia Griggs Fleming, *Soon We Will Not Cry* (1998), tells the life story of a little-remembered activist, Ruby Doris Smith Robinson. Paula Giddings, *When and Where I Enter* (1984), examines the role of black women in the movement. There are two excellent collections on black women activists: Bettye Collier-Thomas and V.P. Franklin, *Sisters in the Struggle* (2001), and Vicki Crawford *et al.*, *Women in the Civil Rights Movement* (1993). In this same vein, Lynne Olson discusses black and white women leaders from 1830 onward in *Freedom's Daughters* (2001). Constance Curry *et al.*, *Deep in Our Heart* (2000), looks at nine white women who joined the struggle. In *Freedom Song* (1987), Mary King, a SNCC member, chronicles and criticizes that organization's evolution. In *Going South* (2001), Debra Schultz tells of northern Jewish women who joined the movement. Sara Evans, *Personal Politics* (1979), connects the civil rights and feminist movements.

Organizations

Scholars have lavished attention on groups that promoted equality and organized many of the protests. Aldon Morris's *The Origins of the Civil Rights Movement* (1984) is a first-rate study that emphasizes the local black church.

Thomas Kreuger, *And Promises to Keep* (1968), and Linda Reed, *Simple Decency and Common Sense* (1991), look at the pioneering Southern Conference Movement.

Merl Reed, *Seedtime for the Modern Civil Rights Movement* (1991), examines the FEPC.

Langston Hughes, *Fight for Freedom* (1962), and Charles Kellogg, *NAACP* (1967), relate the vital contributions of the NAACP. Robert Zangrando, *The NAACP Crusade Against Lynching* (1980), traces the organization's most important goal. Mark Schneider, '*We Return Fighting*' (2002), looks at the NAACP's crucial, but forgotten, work in the Jazz Age. Walter White, *A Man Called White* (1948), and Roy Wilkins, *Standing Fast* (1982), recount their leadership of the NAACP. Denton Watson, *Lion in the Lobby* (1990), credits the NAACP's Clarence Mitchell with getting major civil rights bills through Congress.

Jesse Moore, *A Search for Equality* (1981), looks at the quiet contributions of the Urban League. Dennis Dickerson, *Militant Mediator* (1998), is a biography of Urban League president Whitney Young who blended interracial mediation with direct protest (1998).

August Meier and Elliott Rudwick, *CORE* (1973), studies that organization for a generation after its inception.

James Dickerson, *Dixie's Dirty Secret* (1998), Yasuhiro Katagiri, *The Mississippi State Sovereignty Commission* (2001), Neil McMillen, *The Citizens' Council* (1971), and David Chalmers, *Backfire* (2003), examine organized southern resistance to the civil rights movement.

Two encyclopedic treatments of SCLC are Adam Fairclough, *To Redeem the Soul of America* (1978), and David Garrow, *Bearing the Cross* (1986).

Frank Adams and Myles Horton, *Unearthing Seeds of Fire* (1975), and John Glen, *Highlander* (1988), examine the folk school's vanguard role. In *Sing for Freedom* (1990), Highlander music director Guy Carawan and Candie Carawan collect songs that made the movement.

Clayborne Carson, *In Struggle* (1981), provides a balanced study of SNCC while Howard Zinn's *SNCC* (1964), and Jack Newfield, *A Prophetic Minority* (1966), capture the fervor of the young militants.

James Findley, *Church People in the Struggle* (1993), examines the close relationship between the National Council of Churches, the largest Protestant ecumenical organization, and the civil rights movement.

For important organizational journals, see the *Crisis* (NAACP), *Opportunity* (Urban League), *Fellowship* (FOR), *Southern Frontier* (CIC), *New South* (SRC), *Southern Patriot* (SCHW), *Student Voice* (SNCC), *CORElater* (CORE), *Muhammad Speaks* (NOI), and *Black Panther* (BPP).

See David Garrow, *The FBI and Martin Luther King, Jr.* (1981), Kenneth O'Reilly, *'Racial Matters'* (1989), and Richard Gid Powers, *Secrecy and Power* (1987), for J. Edgar Hoover's war on black America.

Black Power

Any study of black power in America must begin with its foremost modern champion. See Malcolm X's searing autobiography, ghostwritten by Alex Haley (1965), and a brilliant biography by Peter Goldman, *The Death and Life of Malcolm X* (1979). George Breitman, *By Any Means Necessary* (1970), reprints Malcolm's speeches and interviews. James Baldwin, *The Fire Next Time* (1963), angrily condemns the racial state of America and finds Malcolm's ideology attractive. Michael Eric Dyson lucidly analyzes the contemporary legacy of Malcolm X in *Making Malcolm* (1995).

A Caribbean/Algerian radical named Frantz Fanon also inspired black nationalists in *The Wretched of the Earth* (1963). Stokely Carmichael and Charles Hamilton, *Black Power* (1967), define the potent term and criticize interracial coalitions. The changed mood is expressed in Robert Williams, *Negroes with Guns* (1962), Floyd McKissick's *Genocide USA* (1967), and Julius Lester, *Look Out, Whitey!* (1968). See Timothy Tyson's *Radio Free Dixie* (1999) for a look at the radicalism of Robert Williams. Black Panther leaders Huey Newton, *Revolutionary Suicide* (1973), Bobby Seale, *Seize the Time* (1968), and H. Rap Brown, *Die Nigger Die!* (1969), describe the party's philosophy. Hugh Pearson, *The Shadow of the Panther* (1991), studies Huey Newton's topsy-turvy life. Two BPP histories are Michael Newton, *Bitter Grain* (1991), and Hugh Pearson, *The Shadow of the Panther* (1994). Cleveland Sellers, *The River of No Return* (1973), is the life story of a SNCC militant. Herbert Haines, *Black Radicals and the Civil Rights Mainstream* (1988), finds that white support for civil rights grew as black radicalism emerged. William Van Deburg, *New Day in Babylon* (1992), is a comprehensive account of the black power movement. James Forman, *The Making of Black Revolutionaries* (1972), recounts his evolution from integrationist to black nationalist. Komozi Woodard, *A Nation within a Nation* (1999), is a good biography of Amiri Baraka and the black arts movement. Martin Luther King's critique of black power is advanced in *Where Do We Go from Here: Chaos or Community?* (1967).

Riots

Thomas Sugrue analyzes Detroit to understand *The Origins of the Urban Crisis* (1996). Robert Conot, *Rivers of Blood, Years of Darkness* (1968), and Gerald Horne, *The Watts Uprising and the 1960s* (1995), examine the bloody Los Angeles riot. Joe Feagin and Harlan Hahn, *Ghetto Revolts* (1973), and Robert Fogelson, *Violence as Protest* (1971), are the better treatments of race riots in the 1960s. The federal government's study, *The Report of the National Advisory Commission on Civil Unrest* (1968), probes ghetto life and the bloody race riots of the 1960s.

Today

Andrew Hacker, *Two Nations* (1992), and Jonathan Coleman, *Long Way to Go* (1997) see little progress since the Kerner Report. Orlando Patterson, *The Ordeal of Integration* (1997), offers solutions to the paradox of racial integration. In *The Declining Significance of Race* (1980), *The Truly Disadvantaged* (1987), and *When Work Disappears* (1997), William Julius Wilson sees structural economic factors as principally responsible for black poverty. Cornel West, *Race Matters* (1993), addresses several timely topics. Randall Kenan, *Walking on Water* (1999), astutely examines black life at the turn of the twenty-first century.

INDEX

182

Seigenthaler, John, 64–65
Selma, AL, 58, 108–117, 119–120
Selma-to-Montgomery march, 113–118
Sellers, Cleveland, 53, 57, 104
Separate-but-equal doctrine, 9
Serfs, 1
Shakespeare, William, 2
Sharecropping, 27–28, 54, 99
Shelton, Robert, 63, 80
Sherrod, Charles, 75, 119
Shivers, Al, 27
Sholes, Arthur, 89
Shriver, Sargent, 92
Shuttlesworth, Fred, 49, 63, 65, 77–80, 91
Silver, James, 74
Simmons, William, 25
Sims, Larry Joe, 90
Sit-down strike, 16
Sit-ins, 16, 52–59, 60–62, 75, 79, 86, 97,
    100, 105, 108
Skin color, 1–2, 4, 8, 14, 117
Slavery, 1–4, 7, 57, 130
Slavery reparations, 127
Smiley, Glenn, 49
Smith v. Allwright (1944), 18
Smith, Howard W., 64, 90
Smith, Kelly Miller, 54
Smith, Lamar, 25
Smith, Lillian, 17
Smith, Ruby Doris, 56, 97
Smith, Wofford, 73
Smitherman, Joe T., 109–110
Socialism, 14, 63, 127–128
Socialist party, 15
Soul food, 127
Soul music, 127
Souls of Black Folk, The, 13
South Carolina, 8–9, 17, 21, 23–24, 28, 31,
    43, 53, 57, 62, 74, 105, 119
Southern Baptists, 29, 41–44, 49, 54, 75, 77,
    109, 113, 126, 130
Southern Christian Leadership Conference,
    49–50, 53–54, 57–58, 62, 68, 76–79,
    84–85, 91, 97, 99, 105–106, 110–113,
    117, 120, 125–126, 129
Southern Conference Educational Fund, 16,
    47, 58
Southern Conference for Human Welfare,
    16
Southern Democrats, 8, 23–25, 27, 30–37,
    48, 50, 64–68, 70–72, 74–75, 80–83,
    90–91, 100, 103, 105–107, 113–120,
    124–125, 128, 131
Southern Manifesto, 24, 30
Southern Poverty Law Center, 130
Southern Regional Council, 16, 68
Southern Tenant Farmers' Union, 15
Soviet Union, 19, 33–34, 64, 80, 85, 88
Spelman College, 56, 105
St. Augustine, FL, 91, 109

Standing in the door, 75, 81–82
Stanford University, 101
State highway patrols, 63, 65, 73, 80–81,
    100, 113–115, 117
State sovereignty (*see* states' rights)
State sovereignty commissions, 30, 96, 101
States' rights, 24, 31, 34, 70–71, 74
Steele, C.K., 49
Steptoe, E.W., 97
Stereotyping, 1–3, 8–9
Stokes, Carl, 119
Strange Fruit, 17
Student Nonviolent Coordinating
    Committee, 57–58, 65, 68, 75–76, 82,
    84, 86–88, 97–104, 106–111, 113, 115,
    118, 120, 126–127
Students for a Democratic Society, 58, 102
Swahili, 126
Swann v. Charlotte-Mecklenberg (1971), 130

Talmadge, Herman, 23
Taney, Roger, 4
Television, 19, 31, 33–34, 37, 53, 79,
    81–82, 88, 105–106, 112–115, 123,
    127, 132
Ten Commandments, 4
Tennessee, 13, 24, 27–28, 32, 42, 54–57,
    65, 108, 125, 129
Terry, Adolphine Fletcher, 36
Texas, 24, 27, 32, 36, 50, 57, 60–61, 102,
    115
Texas Rangers, 27
Third World, 19, 80, 127
Thomas, Clarence, 131
Thomas, Henry, 63, 67
Thurman, Howard, 45
Thurmond, Strom, 24, 106, 120, 129
Till, Emmett, 26–27, 43, 98
Tillman, Ben, 8
To Secure These Rights, 17
Trotter, William Monroe, 13
Truman, Harry, 17, 22, 90, 105
Tubman, Harriet, 82
Turnbow, Hartman, 98
Turner, Albert, 112
Tuskegee Institute, 13, 119–120
Twain, Mark, 7

Uncle Tom, 24, 124
Underground railroad, 82
Unemployment, 14, 77, 82, 84, 123–124,
    132
Unitarians, 115
United Negro College Fund, 18
U.S. Commission on Civil Rights, 50–51, 64,
    130
U.S. Congress, 7, 14, 17–18, 24, 50, 64, 68,
    77, 84–86, 89–91, 106–107, 111,
    114–115, 128–129, 132
U.S. Constitution, 23

STUART BRITAIN

Social Change and Continuity: England 1550–1750 (Second edition)
Barry Coward   0 582 29442 8

James I (Second edition)
S. J. Houston   0 582 20911 0

The English Civil War 1640–1649
Martyn Bennett   0 582 35392 0

Charles I, 1625–1640
Brian Quintrell   0 582 00354 7

The English Republic 1649–1660 (Second edition)
Toby Barnard   0 582 08003 7

Radical Puritans in England 1550–1660
R. J. Acheson   0 582 35515 X

The Restoration and the England of Charles II (Second edition)
John Miller   0 582 29223 9

The Glorious Revolution (Second edition)
John Miller   0 582 29222 0

EARLY MODERN EUROPE

The Renaissance (Second edition)
Alison Brown   0 582 30781 3

The Emperor Charles V
Martyn Rady   0 582 35475 7

French Renaissance Monarchy: Francis I and Henry II (Second edition)
Robert Knecht   0 582 28707 3

The Protestant Reformation in Europe
Andrew Johnston   0 582 07020 1

The French Wars of Religion 1559–1598 (Second edition)
Robert Knecht   0 582 28533 X

Philip II
Geoffrey Woodward   0 582 07232 8

The Thirty Years' War
Peter Limm   0 582 35373 4

Louis XIV
Peter Campbell   0 582 01770 X

Spain in the Seventeenth Century
Graham Darby   0 582 07234 4

Peter the Great
William Marshall   0 582 00355 5

EUROPE 1789–1918

Britain and the French Revolution
Clive Emsley   0 582 36961 4

Revolution and Terror in France 1789–1795 (Second edition)
D. G. Wright   0 582 00379 2

Napoleon and Europe
D. G. Wright   0 582 35457 9

The Abolition of Serfdom in Russia, 1762–1907
David Moon   0 582 29486 X

Nineteenth-Century Russia: Opposition to Autocracy
Derek Offord   0 582 35767 5

The Constitutional Monarchy in France 1814–48
Pamela Pilbeam   0 582 31210 8

The 1848 Revolutions (Second edition)
Peter Jones   0 582 06106 7

The Italian Risorgimento
M. Clark   0 582 00353 9

Bismarck & Germany 1862–1890 (Second edition)
D. G. Williamson   0 582 29321 9

Imperial Germany 1890–1918
Ian Porter, Ian Armour and Roger Lockyer   0 582 03496 5

The Dissolution of the Austro-Hungarian Empire 1867–1918 (Second edition)
John W. Mason   0 582 29466 5

Second Empire and Commune: France 1848–1871 (Second edition)
William H. C. Smith   0 582 28705 7

France 1870–1914 (Second edition)
Robert Gildea   0 582 29221 2

The Scramble for Africa (Second edition)
M. E. Chamberlain   0 582 36881 2

Late Imperial Russia 1890–1917
John F. Hutchinson   0 582 32721 0

The First World War
Stuart Robson   0 582 31556 5

Austria, Prussia and Germany, 1806–1871
John Breuilly   0 582 43739 3

Napoleon: Conquest, Reform and Reorganisation
Clive Emsley   0 582 43795 4

The French Revolution, 1787–1804
Peter Jones   0 582 77289 3

The Origins of the First World War (Third edition)
Gordon Martel   0 582 43804 7

EUROPE SINCE 1918

The Russian Revolution (Second edition)
Anthony Wood   0 582 35559 1

Lenin's Revolution: Russia, 1917–1921
David Marples   0 582 31917 X

Stalin and Stalinism (Third edition)
Martin McCauley   0 582 50587 9

The Weimar Republic (Second edition)
John Hiden   0 582 28706 5

The Inter-War Crisis 1919–1939
Richard Overy   0 582 35379 3

Fascism and the Right in Europe, 1919–1945
Martin Blinkhorn   0 582 07021 X

Spain's Civil War (Second edition)
Harry Browne   0 582 28988 2

The Third Reich (Third edition)
D. G. Williamson   0 582 20914 5

The Origins of the Second World War (Second edition)
R. J. Overy   0 582 29085 6

The Second World War in Europe
Paul MacKenzie   0 582 32692 3

The French at War, 1934–1944
Nicholas Atkin   0 582 36899 5

Anti-Semitism before the Holocaust
Albert S. Lindemann   0 582 36964 9

The Holocaust: The Third Reich and the Jews
David Engel   0 582 32720 2

Germany from Defeat to Partition, 1945–1963
D. G. Williamson   0 582 29218 2

Britain and Europe since 1945
Alex May   0 582 30778 3

Eastern Europe 1945–1969: From Stalinism to Stagnation
Ben Fowkes   0 582 32693 1

Eastern Europe since 1970
Bülent Gökay   0 582 32858 6

The Khrushchev Era, 1953–1964
Martin McCauley   0 582 27776 0

Hitler and the Rise of the Nazi Party
Frank McDonough   0 582 50606 9

The Soviet Union Under Brezhnev
William Tompson   0 582 32719 9

NINETEENTH-CENTURY BRITAIN

Britain before the Reform Acts: Politics and Society 1815–1832
Eric J. Evans   0 582 00265 6

Parliamentary Reform in Britain c. 1770–1918
Eric J. Evans   0 582 29467 3

Democracy and Reform 1815–1885
D. G. Wright   0 582 31400 3

Poverty and Poor Law Reform in Nineteenth-Century Britain,
1834–1914: From Chadwick to Booth
David Englander   0 582 31554 9

The Birth of Industrial Britain: Economic Change, 1750–1850
Kenneth Morgan   0 582 29833 4

Chartism (Third edition)
Edward Royle   0 582 29080 5

Peel and the Conservative Party 1830–1850
Paul Adelman   0 582 35557 5

Gladstone, Disraeli and later Victorian Politics (Third edition)
Paul Adelman   0 582 29322 7

Britain and Ireland: From Home Rule to Independence
Jeremy Smith   0 582 30193 9

TWENTIETH-CENTURY BRITAIN

The Rise of the Labour Party 1880–1945 (Third edition)
Paul Adelman   0 582 29210 7

The Conservative Party and British Politics 1902–1951
Stuart Ball   0 582 08002 9

The Decline of the Liberal Party 1910–1931 (Second edition)
Paul Adelman   0 582 27733 7

The British Women's Suffrage Campaign 1866–1928
Harold L. Smith   0 582 29811 3

War & Society in Britain 1899–1948
Rex Pope   0 582 03531 7

The British Economy since 1914: A Study in Decline?
Rex Pope   0 582 30194 7

Unemployment in Britain between the Wars
Stephen Constantine   0 582 35232 0

The Attlee Governments 1945–1951
Kevin Jefferys   0 582 06105 9

The Conservative Governments 1951–1964
Andrew Boxer   0 582 20913 7

Britain under Thatcher
Anthony Seldon and Daniel Collings   0 582 31714 2

Britain and Empire, 1880–1945
Dane Kennedy   0 582 41493 8

INTERNATIONAL HISTORY

The Eastern Question 1774–1923 (Second edition)
A. L. Macfie   0 582 29195 X

India 1885–1947: The Unmaking of an Empire
Ian Copland   0 582 38173 8

The Origins of the Cold War, 1941–1949 (Third edition)
Martin McCauley   0 582 77284 2

Russia, America and the Cold War, 1949–1991 (Second edition)
Martin McCauley   0 582 78482 4

The Arab–Israeli Conflict
Kirsten E. Schulze   0 582 31646 4

The United Nations since 1945: Peacekeeping and the Cold War
Norrie MacQueen   0 582 35673 3

Decolonisation: The British Experience since 1945
Nicholas J. White   0 582 29087 2

South Africa: The Rise and Fall of Apartheid
Nancy L. Clark and William H. Worger   0 582 41437 7

The Collapse of the Soviet Union
David R. Marples   0 582 50599 2

WORLD HISTORY

China in Transformation 1900–1949
Colin Mackerras   0 582 31209 4

Japan Faces the World, 1925–1952
Mary L. Hanneman   0 582 36898 7

Japan in Transformation, 1952–2000
Jeff Kingston   0 582 41875 5

China since 1949
Linda Benson   0 582 35722 5

US HISTORY

American Abolitionists
Stanley Harrold   0 582 35738 1

The American Civil War, 1861–1865
Reid Mitchell   0 582 31973 0

America in the Progressive Era, 1890–1914
Lewis L. Gould   0 582 35671 7

The United States and the First World War
Jennifer D. Keene   0 582 35620 2

The Truman Years, 1945–1953
Mark S. Byrnes   0 582 32904 3

The Korean War
Steven Hugh Lee   0 582 31988 9

The Origins of the Vietnam War
Fredrik Logevall   0 582 31918 8

The Vietnam War
Mitchell Hall   0 582 32859 4

American Expansionism, 1783–1860
Mark S. Joy   0 582 36965 7

The United States and Europe in the Twentieth Century
David Ryan   0 582 30864 X

The Eisenhower Presidency, 1953–61
Richard V. Damms   0 582 36818 9

The Civil Rights Movement
Bruce J. Dierenfield   0 582 35737 3